AKRCN HEAD START
902 E. First St.
Akron, CO 80720
(970) 345-2695

The Involved Father

The Involved Father

Family-Tested Solutions for Getting

Dads to Participate More in the

Daily Lives of Their Children

Robert Frank, Ph.D.

with Kathryn E. Livingston

Produced by The Philip Lief Group

St. Martin's Press ≋ New York

THE INVOLVED FATHER. Copyright © 1999 by The Philip Lief Group, Inc. All rights reserved. Printed in the United States of America. No part of this book may be used or reproduced in any manner whatsoever without written permission except in the case of brief quotations embodied in critical articles or reviews. For information address St. Martin's Press, 175 Fifth Avenue, New York, N.Y. 10010.

Designed by Richard Oriolo

ISBN 1-58238-051-1

First Edition: September 1999

10 9 8 7 6 5 4 3 2 1

To my parents, Fern and Jerome Frank,
my wife, Linda,
and my children, Kevin and A.J.

Contents

Acknowledgments

I GATHERED MY INSPIRATION and ideas from so many people. I would like to acknowledge a few here.

To the people who helped me with my dissertation: Linda Curgian, Ron Morgan, Carol Harding, and Mike Helford. To Alan Rubin for giving me my first college teaching job and the inspiration to continue teaching. To Steve Schada and Greg Baldauf for their support with the At-Home-Dads Convention. To my good friends Steve Glink, Mike Shain, and Bob Mishkin for their support. To Dr. Paul Volkman who gave me my start in psychotherapy. To Kathy Gidwitz for her never-ending support. To Elisabeth Kübler-Ross for her inspiration. To Curtis Cooper, Peter Baylies, and Bruce Drobeck, my at-home-dad colleagues, for their friendship and support. To Mrs. Reinhardt, my third grade teacher, who knew I needed extra help and gave me so much. To Janie Isackson, one of my high school teachers, for her support and friendship. To all the parents whose stories are told here. To Kathy Livingston, who brought to the book her great writing skill, tremendous experience derived from fifteen years as a writer on parenting and child development issues for national magazines, and many contributions of her own. To Jamie Saxon for her editing, support, and persistence in getting this book done. To my editor at Golden Books, Cassie Jones, and to Golden Books for giving me the opportunity to publish my views.

My deepest gratitude to the two people who had the biggest influence on my life, my parents, Fern and Jerome Frank. Thanks for the parenting skills. Thanks to my brothers, Mike and Bruce, who taught me so much as we grew up together. And I give special thanks to my wife, Linda, and children, A.J. and Kevin. Without them I wouldn't have had the opportunity to be a parent or the inherent desire and experience on which this book is based.

—BOB FRANK

Heartfelt thanks to my husband, Mitch Kriegler, and our children, Aaron, Sam, and Ben, who offered support, time, and patience. I thank my mother, Virginia Livingston, who is a treasured source of parenting wisdom; and I'm grateful to live and learn with the memory of an involved, caring father, Abram F. Livingston. My deep appreciation to Bob Frank for remembering me when he needed a writer—and for being such a joy to work with. Many thanks to my agent, Elizabeth Ziemska. And thanks to Jamie Saxon at The Philip Lief Group, who guided us with exuberance and skill.

—KATHRYN E. LIVINGSTON

Introduction

I **FIRST BEGAN THINKING** about writing a book on balanced parenting when I became a stay-at-home father after my son, Kevin, was born. As the parent at home I became keenly aware of how important it is for couples to share participation in raising their children on a daily basis—for the well-being of the kids and for the health of the marriage and the parents as individual adults with needs and goals of their own. With my expertise in child development and my wife's budding career, staying home was a natural choice for me. Linda and I decided together that this was the best route for our family. Having a private psychotherapy practice, I had flexibility in how I arranged my hours, while my wife was more locked into a nine-to-five position. The arrangement worked very well for us. My wife was very invested in her career and preferred to continue working full-time. I soon realized that I was quite capable of caring for our baby. (What a lot of dads don't realize is that caring for a baby is on-the-job training—you learn as you go; it's not an inherent skill that only women possess.) There was no real reason why I should necessarily be the one to go to work and my wife the one to stay home.

Two years later our daughter was born, and again my wife and I decided that I would be the primary caregiver, arranging my own work schedule around the demands of running a home and caring for the children. As the years passed and I continued as the at-home parent, I began to think more and more about the issues of balanced involvement and responsibility. Concurrently, I noticed in my practice that more and more women—those who were at home full-time as well as those who worked—were expressing frustration, anger, and resentment that their husbands weren't involved on a daily basis in the lives of their children. Many of the fathers privately told me that they actually wanted to be more involved but didn't see clearly how they could fit into the picture because of their work schedule or because they felt inexperienced in child care or because they felt a push-pull when it came to more traditional parental roles their own parents had played. Other men did think they were doing enough, but clearly there were still unresolved issues wreaking havoc on their marriage and on their children's day-to-day lives. I began to see that, in many families, issues of balanced involvement with the children were at the root of deep feelings of dissatisfaction.

I began to suspect that I viewed this topic from a rather unique perspective. First, I am a stay-at-home father, so I understand the extraordinary demands of taking care of children on a daily, ongoing basis and can empathize with stay-at-home mothers. But, married to a woman who is extremely dedicated to her career as well as to her family, I also respect and understand the needs and goals of mothers who have chosen to work. Further, because I do have a private practice in marriage and family counseling and also teach courses at several area colleges, I know how difficult it can be to juggle child care and two careers in one household (and I have the professional training in psychology and child development to dig deeply into the topic). And, of course, because I'm a father, I know what it's like to look at these issues from a male perspective and to try to balance the needs of my children with my own career desires and personal goals.

My intentions were to do what was best for our family and to spend as much time as possible with my kids. In the process, I have discovered that children in a home where two parents are present thrive best when both parents are involved in the lives of the children on a daily basis. I have also discovered that just as there are an infinite number of ways to hold a baby or to get a toddler to try a new food, there are hundreds of creative ways to achieve a more balanced, equitable parenting relationship, whether one parent stays at home or both work, and even when one parent is reluctant or resistant. Yes, it takes good communication, maturity, compromise, negotiation, and sometimes a thorough reassessment of priorities—but it's not as difficult to get started as many couples or mothers who first walk into my practice think it will be. It is my hope that this book tells the success stories of many of these families and that it inspires you to create your own positive outcomes—as a team with your spouse. I offer family-tested solutions to balancing problems and talk at length about how to improve communication with your partner so that you both may feel fulfilled as parents and as individuals.

I never dreamed I would gain national attention as a cofounder of the At-Home-Dads Network or that my doctoral dissertation on the subject would be covered in the media from coast to coast. But when I think back, the media attention is not what sticks out in my mind. The times I remember most are the days I spent walking with my son, Kevin, just the two of us together for hours, and ice skating in the park with my daughter, A.J. I can't think of anything that has been more rewarding in my life than the experience of watching my children grow up—one day at a time—and sharing that experience with my wife.

As one of my favorite theorists, Erik Erikson, says, I believe that what I have to offer is "a way of looking at things." I hope you enjoy my "way of looking at things" as much as I've enjoyed the experience of living my life as an actively involved dad.

How Did We Get

to This Point?

As an educational psychologist, family counselor, and leader of parenting seminars, I've seen hundreds of couples struggle to balance their lives as parents. Frequently, it's the woman who is most frustrated and torn by the demands of juggling her roles as a mother, wife, and, very often, breadwinner. Even though she's married, she feels she's doing it all herself. Sometimes it's the dad who can't seem to figure out how to prioritize the needs of his children, his wife, and his own career aspirations and personal goals. I think one of the greatest challenges of parenting is reaching and then maintaining a sense of balance between parents—but I also know that it *is* possible. In my practice I've watched many couples evolve from two disparate, resentful, angry partners to communicative, caring individuals in a balanced, "fair share" parenting relationship.

The norm, in so many families, is that the responsibility for the children and for the running of the house remains dramatically out of kilter. A common scene looks like this: Janet, a working mother who is employed full-time as a civil engineer, and her husband, an investment banker, have two children who are in day care. The differences show up at the end of the day. When Bill comes home from work at night, he takes a hot shower and a nap before coming down to dinner. Janet, on the other hand, picks the kids up at day care, rushes home to make dinner, gives the children their baths, reads to them, puts them to bed, and then catches up on the laundry and housework. Virtually on her own, Janet handles what author Arlie Hochschild calls "the second shift." While Bill may pitch in here and there, his sense of responsibility for home and children is nowhere near as deeply ingrained as Janet's. Like many women who work outside the home all day, Janet feels compelled to "make up for lost time" when she gets home. As a result, she never has time for herself and carries deep feelings of resentment and anger toward her mate.

When both parents work, mothers typically take over the domestic responsibilities when they get home, while fathers help out as much as they can—or want. When a mother is home with the children all day, a father may be even less eager or willing to be involved with the children at the end of his workday. "After all," these dads may be thinking, "it's my job to make the money and hers to care for the kids." With this type of attitude, stay-at-home moms get even less help from their mates than moms who work outside the home because their husbands feel that their role as the main breadwinner excuses them from sharing equally in child care. I haven't met a mom yet, working or not working, who wouldn't like her husband to more willingly and equally join in the parenting.

This imbalance of parenting responsibility is detrimental not only to mothers—who feel tired, stressed, frustrated, and quite often angry—but also to fathers who are missing out on the rewards of active involvement with their children and an undoubtedly happier marriage. And uppermost in my mind is the fact that the children in so many of these families where the balance is skewed aren't getting the best of both worlds—daily interaction with their mom and dad.

In addition to my work as a counselor and educator, I also have another unique perspective on this issue. From the time my children, Kevin, age eleven, and Alexandra (whom we call A.J.), age ten, were born, I have served as the primary caregiver, as a stay-at-home dad, while my wife works full-time as a hospital administrator. After completing my dissertation, I continued to conduct research on topics related to fatherhood and parenting, to see patients in my private practice, and to teach university courses in child development and psychology. My wife loves her work, and we are happy with the way we have made it a priority to achieve a good model of balanced parenting. Coming from this multifaceted vantage point, in many ways I feel I can "see it all": I relate to stay-at-home moms (because I'm home most of the day!), working moms (I'm married to one), and dads (after all, I'm a dad, too!).

Over the years I've met hundreds of couples from many walks of life and all types of households coping with the common struggle of how to deal with their parenting responsibilities in a fair and rewarding way. What I see happening is that most are applying an outdated set of expectations to today's realities. Yesterday's cookie-cutter family-structure stereotype of "dad's the breadwinner and mom takes care of the kids" does not reflect current trends in the workforce or current child development research. Even women today who choose to stay at home with their children for a couple of years or until the children grow up are not looking for a husband who is only the breadwinner; they are looking for a partner who is involved on a daily basis.

The bottom line is, the parenting model of yesterday simply doesn't work anymore. In fact, did it ever really work well for women and children? On the surface it may have appeared that families back in the fifties, say, were running smoothly. But how many of those children really knew their fathers well? How many women were able to pursue their own careers and interests? How many fathers from those days have memories of long hours spent cradling their newborns or afternoons in the park with their toddlers?

Things were different then: Society didn't *expect* men to be involved in the daily care of their children. But today, new research reveals and confirms how very important fathers are to the emotional, social, and cognitive (intellectual) development of children when they are involved in their lives on a consistent, if not daily, basis. Moreover, as we discover how kids benefit from involved fathers, we are also discovering the crucial difference that involved dads can make in maintaining a healthy, equitable marriage.

I think today's society puts an enormous amount of pressure on women to shoulder the bulk of child care and household responsibilities, regardless of whether they work in or out of the home or have chosen to be a stay-at-home parent. It is no wonder that mothers are often overwhelmed, to say nothing of being physically and emotionally exhausted, a great deal of the time. While society has finally given the nod that it is acceptable for moms to also be breadwinners, they are still expected to spend a great deal of time with their children. On the other hand, fathers can continue to be breadwinners, society seems to be saying, and spend a *little* time with their kids, and that's okay. Therefore, the bulk of the pressure is really on mothers: They are expected to plan what the family is having for dinner, schedule the kids' doctors appointments, arrange all the play dates, and basically run the show, often in addition to a job. No wonder many women feel that their lives are out of balance and that their husbands just aren't doing their share.

Looking at the other side, many men who want to be more involved find that their desire to be a good father and husband doesn't always mesh with the demands of the workplace. Or they feel confused because they're consciously or unconsciously fighting against the more stereotypical parental roles they themselves grew up with. Or their inclination is to hang back because their wives seem so good at it and they think their help isn't needed. Some men see no reason to expand beyond the work arena where they feel in control—or, if they feel out of control in the work arena, they often feel just as lost at home. Others who want to be involved with their children may not know how to go about it, so they stick with the old "comfortable" roles. Others worry that their efforts will be criticized or ridiculed either by their peers or sometimes even their spouses. If you think about it, parents—mothers and fathers—rarely have any training for parenting, but men tend to feel more hesitant than women in this "traditionally female" circle. (Many men would be amazed to know just how much their help, input, and ideas would be welcomed by their spouses, who may feel equally shaky in the child care arena—especially when a newborn cries inconsolably or a teenager clams up.) Still other men fear, even with all the media focus on men becoming more comfortable with their emotions, that as nurturers they will somehow be emasculated.

Here are just a few of the scenarios that are common as I listen to parents coping with their changing roles:

- Annalise, a stay-at-home mother of three, is frustrated because her husband doesn't expect to have to help with the child care. If a woman makes the choice to stay home with her child, deciding either not to pursue a career or to put her career temporarily on hold, does that mean that Dad is excused from domestic detail? For Annalise and many women like her, that's exactly the case. She is married to a man who, like the guys back in the fifties, expects dinner on the table, his shirts pressed, and Mom to care for the kids since, after all, he's the breadwinner. The fact is, whether Mom works outside the home or works solely in her role as a mother, she is also an adult—and a working adult at that—who needs time to herself and who deserves a supportive parenting partner who will do his fair share.

- Denise, a real estate agent, has flexible hours and is a busy volunteer at her church and her kids' school. As the mother of two girls and a community member, it seems that she can do no wrong. But her husband, Colin, who manages a chain store, never seems to meet her expectations. While she claims she wants him to be an involved, active father, Colin perceives that Denise criticizes his every choice with respect to caring for their daughters, including how he gives them a bath, how he dresses them, what activities he chooses to do with them, and even what picture books he reads to them. He is afraid she thinks she is the "expert" when it comes to the children and that her way is the only way. Their marriage is fraught with tension; it seems that no matter what Colin does with his daughters, it's never the right thing or good enough. When Colin confronted her about the criticism one evening, Denise said, "You know, I didn't even realize I was doing that. That's not how I really want things to be between us."

■ Jeb, a graphic artist, takes a great deal of pride in his work, and when he gets home, he wants to be the best he can be as a father. His twins, now four, are his responsibility from dinner until bedtime; his wife, a nurse, works the evening shift in a city hospital. Unlike his own father, a traveling salesman who was virtually absent while Jeb was growing up, Jeb wants to be a positive, dependable part of his children's lives. But while his intentions are good, Jeb is plagued by self-doubt. How, he wonders, can he be a good father when his own role model was absent? The weight of the responsibility and the fear that he will somehow fail are constant sources of self-doubt in his life. Yet he is determined to let his children know he'll be there for them, as his father was not.

■ Eric has just become a new father, and he's proud of his wife and daughter. What he can't figure out is why he feels so distant from his family. While Julie was preparing for child-birth, reading every book she could get her hands on, Eric began to feel like an observer. Even though he attended the birth, he now feels somehow disconnected, as though he has lost the sense of equilibrium he had when it was just he and his wife. Now their family has become a trio instead of a duo, and he is surprised at how distant and unincluded he feels. Sometimes he feels like just "checking out," at least on an emotional level.

What do these families, along with Janet and Bill at the beginning of the chapter, have in common? A balancing problem and, in many cases, a communication problem. Each and every couple must devise a method or system that will work for them based on the unique variables of their household. Both men and women are experiencing a great deal a pressure as we enter the next century, and as gender roles and working roles change and evolve, so must our parenting roles and responsibilities.

For the past ten years I have been helping families find the answers to these questions:

- How can we as parents arrive at positive, fair solutions to child rearing?

- How can we learn to respect one another as parents and adults, and thus as equal partners, in the care of our children?

- How can we be sure that the needs of our children are being met, that the needs of our marriages are being fulfilled, and that our personal goals and aspirations are being addressed?

- How can we motivate and support fathers to pitch in and help (not as water boys but as key players) and really take an active role in the daily lives of their children?

- How can women encourage their spouses to become the involved, essential fathers that both they and their kids want them to be without encountering a negative reaction?

- How can men more effectively manage the conflicts of work and home, and break out of traditional fathering roles?

- How exactly can we end up with those happier, healthier children that research shows are the outcome when fathers play a positive role?

- In short, how can we learn to balance our lives in a world that pulls us—both men *and* women—in so many directions?

These are the questions I will confront head-on in this book in order to help you as a family arrive at a solution that will bring balance and fairness to your lives. Whether you're a working mom, a stay-at-home mom, a mom whose husband travels a lot, a new father, or a dad with teenage kids, this book will help you identify, practice, and implement balancing skills that will make your careers more fulfilling, your time home more rewarding, and your marriages more communicative. Though I sympathize greatly with fathers (after all, I'm a father myself), I feel that women in our society have been wrongly called upon to "do it all," and therefore my message may sometimes seem skewed in their direction. According to the Bureau of Labor Statistics, in 1997 approximately 72 percent of working mothers had children who were either infants or between the ages of one and seventeen. I see as well that women who stay home to raise their children need equal partners, as do women with careers. Not only do I want to help women get the involvement and support they need from their spouses and men to get the encouragement they need from their wives, but I also want this generation of children to reap the benefits of having two actively involved parents.

Just as we've been striving to increase fairness and balanced opportunities for women in the workplace, we must bring a sense of fairness and equality to men's roles in parenting and home life. I have spent my career studying fathers and the evolving roles and definitions of fatherhood—and, of course, I've experienced firsthand what it is like to be a father in this day and age. This is an exciting, pivotal time to be a father, a time in which society is poised to accept and encourage men's increased involvement in their children's lives. Just as I see the frustration and the anxiety that our changing roles have produced, I also see clearly the hope and potential for a new kind of parenting order. It's my belief that we can make things more fair and more successful as we go along, that we can make things better for our children, for our marriages, and for our personal goals and careers. I believe we can do this by replacing the habits and roles of the past with more appropriate solutions. At last, it seems, both men and women are ready for this change.

The Rules Are Changing

The rules of the parenting game are changing. You could even say there aren't rules anymore. More and more, as even the average American family becomes increasingly difficult to define, families are recognizing that it's okay to set their own rules and priorities. One thing is certain: More and more women continue to play a vital role in the workforce and to contribute substantially to the family income. In contrast, however, fathers as a whole don't seem to be pitching in when it comes to child care and housework with nearly the same level of zeal. In fact, too many men have been dragging their feet when it comes to embracing their equal share of child rearing and housework. (I know, of course, that there are many men who are exceptions to this rule, and I'm happy to say I'm one of them.) The first step in changing the rules is to recognize that in most families parenting is not shared equally. Once we've acknowledged the existence of that disparity, we can move toward a solution.

To start, it is important to understand the many ways in which stereotypical parenting roles evolved and why many fathers are still uninvolved or insufficiently involved. How did we get to this point, anyway?

Child Care Has Little to Do with Biology

Keep in mind that mothering and fathering are largely activities created and defined by culture and society, based on gender and biology. Long ago, in the days of the hunter-gatherer society, the men, who were physically larger and stronger than the women, were the ones who wrestled and killed large animals for food. That's not quite the same kind of work as being a systems analyst or bank teller or lab technician; in the majority of today's occupations, physical prowess is not a key qualification. As the centuries passed into agrarian and then industrial societies, women were stuck in the nurturer-only role, and their intellect, creativity, inventiveness, resourcefulness, or other special skills or knowledge were never seen as qualifiers for employment in the work world. Society just perpetuated the stereotypes—first physical, then intellectual—and continued to issue the message that fathers should work and mothers should stay home with the children.

But beyond childbirth and breastfeeding, many of the roles we play as parents have virtually nothing to do with our biological makeup. Anyone can give a child a bath or a bottle, change a diaper, read a story, take him or her to the park or a children's museum, cook a meal, choose a theme for a birthday party, or take a high school junior on a road trip to look at colleges. There is absolutely no ongoing caregiving responsibility that a man can't physically do. There may be emotional, psychological, or societal barriers, but, trust me, those can be overcome. I've worked with thousands of families who started out in a very imbalanced situation and took the initiative to try something new.

I'm reminded of a man who went clothes shopping at a large department store with his three young sons. While there, he ran into several women—mothers of his children's friends—who openly expressed their shock and disapproval that this dad, rather than his wife, was fitting the boys for their back-to-school clothes. What law states, after all, that a dad can't be the one to take his kids to shop for clothes or shoes? The dad in this story was an involved dad; his wife wasn't slapping any stereotypes on him, and she was probably getting some important work done at home or in the office or, hopefully, relaxing with her feet up or playing tennis with three other moms!

We Need to Stop Blaming Mothers for Everything

Unfortunately, it is all too common for the mother to be blamed when a child has problems, when a child grows up insecure or displays delinquent behavior. To me that's just another distorted aspect of how society puts exorbitant pressure on moms. The psychologist Diane Eyer critiques what is referred to as attachment theory, which she says places too much emphasis on the mother-child bond. (Other critics of the attachment theory include Jerome Kagan, a Harvard child psychologist, who asserts that inborn temperament has as much if not more to do with how a child turns out as the maternal relationship.) While nobody questions that infants learn trust and self-comfort through trusting and comforting primary relationships, Eyer argues that attachment theory detracts from society's shared responsibility for its influence on shaping happy, healthy children. While Eyer focuses on the many facets of the outside world that influence children—including food, music, TV, and school—I think that a logical starting point is to look at attachment theory as *a shared responsibility* between mother and father toward the child. If the "village" gets positively involved, too, so much the better.

Before we do anything, we need to remove blame from the picture and see families as working systems to which all members contribute positive and not-so-positive qualities. Working mothers, stay-at-home mothers, mothers whose children are in preschool or day care, divorced mothers, mothers whose children have a nanny, or single mothers who are raising their children alone are all too often the object of blame (and behind blame rears the ugly head of guilt). It is important that we let go of blame and move on to learn how to balance the responsibilities of children's development more equally between mothers and fathers.

Look at Your Own Childhood

Think back to your own upbringing. If you grew up in the fifties, the sixties, or even the seventies, how involved was your father in your daily life? Was he nearly as involved as your mother? Can you name any activities he did with you on a *daily* basis? What particular memories do you have of him in a fathering role?

Chances are you'll have memories of your father rushing out the door on his way to work or coming home and heading straight for the dinner table. But do you also have memories of him taking you to the park, folding the laundry, cooking dinner, or having a "day out with Dad" while your mom pursued her own career or outside interests? Many of today's parents grew up in a world in which fathers weren't really around much. Dad may have done minor repairs around the house or played ball with the kids after dinner, but on a daily basis he didn't have much input into child care and family management. In many households, this still holds true.

If you look back at your childhood and see this kind of scene, remember: That was then, this is now. Today we know that it's better for everyone—kids, moms, and fathers—when dads are more active in family life. Society's expectations of fatherhood are changing, but, of course, change rarely comes without struggle. Unfortunately, the role models that shaped today's fathers were different from those we have in today's world, a world in which we continue to gain more and more knowledge about how involved fathers influence a child's future success and happiness. Let's take a look at how two fathers have reacted to being raised by "traditional" fathers:

Sam, a thirty-five-year-old construction worker, followed in his father's footsteps. Sam's father retired after forty-two years with the same construction company and died a year later. Like his father, Sam worked six days a week. Sunday was his day of rest, but rather than spending time with his family, he used his one day off to relax. During the week he expected dinner on the table when he got home at 6 P.M. He rarely changed a diaper or helped his wife with any sort of child care; in fact, he openly admitted that he wondered what his wife did all day as a stay-at-home mother. His three children saw him as a distant man whom they feared and respected but didn't know very well.

Sam and his wife came to see me because their marriage was in trouble. Not surprisingly, Sam's wife wanted her husband to be more involved in family life. Though Sam didn't really agree that he should be more involved, he was willing to make some small compromises to improve the couple's relationship because he did love his wife. However, his own father had modeled a distant, hardworking role, and it was difficult for Sam to accept change.

Andrew, another client in his early forties, had also been raised by a "traditional" father, but he didn't want to be anything like his dad. When he came to see me, his wife was pregnant with their first baby. He said he wanted to be more involved with his child from the very beginning, but he didn't know how to go about it.

I came to learn that because Andrew's own father had been nearly invisible to him when he was a child, Andrew felt hesitant about his own capabilities as a father. When I explained to him that he could be involved with his baby from the very start, he seemed surprised yet genuinely committed. Like my story about Eric, the new father earlier in this chapter, Andrew also began by joining his wife in reading books about pregnancy, childbirth, and infancy. What was different in Andrew's case, though, is that he shared his feelings with his wife, and they spent lots of time discussing how Andrew could take an active part both before and after the baby was born. Andrew was a carpenter and came up with the idea that he would design and build a custom bureau/changing table/shelving unit along one short wall of the nursery, indicating a bona fide commitment to that child even before the baby was born. In addition to being present at the birth, Andrew was a hands-on father right away—changing diapers, cradling his newborn through many a crying spell—and when the baby was four weeks old, he started taking on at least one of the night feedings with a bottle of expressed breast milk. Having made this connection with his baby from the start, Andrew continued to be emotionally and physically "there" for his wife and child.

These two examples reveal how our past experiences—how we ourselves were parented—can work either to perpetuate the dated roles with which we grew up or to motivate us to do things differently. While Sam had no inclination to question his father's style, and indeed intended to emulate him with his own children, Andrew reacted to his uninvolved father in an entirely opposite way.

Let's also consider the family in which the mother may have grown up thinking that it would be her primary job to take care of the kids. Maybe her mother always watched the children while her dad worked, always made a big dinner on Sunday night, or insisted on making all the kids' Halloween costumes. Maybe her reason for dominating the domestic scene was that she agreed with society's placing the responsibility of child care on females, and while she would have welcomed some help, she felt doing so would make it look as if she was shirking her responsibility. A woman also brings her own personal history to a marriage and to her perception of how a mother and father should behave.

Who Works and Who Stays at Home (If Anyone)

Along with our past experience, we need to consider how economics affects the decisions we make as parents. One of the questions I ask fathers in my parenting seminars is "How did you decide who would stay home with your baby and for how long? Was it a financial decision or a philosophical decision?" Deciding who works and who stays at home, or if both parents will continue to work after the mom's maternity leave, can set a precedent for how balanced the parenting will be. It is a decision best made by the father and mother *together* after careful consideration of a number of factors, including finances, dedication to and philosophy about work, dedication to and feelings about children's needs and child development, whether one parent may wish to start a new, different career from home or telecommute part-time, and so on. When just one parent drives the decision, resentment may not show up right away, but it will surface sometime. I'll discuss how to make this decision in the most emotionally healthy way in chapter 5, but for now, let's look at how who stays at home and who works can affect the balance of parenting in the family.

The economic picture has changed dramatically in the last twenty years. Dual-career couples are now the norm rather than the exception, and many families make the decision to place infants and young children in some form of child care. (Indeed, most of the working women I know say finding a loving, supportive day care arrangement is one of the biggest challenges about working, but once found, it enables them to pursue their careers without anxiety, knowing their children are being loved and nurtured by competent, caring adults. I'll talk more about day care issues in chapter 5.) In addition to working for the income alone, most men and women work to fulfill personal and intellectual goals, and because they love what they do. Working shows our children that we are important, integral parts of our community, that we contribute not only to the family finances but to the day-to-day operations of a larger world outside the home.

Many working women feel strongly about wanting their children to see that Mom is smart, capable, accomplished, and can contribute in lots of ways to the family. In order to be a successful working mother, it's crucial that a woman has an involved husband who has some flexibility at his own work and that she, too, has flexibility at her own job. For parents who both have careers, the balancing issue is particularly intricate and challenging.

For the mother (or father) who stays home to care for the kids while their spouse goes into the working world, the balancing issues are different—though no less critical. The stay-at-home parent needs relief and support, as does the working parent. Each and every family needs to establish a support system; maintaining the system fairly and successfully takes some real effort on the part of both parents.

In a growing number of households, some parents solve the problem of who works and who stays home by dividing their work and child care right down the middle. For example, in many households in which one or both parents do shift work (such as working for a hospital, motor vehicle manufacturer, food processing plant, or restaurant), Mom may work during the day while Dad watches the children, and Dad works at night. Or vice versa. I call this "tag-team parenting." In these cases, the time spent with children may be fairly divided, but other pressures take their toll. When do the families spend time together? When do the couples spend time alone? When do Mom and Dad get to interact as parents with their children? While in a very real sense each parent does his or her fair share, the drawbacks come into play in terms of couple time, "downtime," and family time.

With flextime, telecommuting, on-site day care, and other advancements in the workplace, the picture continues to change in a positive manner. For example, the Bureau of Labor Statistics reported that in 1997, 27.6 percent of employees had flexible work schedules (compared with 15.1 percent in 1991); by the year 2000 that percentage is projected to increase to 31.7 percent. It is wonderful when working couples can take advantage of these options, for they really have helped solve many families' balancing issues. Some working parents, unfortunately, do not take advantage of these options. For example, some fathers opt not to take leave time granted by the Family Leave Act because of fear of subtle or indirect reprisal from superiors or disapproval from colleagues.

Other working parents do not work for companies or organizations that have such options. I am reminded of a wonderful story I saw in the Metropolitan Diary section of *The New York Times,* which reprinted a letter a six-year-old girl wrote to her father's company. The little girl addressed the letter to no one in particular, but the mailroom opened the letter and, seeing who had signed it, routed it to the girl's father. It read: "Dear People who work with my Dad, I don't think it's fair that my Dad has to work on the weekends. Could you please pick a good job for him so he doesn't have to work on the weekends, please. If you could I will give you 10 dollars."

It is important that employees who work for companies that don't offer family-friendly policies push for the working world to grow along with the changing needs of families. Many employers have yet to make family-friendly options available, despite research which shows that workers would be happier and more productive if they did and that companies actually save money from such programs by way of reduced sick leave and lower turnover. The Families and Work Institute in New York recently surveyed three thousand American workers and found that those with more control over their schedules are more productive and more loyal. Another study conducted by researchers at the University of Miami and published in the *Journal of Organizational Behavior* arrived at similar conclusions. A study conducted by Boston College's Center for Work and Family found that smaller, entrepreneurial companies are touting their family-friendly policies to attract and keep top talent. And a recent front-page article in the *National Law Journal* focused on how law firms are trying to reduce turnover in the ranks by offering associates paternity leave. Increasingly, men and women are giving employers the message that they want to be "whole" people, that they are not only workers but also parents whose children need to be supported not only financially but also emotionally, socially, intellectually, and physically by active, consistent parental involvement. Employers, I say, please hear this message.

When Work Takes Over

For the most part I see that while fathers and mothers who work full-time may see less of their children, they make a careful effort to prioritize their time away from work for their children. They make sure that the time spent with their children is focused and meaningful—even if that just means hanging around the backyard for a whole Saturday or reading stories or working on projects together instead of watching TV. Many working parents I know make a tremendous number of sacrifices (for example, filling lunch hours with errands and grocery shopping) in order to spend time outside of work with their children.

On the other hand, I also see a lot of parents who feel that they must both work full-time—and even overtime—not to make ends meet or to attain important professional or personal goals but to get ahead socially, to keep up with the Joneses, or to show their own parents or peers just how "successful" they are. These are parents who are doing better financially than many couples, yet for some reason they feel compelled to keep searching for more in terms of financial reward, at the expense of their families. Some of these couples may find their balancing issues skewed to the point where neither parent is involved enough with the children. These are couples that need to take a look at identifying changes they can make that will accommodate work but also increase their personal time with their families.

Here is an example of a couple whose family time had been completely overshadowed by their working lives.

Joe and Eileen were two successful attorneys who were totally caught up in the rat race and worked strenuous hours in a prestigious law firm. Their two-year-old son, Billy, was experiencing problems. He wouldn't go to sleep at night, awakened often, and seemed to be afraid that he'd be left alone. Billy was with his babysitter from seven in the morning to seven or eight at night; he rarely saw his parents.

When Joe and Eileen came to see me, they were fighting a lot, and in front of Billy. They were both shaken and strung-out and felt that their work lives had gotten out of control. Eileen found herself snapping at the babysitter—and realized her anger was coming from not feeling more connected to her son. Joe saw the problems going on but just didn't feel he had any options at work to make a change. We discussed their priorities and the direction they wanted their family to take, and they came to the conclusion that Billy and any future children they might have really needed their attention a whole lot more than the high-pressured law firm. Eileen decided to get a job at a different law firm, and by networking with other women lawyers she knew, found a firm that allowed her to cut back her hours to three days a week, with the understanding that she could increase her hours if she wished once Billy entered school. Joe remained with the same firm but opted to forgo partnership in order to better control the time he could leave work each evening; he remained an attorney but took less of a leadership role. The family even decided to move to a less expensive house to reduce their living expenses.

Many of my clients stumble into the realization that their career choices may not fairly consider their families or that their choices reflect not their own priorities but rather someone else's expectations (an overbearing or overachieving parent or peer pressure, for example). For those clients who are basically happy with the companies they work for, I find that once I tell them about the flextime and telecommuting options other clients of mine have negotiated in their own workplaces, they are often more motivated to ask for the same or similar changes.

Grandparents and Other Family Members Don't Live Nearby Anymore

As recently as the first half of this century, it wasn't unusual to find grandparents living nearby or even in the same home as their children and grandchildren. Aunts, uncles, or cousins might live in the same neighborhood or, at the farthest, the next town over. They would often stop by to babysit or take the children for a while. Today, however, that kind of situation is the exception rather than the rule. Many couples live hundreds of miles away from their relatives—they live in different states, on different coasts, even in different countries. Getting together with grandparents and other relatives often requires a plane trip and complicated planning and scheduling. It's no longer a given that parents can call on family for help when a child unexpectedly comes down with the flu or when someone is needed to babysit after school until Mom or Dad gets home from work.

Without extended family support, the need for balanced

parenting becomes even more pronounced. Couples who can rely on Grandma or Grandpa, an aunt or an uncle nearby to help out with the kids may have an easier time of balancing their family's needs. But the more common picture is that most parents today have the added pressures of going it alone, which is all the more reason that both parents should contribute their equal share to the raising of their children.

Yvonne, the mother of two young children, came to see me. She explained that she felt very anxious and depressed even though, with two healthy kids and a husband she loved, she believed she should be happy. It turned out that her mother, who had been a tremendous help with the kids, had recently moved to Arizona for health reasons and was no longer available. The children's father, Tod, worked a sixty-hour week. He saw no reason to come for therapy. (This, by the way, is a common phenomenon. Often it's the mother who seeks help alone or makes the decision to see the therapist because the child is misbehaving. Rarely do men come to me first or alone to talk about family-related issues; some, however, come to talk about stress or their careers, later realizing that family problems are at the root of their dissatisfaction.)

After talking with Yvonne, it became clear that her loss of personal time due to her mother's departure was creating her feelings of anxiety and depression, and she yearned for more input from her husband in terms of time with the kids. I asked Yvonne to make a list of her needs, and we discovered that time alone—to pursue her own interests, to go out once or twice a week with a girlfriend to a movie, or to join a health club to work out was of great importance to her. Now, because her mother had moved away, Yvonne needed to communicate to her husband that he would have to be more available to his family, which wasn't an easy thing to do since Tod felt things had always run smoothly without his making any adjustments. Yvonne and I talked about how Tod might contribute more time to his family and what Yvonne really needed was a pep talk to help her sort out what she wanted to say to Tod.

Soon afterward, Yvonne told me that Tod was beginning to see that his children and family did need more of his attention, and he made an effort to get home early several nights a week so his wife could have some time to herself. Examining your communication style, exploring ways to become more assertive in verbalizing your needs, and figuring out tactics to avoid arguing about involvement issues—these are the keys to establishing and maintaining a more balanced parenting team in which fathers are involved in the daily lives of their children. Chapter 3 covers this topic in depth.

Some Women Say They Are Tired of Being the "On-Call" Parent

The most universal stressor that my clients who are moms talk about is what I have come to call being the on-call parent. In every family it is typically the mom who is "preordained" or "predetermined" to be the on-call parent, the person who is primarily responsible for the children's care. This is typically never discussed between the two parents, it is just naturally assumed. "I'm always there to care for the kids," I often hear my female clients say. "Even when I'm at work, I'm the one who has arranged day care and picks up the kids from day care. I'm the one who gets called if a child gets sick or something happens at school."

There is a child who attends my summer camp whose parents both work at the same company. The mom is the CEO and the dad is a VP. The primary emergency contact for the child is the mom, so in an emergency if we called the company and both parents were in the same meeting, we would be asking for the mom! In my family, I am the on-call person. If I'm not going to be at home in the afternoon when my kids come home from school, I give them my schedule with phone numbers in case they need to contact me. I'm also the one who buys the paper towels, laundry detergent, and all that; this may seem a minor point, but what I'm saying is that the parent who is *not* the on-call parent makes broad assumptions that "all that stuff, from child care to laundry detergent"—in other words, all the stuff that makes the house tick on a daily basis—is not his or her responsibility.

Everyone agrees that the good side of having an on-call parent is that it gives kids an important sense of trust and comfort. They know that at least one parent will always be there or be able to come quickly if need be. The bad side is that the on-call person—and it's usually the mom—has a tremendous amount of pressure on her because of that role, pressure she must essentially carry twenty-four hours a day. Redefining the on-call role so that the mom does not have to be the default person all the time is one of the first things I work on with couples who are trying to achieve more balanced parenting. What we aim for instead is to have that role "flex" between the two parents. Good communication between spouses helps this process, as does spending time discussing the feelings that go along with being the on-call person. Flexing that role generally frees the mom from any negative feelings she had about being the on-call parent. I will show you how to do this in chapter 4.

Some Women Say They Don't Ask for Help Because They Don't Want to Hear "No"

Many issues can stand in the way of a couple's reaching a balance as parents, and though it seems easy to pin it all on the father (who often takes the attitude that child care issues are the woman's "problem"), that is too simplistic a route to take. While I agree that too many men are quick to delegate all child care to their wives, frequently women don't realize that some of the values instilled in them by society contribute to the situation. When I hear a mother say she doesn't ask her husband for help because she doesn't want to hear "no," more often than not what she means is she doesn't know *what* to say to ask for help, *how* to say it, and *when* the best time would be to bring up such discussions with her spouse.

A woman may feel as though parenting is her job first and her husband's second; this is what society has told her. The fact is, raising the children is the responsibility of both parents, and society is moving more and more toward reassessing outdated concepts. A mother no longer needs to feel that parenting is her responsibility alone, and she needn't feel guilty about wanting a fair share of input and assistance from her mate. All the research points to the fact that it's better for everyone in the family if Dad is equally involved.

Some Women Say They Feel They Don't Deserve to Ask for Help

Some women may feel that they *should* be able to do everything. The media and our society in general have perpetuated this idea that moms can handle it all, and many of them try to do just that. One of my clients told me that she didn't like to ask her husband to give the kids a bath or to read them a story because he worked so hard all day as a mechanic. Maybe he *was* able to rest on the couch and watch TV at the end of the day, but he missed out on those close bedtime moments with his children—and his wife missed out on valuable downtime. Perhaps this mom felt she shouldn't want to share these responsibilities. Or perhaps she really had the misguided perception that Dad couldn't possibly muster up the energy to read a story at the end of the day (even though she, a teacher, managed to do it).

In my studies of stay-at-home fathers who act as primary caregivers for their children, I found that when working moms come home, they pitch right in with making dinner and child care. So why do women think they can't ask the same of working husbands? Chances are Mom has had just as hard a day—whether she watched the children at home or worked at a job outside the home.

I'm not pointing any fingers here; we're all guilty of these kinds of behaviors. To be honest, during the summer when I run a summer day camp for two hundred kids, my wife and children really bend over backward to let me relax after work. Of course, my wife, a hospital administrator, has been working all day, too—managing people and projects, budgeting, communicating with different departments, taking on all sorts of serious responsibilities. Yet she comes home and dives right into our domestic chores while I'm allowed to take it easy after a day supervising camp staff. One morning she asked me, "Why is it that you get so tired in the summer from working all day, and I'm not supposed to get tired even though I work full-time outside the home all year round?" I realized I had played into that "poor me" syndrome that some working males seem to savor.

Some Women Fear They'll Lose Their Connection to Their Children If They Ask for Help

A lot of women really want their husbands to be more involved with the children but hold back because a part of them believes that if their wish comes true, they might also lose their connection to their children. In some extreme cases they even fear they will lose their children's love.

Marvin, an electrical engineer, and Angela, a human resources consultant, had one daughter, Eliza, who was a sophomore in college. A big issue in their marriage had arisen when Eliza went off to school. Marvin complained that when their daughter called from college and he answered the phone, Angela immediately yanked the receiver away. On the other hand, Angela complained that Marvin didn't care about Eliza now that she was away at school. For a long time Marvin shrugged off the situation, saying, "Well, I'm not a phone person anyway," and seemed convinced that Eliza just wanted to talk to her mother.

It turns out that Angela was worried that if Marvin talked to Eliza on the phone, Angela would lose her strong connection to her daughter, as if the umbilical cord had been replaced by the phone cord. Then, during one counseling session, Marvin revealed that for years he had felt left out and jealous that the two females seemed to converse so easily. It also turned out that Angela assumed Marvin didn't like talking on the phone when in fact that was untrue. It's just that he hadn't been given the chance to practice. I tried to help Angela understand that it was counterproductive to complain that her husband wasn't involved in their daughter's life and then prevent him from talking on the phone to her.

I encouraged her to let Marvin talk to their daughter for at least five minutes if he answered the phone when she called, and I then asked Marvin to make sure he passed the phone on to his wife when he felt his conversation was finished. When he looked at me blankly and said, "I'm afraid I won't know what to talk about," I suggested that he ask his daughter just one open-ended question about school or share one piece of family news. That way he didn't have to talk for a long time, and his daughter would feel that she was getting attention from her father. Over time, father and daughter had longer conversations and the awkwardness was gone. Angela gradually let go of her power play and admitted to enjoying Marvin's replay of his conversations with their daughter.

I'm not in competition with my wife; marriage isn't a tennis match. For example, my ten-year-old daughter recently told me point-blank that my wife is her best friend. She also once said to a reporter who was doing a story on me and interviewed both my kids, "My Dad's on the phone a lot. I can't wait for my mom to get home." These comments don't bother me; I'm not jealous, even though I'm the one who has been at home as the primary caregiver for the past eight years. I think it's great that my wife and daughter have this singular bond, and there is no reason to feel threatened by what is probably a very healthy attachment on my daughter's part. I'm not competing with my wife over which one of us our kids like better; we're both doing our part to raise the children. But many women (and men, too) may fear that the preferred parent of the day is the one who is more loved by the child. That should be a red flag for a parent whose identity is perhaps a little too caught up in competitive issues. When I have a client who feels threatened by the idea of her husband, say, taking the child to the movies without her, very often the best progress is achieved when we spend time looking at how she defines her own self-worth, how she shapes her identity, and how she can work to build up her self-esteem and identity through avenues that don't include only her children.

Some Women Say They Feel Guilty If They Ask for Help

Guilt can also be an issue, particularly when it comes to tasks that are traditionally associated with females. One mom, a freelance technical writer who worked out of her home office, said she felt horrible when she sent her husband shopping for her child's birthday presents, even though she was working and he was free. She was certain he could locate and pay for the items they'd agreed on just as well as she, but nevertheless this mom fretted all afternoon about whether she should have taken the day off and gone to the toy store herself. It just didn't seem, she said, that a "good mother" wouldn't shop for her child's birthday—but at the same time she found it perfectly acceptable for a father to leave this task up to his wife! Letting go of guilt is not only personally liberating, it also does wonders for a father's sense of competence with and enjoyment of his children.

Some Men Say Child Care Emasculates Them

I've spent a lot of time talking about the reasons some women have difficulty asking for more involvement from their husbands. Men, too, have issues that create obstacles to fair-share parenting. There are plenty of fathers who aren't willing to take on the child-related tasks women have shouldered for years. These are the guys who still think feeding, bathing, driving the kids to lessons, and so forth are somehow emasculating. One father I know refused outright to accompany his young son to a friend's birthday party, so the mom, who had to be somewhere else at that appointed hour while her husband was at home, was forced to find another mother to accompany her child.

In certain cultures, child care is definitely considered women's work. But American culture is such an evolving mix of values and customs that we need to find a perspective suitable for contemporary families. A man in one of my parenting workshops told me that his brothers would be horrified if he were more involved with the kids. Dads like these are missing out on the rewards of fatherhood. When parents make involvement decisions based on what is best for their immediate family, they can begin to override cultural rules that have a limited place in today's households. After all, this man needed to support his own wife and children first and foremost—not answer to his brothers, his great-grandmother, or his cousins.

Some Men Say They Think Work Is Easier Than Being at Home

Most of us know more than a few dads who secretly believe their work is "easier" than involvement at home. So they stay late at the office or work weekends to avoid helping out with the family, using the excuse, "Hey, *somebody* has to make the money!" Certainly, plenty of men work hard and would love to be home enjoying their kids if they could. But others spend a lot of time creating more work for themselves at the office in order to avoid their homes because they don't really know how to deal with domestic life.

Allan, a cameraman at a network TV station, refused to have dinner with his family because he knew his two kids, ages six and nine, would misbehave. Even though he had a scheduled dinner break in between the early evening and late news and lived only ten minutes from the studio, he often ate out alone or with a colleague. On the rare occasions when he did show up for dinner, his wife, Joanne, would bombard him with complaints about how hard she had worked that day at the telephone company and how much needed to be done around the house. The children, who rarely saw their father, seemed so stimulated by his presence that they misbehaved.

Why was Allan hiding in his work? The answer, it turned out, was rooted in his failing marriage, not in his fear of helping out at home. It had been so long since Joanne and Allan had had any time alone together, they'd nearly forgotten how to behave or show affection for each other. I suggested that they spend some time together and try to reframe their marriage as closely as possible to the way they were before they had children. In order to repair the damage that had accumulated over the years, this couple needed to step back and spend some time remembering what had brought them together in the first place. Many couples who dig this deeply into their emotional lives find that they really have grown in different directions and do not have much in common anymore— but happily for this couple, time together resulted in a rediscovery of their initial attraction. The kids, thrilled that their parents seemed so happy again, began to behave more appropriately.

Some Men Need to Be Masters

In their offices or places of work, a lot of men are masters; they feel competent and in control in their work environment. At home they feel incompetent or that their role is less clearly defined (and women who work long hours away from home may feel this, too)—and children seem to turn order into chaos with very little effort! Avoiding the home and delegating the child care tasks to a wife or a nanny may be a lot easier than stepping into the fray. It is surprising, though, how many men can very quickly learn to braid their daughter's hair, prepare infant cereal, or come up with a way to pack for the beach in under twenty minutes once they've done it a few times.

When Dads Are Involved on a Daily Basis, Parenting Is More Rewarding—Now and When Your Kids Are Grown

The solution, I believe, to many of the balancing problems in today's families is to bring fathers to a place where they are able to and want to share more equally in not only the demands and responsibilities but also in the joys and rewards of caring for children. Time and time again, in the families I've counseled over the years, I've seen mothers who are depressed, overburdened, and feel as if they are in this child-rearing phase of their lives alone even though they are "happily" married.

If dads put off becoming involved in their kids' lives until, say, the age of seven or eight, when the child can bat a ball well or learn the art of fishing, for instance, they're missing out on so much. They may also be disappointed to find their kids are not all that interested in "dad time" since the dads weren't involved from the very beginning. When my kids leave for school in the morning, I want to feel that I've done my best to be part of their lives, to live my life as a parent to the fullest. I don't want to look back and know that I've missed these years with my children.

I've been greatly impressed by the work of Elisabeth Kübler-Ross, who pioneered much of our understanding of death and the way people die in our society. Working with the dying, Kübler-Ross discovered that regret was a common theme in individuals who hadn't lived their lives fully. I'd like to apply that principal to parenting: In order to make the most of our years as parents, we need to experience and enjoy them with our children. We can choose to be the kind of parents we want to be, and we can choose to participate in our children's lives. But I know all too well how imbalance in a household can wreak emotional havoc—on the spouse who feels she's handling too much on her own and on the children who miss out on the benefits of having a mom and a dad involved in their lives on a daily basis.

As parents we need to focus on enjoying and making the most of the here and now, on making sure that we don't let those years with our children slip by unattended. If we choose to be involved in our children's lives and make a commitment to setting aright any imbalance we have, these are the years we'll look back on with satisfaction. We won't feel regret because we'll know that we have made the best choices we could have made, whatever our circumstances. One of the most moving stories Kübler-Ross tells is of the dying man who looks back on his life as a renowned physician with sadness. How can that be, he is asked, when he saved so many lives and did such important work? Yes, the man answers, but it wasn't the work he really wanted to do. He'd gone into the medical field because his parents had expected it of him, not because he truly aspired to become a physician.

One common error that parents make is to label normal, everyday tasks as drudgery. I don't see bedtime or bathtime routines that way, and really, in just about anything you do with kids, you can have a good time—if you want to. I try to make everything fun when I'm with my kids. A trip to the store, reading, talking before bedtime—these aren't grueling tasks. When I take my son to hockey practice three times a week, I love to watch the kids skate. I get a big charge out of their energy and enjoyment and the determination they have to get better every time. But most of the parents I strike up conversations with at the rink complain about what a pain it is to take their kids to practice so often, or they have their heads buried in the newspaper until practice is over. They really do look at it as drudgery.

A friend of mine once told me that he used to dread bathtime with his three-year-old—not because his son was a problem at bathtime but because he thought it was a bore. He used to read the paper sitting on the floor of the bathroom while his son splashed and played. One day his son said, "Daddy, can I wash your hands?" My friend grudgingly put down his paper and laid his hands on the edge of the tub. His son made an elaborate game of sudsing them up with lots of bubbles and babbled little songs. He said, "Daddy, does that feel clean?" Before he knew it, my friend was completely drawn into the moment, forgot what he had been reading about, and, in the process fell totally in love with his son all over again. The handwashing ritual carried on for weeks, with father and son making up all sorts of games and songs.

If you convey that you are having fun and relax and enjoy yourself, and add a sense of spontaneity or creativity to every day, your kids will pick up on that and naturally mirror that sense of fun. If you don't, your kids will pick up on that, too. And most parents, I believe, will agree with me once they find out how rewarding being with their own children really is.

From the work I have done with parents of grown children, I know that we don't want to be thinking one day, many years hence, of what we might have done or should have done with our children. This is our chance to parent the way we want to. I can say without a doubt that if you have imbalance in your marriage with respect to caring for the children, there are many different solutions I can share with you. Some will be right for you, and others you may decide are not.

Making Everything Fifty-Fifty Is Not the Goal Here

When fathers are as involved as their spouses in their children's daily lives, that doesn't mean all the responsibilities and duties regarding their kids must be split fifty-fifty like a non-negotiable contract. Perhaps fifty-fifty sounds fair in theory, but it is definitely not a realistic goal for most families. More likely one parent does work longer hours or leaves in the early morning for a commute and isn't available during the morning, or maybe one parent really feels stressed at the children's bedtime and doesn't want to take that on. A good goal is achieving a logical, balanced use of both parents' available time and an equitable compromise of personal preferences. As long as a child is getting a fair balance of involvement from his mother and his father, and is forming and strengthening attachments to both, and Mom *and* Dad feel comfortable with the arrangement, that's balance.

But when Mom (or Dad) has shouldered 90 percent of the care and the other parent is excluded from both the fun and the work of parenting, changes need to be made to bring the parenting partnership into a more balanced alliance. I plan to show you how this can be achieved, even when one parent (usually Dad) seems reluctant or unable to do his fair share. I've filled this book with lots and lots of practical tips that you can start doing right away, tips and strategies that will help you and your spouse achieve fair-share parenting in these and many other areas of child care—even when you feel the effort is against all odds:

- the dreaded "second shift," including mealtime, bathtime, and bedtime routines

- morning routines

- finding and managing day care routines

- homework

- negotiating downtime with your spouse

- handling stressful schedules

- what to do when one spouse travels a lot

- shopping and errands

- communicating with your spouse

- divvying up housework fairly

- weekend activities

Balanced Parenting Lets—and Insists That—Men Be Nurturers, Too

A key goal of equal-balance parenting is to bring men more clearly into the picture as nurturers. There is absolutely no evidence that men can't nurture children just as well as women. In my research, in my practice, at my parenting seminars, and even at the camp I run in the summers, I have found that fathers who let themselves be nurturers are happier, more understanding, more pleasant to be with, more flexible, more in tune with their wives' and children's needs, and better communicators than men who refuse to nurture. They say that sharing a new picture book with their children, helping them feel better after a spill on the playground, seeing them eat a whole meal they've made for them, or comforting them after a bad dream is more rewarding than almost anything else they do.

Watch Out for the Band-Aid Approach

Too many couples make the mistake of using a quick-fix solution that doesn't really resolve the underlying issues or change old behavior patterns. I call it the Band-Aid approach. Instead of sitting down to really discuss and work out a problem, they slap on a Band-Aid, something they can do right away and quickly, but it won't really help all that much in the long run. Eventually the problem will resurface. Watch what the Band-Aid approach looks like:

Candace and Arturo both worked outside the home, but Arturo worked only part-time. Since their seven-year-old daughter, June, was in school, he had plenty of opportunity to pursue his interests in music and computers. But Candace never seemed to have any time to herself; between her full-time work as a teacher, her volunteer work, and care for June at night, she never seemed to have a moment's rest. As a result, she was growing increasingly resentful and dissatisfied with her marriage, but whenever she mentioned to Arturo that she'd like to get out or have some downtime, he came up with an excuse. Finally, in exasperation, Candace scheduled a three-day weekend for herself with a girlfriend. She packed her suitcase, told Arturo point-blank that she was leaving for three days, and left. Arturo had no choice but to take care of June full-time while his wife was gone. When Candace returned, she felt temporarily refreshed, but Arturo was somewhat hostile. And within a few weeks everything was back to the way it had been before.

The Band-Aid approach (Candace's three-day trip) might have solved the problem temporarily, but it didn't really help matters all that much in the long run. Little had really changed; Arturo still needed to learn that his wife was working overtime while he wasn't doing his fair share. And June, who might have loved to spend her evenings engaged in reading and conversation with her dad, was still missing out on the benefits of a truly involved father.

Here is a family that avoided the Band-Aid approach:

Deana, a stay-at-home mother, had three young, demanding children, all boys. Though her husband had always been very involved with the kids, Deana complained that she never seemed to have any time alone. Karl, a carpenter, was home most nights for dinner, and though Deana had an at-home business that she operated around the family's schedule, she felt that she rarely had a break. She expressed her concerns to Karl, who at first thought that his wife had plenty of time to herself. In looking at her actual schedule, he realized she had a meager amount of time when she wasn't responsible for either work or children. Karl suggested that on Monday evenings, his night off from work, he take the children out for dinner, sort of a "boys night out" for Dad and the kids.

This solution gave Deana a few hours every week when she could read, fix herself a sandwich for dinner, or go out herself, and not have to worry about the family for a while. It also gave Karl and the kids a private ritual they all looked forward to every week. Best of all for Deana, it was an ongoing solution to a common problem; the nagging feeling that most moms have—that they're never really "off duty."

Balanced Involvement Improves Your Relationship as a Couple

Perhaps the most important outcome of balanced parenting is that two parents who are equally involved in the care of their children are closer as a couple. Not only do they have common interests (their children), they also develop better ways of communicating with each other about other topics. As communication opens, couples often find it easier to spend valuable time together and to resolve other issues not directly related to caring for the children.

I always advise parents to get their kids to bed at a reasonable hour. Not only do kids need their sleep in order to stay healthy, grow properly, and do well in school, but parents need private time together as a couple—and it makes sense for most families that this occur in the evenings. Most wives (and probably most husbands if they thought about it) would agree that "You give the bath, I'll do the story, and we'll meet downstairs at nine o'clock" is a better way to be together than "You sack out on the couch while I do everything!"

Involvement in the Daily Lives of Children Improves the Father-Child Relationship

All the research points to the fact that greater father involvement is a positive factor in children's lives that leads to better self-esteem, their doing better in school, enhanced social development, breaking gender stereotypes, and one day becoming better parents themselves. I cover this topic in detail in the next chapter. In chapters 5 through 9 I'll talk about ways fathers can become more involved in children's lives throughout all their ages and stages of development, from infancy into the teen years and beyond. But for now, note that equal-balance parenting helps a father keep a finger on the pulse of his family, thereby enhancing the life of the child and increasing the rewarding feelings that fatherhood should bring.

Equal-Balance Parenting Enhances Family Communication

Not only are Mom and Dad happier in a more equal arrangement but also, based on the families I've seen in my practice, kids really open up when they see that both parents are making an equal effort to know about their lives each and every day. Especially during the preadolescent and adolescent years, it is essential for children to feel they can talk to their parents and that their parents know how to talk to them in a manner that helps them feel comfortable talking and sharing information. Good parent-child communication can mean the difference between a kid who slips through the cracks and a kid who has the self-confidence and emotional reinforcement at home to rise successfully to the challenges of the teen years and beyond. Indeed, learning how to communicate well in childhood is one of the most important social skills we learn. The ramifications of an emotionally distant or verbally uncommunicative father—or mother, for that matter—often play out in very negative ways after children have grown up and entered into adult relationships and the workplace.

Equal Balance Parenting Lets Moms Become ''Whole'' Again

Many of my female clients complain that they feel not only isolated from their husbands and other adults but that part of them is "missing" or that they've lost their identity. When a mom feels conflicted at work, doesn't get out with friends anymore, has difficulty making a routine medical appointment or treating herself to a day in the city, can't consider taking a course at night or doing some volunteer work, she begins to feel cheated and unfulfilled. This can spell big trouble for a marriage. Some moms compensate for this by getting up at 5 A.M. to read a novel, exercise, or even clean the house. But I don't believe mothers should sacrifice essential sleep in order to get the time alone that they need. When a woman feels "whole" by pursuing outside interests or having enough private time and time with adult friends, she remains the vibrant, multifaceted woman her husband married. In the present, conversation at the dinner table or over an evening cup of coffee is more dynamic and interesting, and doesn't just focus on what the kids did or will be doing. After the kids are grown, the marriage continues to benefit from this dimension.

Equal-Balance Parenting Draws Fathers in Even When They Are Reluctant

In this book I'll teach you how to start small (the biggest goals are best reached in small steps), set interim goals, communicate effectively, identify and get rid of unsuccessful behavior patterns on both your part and your spouse's, and prioritize family objectives— all in order to experience success in having fathers become motivated to be more involved. This can and should happen at a pace and with goals that make sense for both parents and for the family. I invariably find that as a father spends more time with his children, he becomes more competent; as he gains more experience with child care, he feels more confident; as he enjoys his children more (and they him), more likely he'll want to do it all the time.

A father I know nearly lost his son when the boy became gravely ill with pneumonia. While his child was in the hospital, the man realized how uninvolved he had been in his son's life even though he deeply loved him. As his son lay in the hospital bed, this father experienced a revelation of sorts and vowed to be an active part in the boy's life if he recovered. Happily, the boy did get well, and the father followed through on his promise. To this day he recounts how closely he came to losing his only chance to be an active father.

This is a dramatic example of how a man changed when a crisis occurred in his family. Obviously, I'm not suggesting that any man wait until it's nearly too late before becoming a dedicated father. Quite the contrary, I use this example to reveal how important it is to make the most of each day with your child and to encourage fathers to take an active part in their children's lives in an ongoing, consistent manner.

There are many reasons that men are hesitant to become active parents; fear of failure, fear that they aren't really competent, poor role modeling on the part of their own fathers, and fatigue are just a few of the common reasons. In this book you'll find solutions that will help draw fathers more deeply into their families and give them the support and encouragement they need to overcome their feelings of fear and inadequacy.

How in the World Could This Work for *Us*?

If you're a woman whose husband doesn't want to be more involved with the kids or if you're married to a man who doesn't see the need to change, you may be thinking that this isn't possible but is an unattainable fantasy that doesn't exist in the real world. But the truth is, many couples are already living this way, and you can, too.

If a father really wants to be involved in the children's lives on a daily basis but just doesn't know how, a more balanced parenting relationship should come quite naturally with appropriate encouragement and support from his wife. But if your spouse doesn't want to change and thwarts your every effort to make him an active father, don't despair. I'll discuss simple ways to help him step into a more active role.

Let's take a look at a family in which the husband was adamant in his refusal to become more involved.

Helen came to see me because her son, Jimmy, a charming but very boisterous seven-year-old, had attention deficit hyperactivity disorder (ADHD), and although Jimmy was on medication, he was still quite a handful. In the course of meeting with Jimmy each week, I began to talk to Helen, too, and discovered that she was very unhappy with the fact that her husband didn't help out enough at home. Kenneth was a successful salesman and thrived in a competitive environment. His company reinforced his competitive nature by giving out incentives and rewards to those who made the most deals. He was on the phone and meeting with clients every day and most evenings, too. Helen worked from their home as an interior designer, and as she often met with clients in the evenings, accommodating everyone's needs was wreaking havoc.

Helen longed for Kenneth to be more involved in Jimmy's life;

he was a troubled child who consumed a great deal of his mother's energy. She tried very hard to be there for him, but she was understandably overwhelmed. After learning of this problem, I suggested that we begin to identify specific ways for Helen to draw Kenneth gradually into the family. The first tactic we tried was to ask him to meet his wife and child at a restaurant for dinner one or two nights a week so that the family could have a little time together before he went back to his office.

This worked for a few weeks, but then Kenneth began calling to cancel or he'd arrive late and stay for only a few minutes. Next, I suggested to Helen that she try to arrange some father-son outings, both to give Kenneth and Jimmy a chance to spend some much needed time together and to give Helen some much deserved time to herself. Kenneth agreed it was a good idea, and they decided to set up a one-day fishing trip one Saturday and an afternoon at the movies the next week. Kenneth canceled both, coming up with an excuse at the last moment; this angered Helen and deeply disappointed Jimmy.

Truly, Kenneth was not budging in the direction of involvement, but I told Helen to keep trying. I remember when A.J. was about four, she kept coming into our bed in the middle of the night. We kept taking her back to her own bed, and this went on for weeks until my wife finally said in despair, "Are we crazy? Let's just let her sleep here." But that very night, A.J. stayed in her bed, and that was the end of the problem. Sometimes gentle persistence is the best road to take, and I suspected that this was the case with Kenneth.

I encouraged Helen to stick to her plan and not to give up. While she was forthcoming with me about her feelings, I knew what she really needed was to share those feelings with her husband and to figure out a way to have a meaningful discussion with him. Helen kept talking to her husband about how important father involvement is. She clipped articles and brought up the topic at different times when she knew Kenneth was his most relaxed and receptive. She talked to him about how she believed it would make a great difference in Jimmy's life if his father could be around more. She loved her husband and wanted this to work without having to nag or complain. She simply kept pointing to the many reasons that involvement would be beneficial. Kenneth listened but didn't respond in any particular way.

One day Kenneth came home for dinner unexpectedly. Helen was surprised, but she noticed he had been talking less and less about work, and seemed to be more interested in how things were going with Jimmy at school. Before long he had stopped working five nights a week. He cut his nights at the office down to two a week and began to take Jimmy on some outings. Because Kenneth was naturally competitive, he found that he actually enjoyed watching Jimmy play soccer, and he volunteered to take him to some baseball games as well. Jimmy had interests that he could share with his dad, and Kenneth began to feel increasingly comfortable around his son. Helen was thrilled that things seemed to be working out for her family. She continued to talk about involvement with Kenneth and to find ways to draw him more equally into the parenting partnership. As he spent more time with his son, Kenneth became a better and better father.

This case was difficult, but the effort spent was well worth it for both parents and child. When two partners are committed to each other, obstacles can be overcome; it's just that it doesn't happen in the "quick-fix" manner our society is so accustomed to. Communication, persistence, patience, hard work, and understanding are all key elements in the process of balancing the inequities in any parenting relationship, as they are in reaching any important, valuable goal such as getting your dream job or losing weight. Helen and Kenneth's story is a realistic one in which a more equitable balance was reached gradually.

What Does Fair-Share Parenting Look Like?

What might your life look like if equal parenting was a reality in your household? Here are some of the components that I discuss in subsequent chapters. These are goals to strive for in your family, too:

- Both parents feel equally connected to their parenting roles; neither feels as if she or he is in this parenting thing alone.

- Parenting is experienced as teamwork, not as a competition. Neither parent feels jealous or as if power has been usurped if the other helps with child care responsibilities such as making meals, bathing, or dressing.

- Time at work feels productive and meaningful, as does time at home. Neither parent feels as if he or she is working harder than ever and not really getting anywhere.

- Parents respect and appreciate one another. Resentment is diminished or nonexistent because help is willingly offered by each spouse on a consistent basis.

- Parents communicate their needs to one another clearly and without guilt or fear.

- Both parents enjoy parenting and don't feel deprived of support from the other.

- Both parents agree on what equal-balance parenting means for their family.

- Each parent is able to pursue his or her career and interests without resentment from the other partner.

- Both Mom and Dad are confident that they're living their lives as parents to the fullest and that their children are reaping the benefits of having two actively involved and committed parents.

Why Is Daily

Involvement Such an

Important Issue?

O CCASIONALLY, MOTHERS AND fathers who sit down to discuss what involvement means to their family pretty much have the same idea of what both Mom and Dad should be doing. But more often the case is not so clear-cut. A woman may think her husband could be doing a great deal more, while Dad feels he's a lot more involved than many of the fathers he knows personally or observes in his neighborhood or community.

Jason and Anne came to meet with me because they were experiencing a great deal of conflict regarding their parenting roles. Jason was completely dismayed by Anne's expression of dissatisfaction. As basketball coach for his nine-year-old's team, he went to practice with his son two nights a week and to all the weekend games, and even coached the traveling team. In his opinion he was doing more than his fair share and was maintaining an active working life as a computer technician. However, when Anne revealed that Joey wanted to sign up for a nature class and an art course when basketball season ended, Jason refused to accompany him. Insistent that this was "not a male thing," he was so offended by the request that he threatened to quit coaching basketball. Anne explained that she wanted her husband to be involved in Joey's other extracurricular interests, not just sports. But Jason felt he was already doing far more than most dads he knew; that, to him, was enough.

In our sessions we talked about some of the positive outcomes of fathers being involved in a variety of activities with their children, and knowing Jason was interested in "facts," I also discussed research confirming fathers can do nurturing-oriented activities just as well as mothers. I suggested that Jason try doing one or two nonsports activities with Joey. Though he initially balked at the idea, when I explained the message he was giving his son—that if he didn't play basketball, he wouldn't merit his father's attention—Jason was stunned and even sorry. Though Jason admitted he loved sports and really hoped Joey would pursue basketball as he grew older, he didn't intend to convey the message that he'd only pay attention to his son if he played sports. Jason agreed to go with Joey to the nature class and to be responsible for overseeing Joey's bedtime routine, including reading a chapter each night of a book of Joey's choice.

Anne, a pediatric nurse, still felt she had more responsibilities than Jason, but she was very happy that her husband had made these steps. In sessions with Anne alone, I talked with her about setting interim goals to bring the balance closer to her ideal (I include a discussion about setting goals in chapter 4). I asked Anne to make a list of three things she wished her husband would do more of. She replied instantly: cooking, cleaning, and grocery shopping. I encouraged her to pick just one of the three and ask Jason to take on partial responsibility for that area. After several weeks, during which Anne often expressed to Jason how happy she was that he was getting involved with Joey in different ways, she broached the subject of cooking. She expressed to Jason that it would be a great relief to her not to have to think about dinner twice during the workweek. She said she didn't care if Jason cooked or bought take-out. Her approach worked. While Jason did purchase a lot of take-out, he and Joey learned some outdoor cooking shortcuts in his nature class and tried them at home on Jason's night to cook. The family began to define what involvement really meant, and Jason made the vital discovery that his idea of involvement had been very different from his wife's.

Define What Involvement Means to You as a Couple

Before we can work toward helping fathers become more involved with their children and families, each couple needs to decide for themselves what involvement means to them. Some partners will be amazed at how differently they look at this question, but that doesn't mean a compromise can't be reached.

Although I've geared this discussion toward married couples, I'd like to point out that increased father involvement is of vital concern to divorced couples as well. All the research points to the fact that children do better when they receive positive, consistent attention and love from *both* parents. Though my discussion is primarily directed toward families with married spouses, many of these principles can be applied by divorced couples as well, as long as they agree that both will do their best (even when living apart and moving on with other parts of their personal lives) to stay actively and mutually supportive of their children.

Involvement Can Mean Different Things in Different Families

Why is involvement such a controversial subject, and why isn't its definition clear to everyone? The answer is as complex as each family structure, and that's why couples must proactively discuss their family's needs. The father who commutes to work may be routinely gone so many hours that daily involvement is nearly impossible. If that's the case, then the parents need to focus on how time for the kids can be built into the weekends. That family's definition of involvement is going to differ greatly from a dual-career couple who both work locally or a couple in which one parent works out of the home. Regardless of the time structure, another part of the definition of involvement is what exactly goes on while fathers and their children spend time together. Let's take a look at how two fathers who spend a comparable amount of time with their kids can differ widely in their approach and attitude.

Scott, a father who is very involved with his two children, really looks forward to Saturday afternoons and the two nights a week when he takes care of Max and Helene, who are now three and six. His wife, who is going back to school to get her master's degree, attends a three-hour class on Saturdays and uses the two weeknights to go to the library and study. Scott takes his responsibilities as a father very seriously, yet he wants to have fun with his kids, too. He plans activities for Saturday afternoons and discusses them with the kids in advance to get input on what they might want to do. Max and Helene are thrilled to spend the afternoon with their dad, and they know they'll be included in the plans even if they decide to rent a video and curl up on the couch together. During the weeknights when he is in charge, Scott makes dinner for the kids, gives them their baths, reads to them, or plays board games. Though he doesn't spend as many hours with his children as his wife does, he is an actively involved dad who takes his role to heart.

Ted, a jazz musician, works irregular hours, and he's home with the children quite a bit while his wife, a teacher, works. When he has a rehearsal, he drops the kids at family day care where they're cared for by a loving middle-aged mother of three whose own children are in high school, and his wife picks them up on her way home. Ted considers himself an involved father since he spends at least three mornings a week with his two children, ages two and four, and he's often home on Sunday afternoons as well. During the week, the kids watch TV or color while he sets up jobs on the phone, and by the time his wife, Heather, gets home from work, the house is usually a mess, which she cleans up after Ted leaves for his evening gig. On Sundays when Heather goes to visit her mother, who is in the hospital with a serious illness, Ted takes care of the kids again. Usually, the kids play outside in the yard on their slide and swing set while Ted practices his saxophone.

Both Scott and Ted consider themselves involved fathers, but the difference is that Scott approaches his role with a positive outlook while Ted is simply trying to get through the hours. Hour for hour, both fathers spend about the same amount of time with their children, but Scott is engaged in activities such as reading and playing games, and he also plans special activities for Saturdays that the kids look forward to; it's their time with dad. Ted is in the same house with his children but doesn't pay much attention to them other than to be sure they are safe and fed, and he never discusses what they might all do together for fun. While Anne feels that her husband is doing his fair share, Heather comes home to find the house a pigpen and the kids listless and irritable. As a result, even though her husband is physically present, Heather doesn't feel as if he is actively involved—and neither do the children.

When discussing what involvement means, it is important for couples to really dig deeply into these issues. How can dads take their role more seriously and use the time spent with the children to really enhance the relationship? Obviously, there are times when we all "zone out" around our children (we'd probably go crazy if we didn't), and my kids often accuse me of talking on the phone too much or burying my head in a book when I'm around the house. We can't always be racing off to the zoo or going to the movies—I certainly don't advocate planning every minute with your children. Spontaneity counts, as does quiet play. Chores, too, have to be done around the house, whether Dad or Mom is in charge. When parents include children in household tasks, they can become learning experiences and help children understand that it takes a team to run a house.

Nevertheless, active dads approach child care in ways that are vastly different from dads who just want to do the "bare bones." The involved father has the emotional maturity to realize that his attitude and actions have a deep effect on his children; if they are old enough, he talks to the children about what they want to do (or, with an infant, decides for himself where they might go, such as running errands or taking the stroller to the park, or what toys they might play with on the floor if they stay indoors). He prepares for the day, looks forward to it and makes the most of the time with his kids, and pays attention to the children. This isn't to say that he isn't sometimes distracted, bored, or tired. All parents wax and wane in energy and attention level, but in general the involved father relishes and makes the most of his role as a dad.

The uninvolved father, even when he's watching his kids, does the things *he's* interested in (watches a ball game or works on his computer), doesn't discuss activities with the children, doesn't plan anything special for their time together, and basically gets through the time with as little effort as possible.

In order to define what involvement means in a family, couples need to examine how much time fathers spend with the children, what fathers do with the children when they're together, and how fathers feel about their role. A father like Ted who is just getting through the day may indeed love his children but might not understand what involvement really means and why it's so essential to children's growth and development. In my practice I have found that many fathers, either because of their own poor role models or other unconscious or conscious reasons, have not actually stepped back to consider how truly important their role is; they have not thought objectively about the messages they are sending their children. Once I bring up these issues, in the context of child development research and other factors such as the influence of the father's own childhood and how it molded him, they are often better able to look at the situation from their child's or wife's point of view. This process almost always motivates them to make the time with their children more meaningful.

Parenting Play Styles

When we do spend time in a play situation with our children, research shows that mothers and fathers relate very differently to children, and this is to the children's benefit. Several studies have shown how mothers and fathers play differently. Mothers tend to use toys more; fathers, their own bodies as they give horsy rides and roughhouse with toddlers and older children. Research by Robert Moradi, a psychiatrist at UCLA School of Medicine, revealed that men tend to encourage their children to "individuate." They're more willing than mothers to let the child out of their sight and explore new situations while they hang back and observe. Women tend to remain in closer proximity to their children and to move closer when they encounter a new situation. While this type of reassuring presence is important, of course, too much direction, Moradi found, actually prevents some children from gaining independence and learning to entertain—and comfort—themselves.

Mom's Style

In general, moms tend to focus on emotional and personal safety. At the indoor play area of our kids' favorite fast-food restaurant, I've seen Moradi's study results in action. I noticed that moms tend to stay near their youngsters, especially the toddlers, who occasionally fall down while negotiating the slide or ladder.

Dad's Style

Fathers make risk-taking, independence, and physical play their priority. When my kids were younger, I observed at this same restaurant, that the moms quickly reacted to a child's cry, whether the child was really hurt or not, by going right to the child. I also observed that the dads (myself included) didn't always spring up out of their chairs right away. We listened and looked but took more time before making a judgment call. One day when I was having a coffee while the kids played, I heard my son, who was then about four, let out a shriek. I knew from experience, without even turning around to look, that not only was this my son, Kevin, but that the shriek was one of his "fooling around" howls. One of the moms swiftly raced over to me and asked, "Is that your child crying?" She didn't know what I knew and was trying to be helpful. My "nonreaction" came from my own style with and knowledge of my son. I don't know whether she thought I was neglectful, but without really knowing about the many differences in how women and men approach children, I can see how someone might have thought I wasn't tuned in to my kid.

Why Kids Need Both Styles

In general, children benefit from both play styles. From moms they learn that they can live and play in a safe haven and that someone they love is always close and watching out for them. From dads they learn to be independent and unafraid, to take risks and stretch their limits a little bit more each day. This enables a child to explore, discover, and grow in the context of trust and an important, vital safety net. This is how the full breadth of a child's development can be nurtured and challenged at once, to help him develop a strong sense of security, independence, individuality, self-fulfillment, and self-esteem. Having both a mother and a father who work in this unspoken but complementary manner, the child's needs to be safe and secure, as well as to investigate the world around him, get met. It is important for parents to realize that mothers and fathers *do* play differently and that there's nothing wrong with that. We need to work with those differences, not against them.

In many ways I feel as if nature intended moms and dads to play differently so that the child would get the best of both worlds. Interestingly, research studies suggest that dads who are around their children more actually begin to expand their "repertoire" of play styles and are more likely to alternate vigorous physical play with more gentle, quiet play. These men also begin to more readily engage in caretaking activities that are usually the mom's arena—bathing, cuddling, story reading, and so on. The researchers found that men who spent a significant number of hours caring for their children were less inclined than other men to rely on rough-and-tumble play as the primary way of making a connection with their children. This suggests to me that in households where both parents are equally involved in child care, the moms and the dads naturally broaden their own perspective of how they can and might interact with their children. It is great for kids to see that moms will join in pillow fights and dads can also read them their bedtime story. That's how the stereotypes of yesterday can begin to be broken.

The Big Dog Test

When I teach a parenting seminar, I use the "big dog test" to reinforce the idea that there is actually an infinite number of approaches to child care, each of which represents, in a way, the parent's "world view," how he or she approaches the big wide world. I describe the following scenario: You are walking down the street with your toddler and you see a German shepherd with big sharp teeth. You have a number of options for how to react, including (1) instantly running to the other side of the street with your toddler and telling her, "That is a scary dog. We must stay away," (2) confidently approaching the dog and saying to your toddler, "This is a big dog. We're going to walk up to him, but we have to be careful and first ask the owner if it's okay to pet him and say hello," or (3) grabbing your toddler's hand, impulsively running right up to the dog, and affectionately scratching him behind the ears. There are even more options than these, but the point is that each option represents a different approach or style to interacting in the world. The person who avoids the dog altogether might be a mother unconsciously holding her daughter back from trying new experiences or developing the confidence to step in and deal with new situations. The person who rushes over to the dog, smiles, and gives it a big hello might be that woman's husband, who wants to encourage his daughter to do new things and meet new people. Just as likely, though, it might be exactly the opposite, with the mom comfortable petting the dog and the father wary. Fathers with daughters need to make sure they don't overprotect them and that they give them the same encouragement to explore as they do their sons.

Try Switching Roles

While men and women have certain play styles and attitudes toward play, I encourage couples to switch roles on occasion and do some of the tasks and activities the other spouse usually does. Though I stay home with our kids, for instance, my wife sometimes does the laundry. Like most people, she may not like this task, but it's valuable for our kids to see that women can do domestic chores— quite a reversal from the traditional family! Likewise, kids in more traditional households who are always observing their mom cleaning, cooking, or taking care of the kids get the erroneous message that these tasks are gender-related. When Mom gets down on the floor to roll around with the kids or goes outside to play catch and Dad offers comfort and reads stories, children learn that it's okay to go to fathers to be nurtured and to their moms for fun.

By switching roles, partners also learn what it's like to be in the other parent's shoes. One of my clients, who always rose early to make the lunches for her four children, said she just had one simple wish: that her husband would take over this repetitious task. Her husband, a busy but easygoing college professor, agreed to make the lunches for two weeks if his wife would take on the job of driving the kids to school. So for two weeks this dad made turkey sandwiches, peanut butter sandwiches, and buttered bagels, which were the only items that the kids would eat. At first he thought this job was easy and fun, but by the end of the first week, this guy was beginning to understand why his wife found it so repetitious and boring. And his wife, who was thrilled not to have to make lunches, was beginning to have sympathy for the man who had to drive the kids to school—in snow, rain, and traffic. At the end of two weeks, the couple happily traded back.

It's Important to Meet Each Parent's Need for Time Off

No parent, whether working outside the home or not, can be "on" all the time they're with children. As a parent, both mothers and fathers are more effective and enjoy parenting more when they have some time to themselves. It's important for each partner to express these needs to the other so they can work out ways to achieve personal goals and time off. Whether the mom or dad needs time to exercise, visit with friends, pursue a hobby, or just "veg," parents must work together to create a feasible schedule. This is especially important for working women who may feel that they need to "take over" the moment they enter the house. Although my wife works full-time outside the home, I encourage her to stop at the gym on the way home. She doesn't always take me up on my offer, but it certainly helps her to know it's an option anytime she wants it.

I tell couples they'll be better parents if they unwind after work with built-in transition time. By that I mean, if you've had a particularly stressful day, it makes more sense to meet a friend for coffee on the way home or to take the scenic route home before going in the house. Better to go home a little later (if you've communicated this to your spouse) and refreshed than to storm in the door, wired for disaster. I know one working mom who arranged to pick up her daughter at the family day care provider at 5:45 each day. She left work at 5:00 and gave herself forty-five minutes "transition time" to window-shop, run errands, or take a short walk in town.

The Payoff for Kids

What are the benefits for children when both parents are actively involved? Most of the research in the past has focused on negative outcomes that emerge when fathers aren't involved—low self-esteem, higher dropout rates, and less success in later life. Instead of underlining the negative results that occur when fathers are absent or uninvolved, the next several sections focus on the often dramatically positive changes that occur when fathers are actively involved in their children's lives.

Roughhousing Has Its Place

Roughhousing, the classic "father's play," helps girls and boys develop in a number of ways. Research indicates that such characteristics as emotional and physical self-control, self-esteem, social competence, and the ability to carry out responsibilities are all positively correlated with activities such as roughhousing that include a high level of father involvement. For example, psychologist Michael Lamb, author of *The Role of the Father in Child Development,* as well as other researchers have found that when dads roughhouse with their kids or gently bounce their babies, children learn to recognize emotional cues. In the arms of her dad, a baby learns to explore and to read such emotions as fear and excitement. She begins to wonder, "Hey, why is this guy who loves me bouncing me up so high, and what am I going to do about it?"

When toddlers and older children roughhouse with their dads, they learn about the connection between setting limits in physical play and emotions. When I was a boy, my father would sometimes take roughhousing too far. We'd be wrestling around on the floor, and before you knew it, things would get out of hand and I'd end up crying. Sometimes dads overstimulate their children without realizing it, or they fail to read the child's cues that signal he's had enough or is really scared. I saw this at the pool the other day. A father was throwing his toddler up in the air and catching him; the kid looked terrified and was protesting with yelps, but the father kept saying, "Isn't this fun?" Both fathers and children need to learn how to adjust their play styles to one another. The more fathers are involved with their babies, the better they will learn to read their baby's cues and signals.

Roughhousing is also one of the first arenas in which kids learn social skills. Children learn how to "fight fair" from their dads, who set, teach, and enforce such rules as no hitting, slugging, biting, or kicking. Early on, it's important for children to learn that even in a struggle, rules of etiquette exist. Kids (boys especially) who don't have this experience and guidance from their dad may never understand what it means to struggle in a humane manner that is respectful of the opponent. Girls, though they may not always engage in as much roughhousing as boys, are nevertheless encouraged to stand up for themselves, face challenges, and develop higher self-esteem when dads are involved.

Roughhousing also has a connection to children's cognitive

development. This type of play challenges children's thinking capabilities—in figuring out how to respond to dad, how to match him, how to compete with him, how to surprise him. Children actually exercise their brains along with their biceps. Being put in a safe but challenging situation gets kids thinking.

Parents Back Each Other Up

When both parents are involved, each parent's effectiveness is heightened by the other's input, and vice versa. For instance, when Mom sets rules with her toddler by saying "no cookies until after dinner," it certainly helps if Dad backs her up. When Dad says his son must wear a helmet when riding his bike, Mom should require the same rule when Dad's not home. Children need limits, rules, and boundaries for safety and to learn self-control. When both parents agree on what these are, the rules will be more effective, and it will be easier for each parent to enforce the rules when they are parenting on their own. Even though moms and dads have different play styles, children learn consistency when parents remain a united front on child-rearing principles such as discipline, family values, house rules, and so forth.

Ellen and Peter were divorced parents whose daughter, Tina, was enrolled in a summer tennis camp. Though the couple had a hard time communicating, each made an effort to get along. At the onset of the summer camp, both parents came to meet with the director and explained their situation. They asked for two sets of schedules and instructions, and made arrangements for the bus to drop Tina at her dad's house two days a week; the other days she went to her mom's house. Both parents provided the camp director with information about where they lived and worked, and each requested to be called if there was a problem or an emergency. On parents' day, both Ellen and Peter showed up to watch Tina's game. These parents really went out of their way to complement each other's efforts and to be there for their daughter's best interest, in spite of the fact that they had been through a difficult divorce.

It is important for divorced parents to make this commitment and to understand that while equal-share parenting may be harder for them to achieve, many of the components are attainable with communication and determination. When couples divorce, it's essential to remember that kids want their parents to be together. Divorced parents need to let their kids know that they are *not* going to get back together and that they *are* going to be together, though separate, in their support and love for their child.

Both Parents Are in Tune with the Child

Think back to when your baby was first born. Early on, parents read their baby's cues and signals. When both parents are in tune with the baby, a strong bond is formed. This creates a sense of trust and security—a greatness in the child. Having two parents who understand and are in tune with the child makes that bond and confidence all the more solid. Children who perceive this unity from their parents get fewer mixed messages, which in turn makes them emotionally healthier and more stable as they form their own self-concept through their childhood years.

Tom, a building contractor, suddenly found himself in charge of his two-year-old daughter when his wife had to fly to Ireland to attend her mother's funeral. An avowed workaholic, Tom hadn't spent much time with Tammy up until now. Left in a pinch, Tom took a few days off from work in order to care for his daughter until he could find a replacement sitter. Tammy, who was just beginning to potty train and who had only recently given up nursing, was whiny and defiant around her dad. Since he didn't really know his daughter's habits or even dislikes and preferences, he found that feeding her and anticipating her need for the potty was a challenge. Tammy, who missed her mother, loved her dad but sensed that something was wrong, and this made her all the more difficult to deal with.

Theoretically, a father shouldn't be the understudy who learns his lines just so he can step in in an emergency. If both parents are in tune with the child from infancy, the child learns to trust both parents equally as competent caregivers. Not only is this an important payoff for the child, but it makes the lives of parents less stressful. Moms who work and mothers who stay at home can be confident that their spouse is capable of stepping in and taking charge of the family.

If Tom had been more in tune with his daughter when his wife had to leave the country, he would have known exactly what foods Tammy liked and what progress she had made in her potty training. He would have been able to pick up Tammy's signals, anticipate when she might need to use the potty, and support her attempts. Instead of feeling panic at having to quickly locate a babysitter to fill in for his wife, he'd have slipped comfortably into the role of primary caregiver, and Tammy's sense of trust and security would have been maintained.

Imagine how it feels for an infant when one parent is out of sync. A baby can't say to his father, "You're not holding me right!" But learning to be in tune with a child needn't start at infancy, though that's the ideal time. Fathers can begin to pick up on their children's cues and signals later in life as well. It's never too late to help build a father's confidence and ability to become close with his children.

John, a general contractor, came to see me because he had recently contacted his daughter, Judy, from a previous marriage, and he wanted to become a part of her life after many years of absence. He wasn't confident that he was doing the right thing by entering his daughter's life so late. This wasn't entirely John's fault; the court system had given his ex-wife full custody, and she had discouraged all contact with the father. As an adult, however, Judy wanted to make her own decisions, and after meeting a few times, the two found that they had a deep desire to get to know each other. I encouraged John to continue to build this relationship, to talk with Judy about her career and marriage plans, to become engaged in the life she was leading now. The last I spoke with John, he seemed much more confident and felt that even though it had been difficult, it was worth finally getting to know his daughter.

Two Involved Parents Can Help Meet Children's Needs Faster

Another significant benefit of having two actively involved parents is that the child's needs are met sooner. This isn't to say that when Johnny screams, both parents should drop everything and go running. But when both parents are equally involved, either one might come up with a solution. Parenting is a difficult job, and it can be very tough to figure out what a one-year-old wants or needs since she isn't talking yet.

A common frustration I hear from mothers whose husbands aren't involved is that they feel they're parenting alone and when there's a problem they can't turn to their spouse. Instead they ask their mothers, girlfriends, teachers, or pediatricians for advice. In addition to consulting friends and others, it's natural for spouses to look to their partner for advice and ideas.

When our children were young and my wife and I were scratching our heads about dealing with common problems such as tantrums and how to introduce new foods, we often said to each other, "Your guess is as good as mine." We both read a lot of parenting books and magazines, and would often share ideas with each other. Sometimes an idea would pop into my wife's head at work, and she would call and say, "Hey, I just thought of something! Why don't you try . . ." Or when she came home, I'd have tried something new and I'd say, "You'll never believe what worked with . . ."

When Kevin was a baby, he'd occasionally get a bad case of gas after eating. My wife's reaction would always be to pick him up and soothe him. She'd then lay him on his back and rub his tummy while whispering comforting words. The result, believe it or not, would always be that Kevin screamed even louder. My wife wasn't doing anything wrong, it's just that we hadn't quite figured out what worked for Kevin in that particular situation. One evening I had an idea that I would hold Kevin against my shoulder so that his tummy was pressed up against my shoulder and his little body sort of slumped over it. Oddly enough, this seemed to calm him right down. I don't know why—whether it was the way I held him, the position I used, the pressure of my shoulder, or what—but whenever he had a tummy ache, I'd gather him up, hold him in that manner, and he'd stop crying. My wife was very relieved that I had come up with a solution, and she has solved many similar problems at other times. We are grateful to each other, not resentful. Again, I have to emphasize here that parenting is not a competition. If anything, it's a team sport. You can't get the ball through the hoop if someone doesn't pass it to you.

One father told me he had much more success than his wife did in taking his preteen clothes shopping. While Mom was very stylish and artistic, she and her daughter would get into a power struggle whenever they shopped, and the teen would return home in a huff. When this dad began taking the daughter shopping, the situation immediately improved. All he had to do was say, "Gee, you look great in that!" and the daughter got the message that she was the apple of his eye. The male perspective was just the ticket in this instance; the daughter didn't engage in power struggles, the father was patient and supportive, and the shopping trips went much better. It also helped the father-daughter relationship because the teen thought the fact that her dad liked the same styles she did made him cool.

Sexuality and Gender Role Modeling

The part that fathers play as a gender role model for their children is intricate and important. Fathers who handle multiple responsibilities in the family, including nurturing and being supportive partners to their spouses while acting as primary or co-breadwinner, show boys and girls that men have a broad range of roles in raising a family. They are good role models for demonstrating how a man positively contributes to marriage and family in a number of ways.

I began working with Louise and her family just after her husband had died of cancer, leaving her alone to care of two children. Though the children grieved for their father, he had been virtually absent in their lives for more than a year. He had lived at home until the last two months of his illness, but because of his increasing debilitation, he had not been involved with the children's care. The children, who were seven and nine at the time of their father's death, were often in trouble at school and with peers, and suffered from low self-esteem. They were constantly challenging authority, fighting in school, and refusing to help their mother at home. Louise remarried three years later, and the children began to benefit from a positive male role model in their lives. Tony, her second husband, was virtually a "rescuer." He wanted to be very involved in the kids' lives and made every effort to give them solid guidelines and boundaries. While the children were reluctant to get close to Tony at first, they gradually realized that the guidelines and boundaries he set were because of his care, affection, and commitment. Tony took the children to the park and on other outings, helped them with their schoolwork, and talked to them constantly about values and how he expected them to behave. After about a year, the children were strongly bonded to Tony, and by the time Louise stopped coming to see me, the kids were beginning to regain a sense of self, with some excellent input from their stepfather.

This was a case in which the children really showed the negative effects of not having a male role model. While the untimely death of a father is not common, it can occur tragically by an accident, a heart attack, cancer, or other disease. There are plenty of single and widowed mothers whose children are happy, healthy, and developing into wonderful adults. These moms should be lauded for their extraordinary efforts and the immense responsibilities they bear on their own. Many single mothers I know have been able to enlist the support of male mentors, friends, uncles, and so forth to contribute a strong male influence on their children.

While fathers communicate to boys what will be expected of them when they become men, fathers can also show children of both genders that masculinity and nurturing can exist compatibly. I often hear fathers complaining that if their boys play with dolls or show interest in cooking, they'll grow up to be homosexuals. Last year a special report on boys in *Newsweek* included commentary from a number of researchers, including Dan Kindlon, an assistant professor of psychiatry at Harvard Medical School, who said: "The feminist movement has done a great job of convincing people that a woman can be nurturing and a mother and a tough trial lawyer at the same time, but we haven't done that as much with men. We're afraid that if they're too soft, that's all they can be." To deny the caring, nurturing side of the male is really to deny men the opportunity to become whole individuals. Boys who are conditioned to shut down positive emotions such as love, stated the report, "are left with only one socially acceptable outlet: anger." Kindlon, who is coauthor with Michael Thompson of *Raising Cain,* says that once these boys enter early adolescence, they step into the "culture of cruelty," and "anything tender, anything compassionate or too artistic is labeled gay. The homophobia of boys in the 11, 12, 13 range is a stronger force than gravity."

Clearly, we still have a long way to go. I firmly believe that it is important for both boys and girls to learn not only that their fathers can nurture but also that their fathers will always be there for them. The benefits of sticking to that kind of commitment and fighting against the more negative norms of our society are borne out in still more research. The *Newsweek* report stated that, especially with troubled boys, "a strong parental bond is the most important protection against everything from smoking to suicide."

For girls, a father who is a positive, involved, nurturing man helps set the tone for later experiences and relationships with males. This is particularly important in the adolescent years, which we'll discuss in chapter 9. My daughter often comes to me and asks me what she should wear on a certain day, and she might make a suggestion about my tie or my sweater. When I tell her, "You look great!" it really means so much; fathers who support their daughters by approving of their femininity as well as by showing support for their schoolwork, their interest in sports and technology, and in all their pursuits and aspirations are really giving their girls the message that women are capable and successful, and deserve the respect of the men they love. A father's disapproval or disinterest can go a very long way in damaging a girl's development of self-esteem and negatively affecting her future relationships with males.

Teaching Kids to Care

Children whose fathers are actively involved are also more empathetic. In their research, R. Koestner, C. Franz, and J. Weinberger found that paternal child rearing involvement was the most important indicator for future feelings of sympathy and compassion for others.

Devon, a third grader, received a letter of commendation from his teacher because he was the most "empathetic" student in the class. Though his teacher may not have been aware of it, Devon was being raised in a balanced parenting partnership. His father, who worked nights, was with him in the mornings before school and in the afternoons after school, while his mother, who worked full-time as a graphic artist, took care of him at night. Devon's father took him on camping trips, hikes, to art classes, on walks, and out to restaurants. In class, Devon's teacher noticed that he was remarkably generous and fair with the other children at an age when the boys in the class were beginning to become competitive and aggressive. He was well liked by his peers and often chosen as a leader even though he didn't seek this role. Many of his classmates turned to Devon when they were having a problem.

Psychologist Norma Radin found that children whose fathers are more involved are also more likely to be accepting of nontraditional gender roles. I find this with my own son, who writes stories in which the captain of a ship is a female. Also, my son's best friend is Sam, as in Samantha. He and Sam met when they were both seven, and at age eleven they are still best friends. It stands to reason that children who see their parents sharing roles and reversing roles will more likely blend roles when they become adults. I think if Kevin becomes someone's boss when he grows up, he won't perceive a glass ceiling regarding the women he works with.

One father I know was hanging his laundry out to dry when he heard cat calls from the nearby high school. "That's women's work!" the teenage boys were yelling from the bike racks in front of the school. This man, whose mother had taught him to do his own laundry as a teen and who respected his wife's career, was shocked to discover that a new generation of boys was being raised with this type of gender bias.

The Payoff for Dads

While much of the focus on having an involved father is on how children benefit, I have found that many people don't realize how positively father involvement impacts on men's lives. We've all heard the stories of men "healing the wounds" of their relationships with their own fathers or their own fatherless pasts. Contemporary men are increasingly coming forward to announce that their own fathers were absent, abusive, detached, or critical. Let's turn that around to see how today's involved fathers will feel in the future about the roles they've played.

Fathers' Self-Esteem Goes Up

I know from my own experiences as a stay-at-home father that actively raising your children makes a man feel good about himself. Women have been experiencing this sense of pride and accomplishment for generations. In the past, men have been able to think of their accomplishments in regard to parenting largely in economic terms: "I worked hard to pay for my daughter's college education." This is perfectly fine (and many working women feel the sense of pride that comes from knowing they are important breadwinners for the family's needs), but what about the other side of the coin? When I teach my toddler to say "thank you" and then he thanks a waiter for handing him an ice-cream cone, and I'm there to hear him say it, I feel good about myself. It's rewarding for a father to know that he has helped teach his child to read, to be courteous, to help others, to install software on the computer, and to make ethical decisions. When a father experiences this sense of accomplishment

("Hey, I taught him that!"), his self-esteem rises. Success is a heady feeling, and when fathers experience the singular pride and sense of accomplishment that comes from teaching their children, they get a valuable dose of positive reinforcement.

Fathers' Work Life Improves

When fathers are involved and happy with their home life, research reveals, they feel less stressed at work and are able to perform better. This is what makes the goal of creating family-friendly workplaces even more important. Society is beginning to recognize that not only does stress at work impact negatively on the family, but lack of support for families by employers only serves to make workers less productive. Employers who don't support family life are in effect really shooting themselves in the foot.

James Levine, director of The Fatherhood Project at the Families and Work Institute in New York, found that far from damaging worker productivity, involvement in family life enhances working life. In *Working Fathers,* Levine reports that when men are comfortable at home, their sense of accomplishment and confidence carries over into the workplace. It's in everyone's interest to make careers and family compatible—for both women and men. Workers who are more satisfied at their jobs are more likely to be positive people in general and to create a better home environment for their children. Fathers who are treated badly at work may have lower self-esteem, which will impact negatively on how they parent. Dads with more autonomy and control at work, and who have supportive supervisors, have higher self-esteem and carry this home; they are more fair disciplinarians and demonstrate a greater acceptance of their children. When fathers are satisfied at work, even their play with their children is longer and of better quality, Levine has found.

Bonds That Carry Dads and Kids into the Future

Bonds that fathers establish with their children early on are carried into the future. I'm hoping that one day when my children call from college, they won't just talk to me about sending some extra cash and to my wife about what's really going on in their lives. I expect that, because of the strong bonds we've nurtured over the years, my son and daughter will talk to me about their experiences and emotions, as they will to my wife. I don't foresee that one day they'll have nothing to say to me or I to them. We've all heard stories about the distancing that occurs when kids grow older, and some of that is a natural, healthy quest for independence and separation. But parents who have solid emotional connections to their children, who have always talked to them and encouraged them to talk to their parents, may very well find that the lines of communication remain open far into the future.

Involved Fathers Have Better Health

Maybe it's not so surprising that, as was discovered by Rosalind Barnett, a research scholar at Radcliffe College and the author of *She Works, He Works*, involved fathers are actually healthier than those who are more distant on the home front. Fathers who had the fewest worries about the relationship with their children, Barnett discovered, also had the fewest health problems. I also suspect that many fathers become even more motivated to stay healthy when they become involved in caring for their children. The desire to keep up with a toddler, to be fit enough to go fishing or sailing or hiking with your kids, or to be around to play with one's own grandchildren is a good incentive to eat right, keep in shape, and stay healthy.

A dramatic example of the physical benefits of being a father is expressed in Art Klein's book *Dad and Son*. Klein, who was diagnosed with a life-threatening neuromuscular disease when his son was born, writes about how his determination to touch and hold his baby carried him through the most difficult time in his life. Inspired by his desire to be a good father, Klein claims he actually overcame his illness. To be sure, Klein's experience was unique, but most parents who are actively involved with their children will understand that being a parent in and of itself provides a deep motivation for health and survival.

The Payoff for the Couple

Father involvement has a dramatically positive effect on marriage. Mothers whose husbands are actively involved with the children repeatedly tell me how much satisfaction it gives them and how much better it makes them feel about their marriage and about men in general. Most men, I believe, do want to make their wives happy and their marriages successful. But they may not realize how crucial their involvement with their children is to achieving this goal.

Many men may still not get the connection between doing their fair share with the children and having a happy love life. Women who feel overburdened, stressed out, and responsible for all domestic duties, child care, and work are probably not going to feel especially positive about the state of matrimony. Although it seems an obvious deduction, many couples aren't aware that unbalance is even their problem. And if they are aware, they may feel a solution is nonexistent or the effort futile. Research supports the fact that when women get more support about their multiple roles, they are happier about themselves and their marriage.

Healthy Marriages Are Healthy for Kids

Researcher Michael Lamb points to the fact that healthy marriages are better for kids—no surprise there—but sometimes even the most conscientious parents need a gentle reminder that resolving marital problems should be attempted not only for the parents' sake but also for the kids'. Lamb asserts that when the marriage is good, parents actually report in research study settings that they think more highly of their children and their role as parents. When it is a strong marriage, parents speak to their children in more complex sentences, child care is more often shared, and there is more agreement between parents on problems that arise. A good marriage creates solid, positive attachments between parents and children, lending a critical sense of both security and sociability. Happy marriages often produce kids who are more outgoing and open than children from troubled marriages. Parents in a good marriage tend to have more positive teaching styles—they listen to and spend more time with their kids—and show greater responsiveness and sensitivity toward their children.

Shared Responsibility Makes for a Better Marriage

Over the years, through my counseling experience and the feedback I get from participants in my parenting seminars, I have determined many factors that contribute to the making and maintaining of a good marriage, but two of the most important ingredients, I believe, are communication and shared responsibility. Sooner or later if one person is doing all the work (either emotionally or in the more practical sense), things are going to sputter or burn out. A good marriage requires positive contributions from two individuals, not just one. In today's society that translates to the fact that sharing of child care and household labor is a must.

What else does a good marriage need? Intimacy and time alone together are essential. Humor, of course, is always a big plus. Other essential elements include nurturing each other with emotional support, helping to make each other's dreams come true, enjoyment, commitment, flexibility (especially for couples with children), and sharing fun. My wife and I joined a volleyball team just to get ourselves out and keep up the enjoyment quotient. We often take walks together as a family; the kids frequently run up ahead of us, and my wife and I get a lot of talking done. Lots of times that talking turns out to be one of us griping about work, but at least we're talking. And speaking of talking, learning how to talk with each other is a skill that always needs honing. Chapter 3 focuses on the communication skills needed to start the journey toward more balanced parental involvement.

The Power of Positive

Communication

T HE OTHER NIGHT my wife got home from work at 5:30, and I departed for a school board meeting at 5:35. As I gave her a brief rundown before rushing out the door of what the kids were up to and what I had planned for dinner, I thought once again about how difficult it is for couples to maintain intimacy and good communication when our lives are so often pulled in different directions. I was mulling this over in the carpool on the way to a school board meeting when one of the other passengers began waving frantically at a car that was passing by. "Oh, there goes my husband on his way home from work!" she exclaimed. I felt lucky that I'd been able to have a short chat with my wife at the end of her workday, while my friend had only managed to wave at her spouse's passing vehicle! And he didn't even see her!

I value the work and ties that I have outside the home, just as my wife does, but sometimes we get so caught up in our other commitments that we don't have the time or the energy needed to nurture our relationships at home. Without sacrificing our autonomy, fathers and mothers need to spend time together one-on-one;

this is really the best way to keep family members connected on an emotional as well as practical level.

In an office setting you wouldn't expect a colleague to throw a stack of papers on your desk and not tell you what they were about. You might need to be "debriefed" or informed; you might need an explanation or a deadline, or to be asked for your input before you proceeded. Running a family is much the same. Parenting together requires both mother and father to be cognizant of what is expected, what has been (and still needs to be) accomplished, what the family's goals are, and so forth. The difference is that in a family situation, many of the issues that arise on a daily basis are emotionally charged and personally significant to your family, no matter how inconsequential they may seem to the world at large. All the more reason why the lines of communication between parents (and between parents and children) need to be consistently maintained. Yes, this takes hard work, but we've all experienced the alternative.

Good communication is a key characteristic of healthy families, but I have found that too many couples believe that communication is a "given" when people love each other. Good communication is a learned set of skills, not something that comes naturally with the wedding-vow package. For many people who didn't have good role models in childhood, communication skills must be learned in adulthood. Effective communication requires that you find your own role models, learn to express yourself, and become an active, receptive listener. In this chapter we'll discuss all the important tactics for opening the lines of communication and keeping them in good working order in your family. How can you be part of a team, after all, if you never even talk to the other players?

Compromise Is an Important Outcome

As pointed out in chapter 1, each adult enters a marriage with a unique family history and his or her own set of values, customs, communication styles, and so on, which become blended over time as the two partners create their own new family. While some couples may confront differences that are more extreme than others, each partner must learn to compromise in order to create a successful, communicative relationship.

In my parenting seminars I illustrate the importance of compromise with a very trivial scenario, which I call the peanut butter example. Let's say the mom likes to store the peanut butter jar in the cupboard. That's the way it was always done when she was growing up. Her husband keeps the jar in the refrigerator, just as his parents taught him. Obviously, they can't have it both ways; not only will the peanut butter end up stiff if it's refrigerated one day and left in the cupboard the next, but this little annoyance may one day trigger a bigger disagreement. So the couple has to compromise and agree to leave the jar in or out, to purchase two jars, or to swear off peanut butter altogether. I use this small example of how a husband and wife must communicate to blend their individual family history into a marriage because it reveals how necessary it is to compromise. Parents who work as a team accept that they must compromise on just about everything. Peanut butter is a trivial concern, but if parents can't resolve minor issues like that, imagine how they will butt heads as they try to resolve larger issues such as child care, discipline, and financial issues.

Sometimes, however, parents confuse compromise with "you get this and I get that." When it comes to resolving parenting issues, nothing is that simple. More often, parenting issues are resolved through a series of small compromises in which each partner feels that some of his or her needs, if not all, are being met. For example, if a working mom wants her husband to pick up their child two out of five nights a week, he might say, "Well, I play basketball twice a week from five to seven so I can't do it." And then the mom needs to say, "I know, but that's Mondays and Wednesdays. I was hoping you would do it Tuesdays and Thursdays. I switched my evening exercise class from Monday to Tuesday when you told me you wanted to join the league, so now I'm asking you to help me out." If the father agrees to the Tuesday-Thursday arrangement, both get to exercise and the mom is relieved of the sole responsibility of picking the child up every night. Both parties also compromised: The mom changed her exercise class time, and the dad agreed to pick up the child on nonbasketball nights.

There are no "quick-fix" solutions to issues of involvement. Quick fixes, the Band-Aid approach discussed in chapter 1, may solve the problem temporarily, but chances are another similar problem will soon arise because a true compromise or resolution was never reached.

Good Communication Requires Openness and Honesty

To be good communicators, we need to speak openly about our thoughts and feelings. This, too, takes practice. Partners shouldn't have to guess about what's troubling the other partner. I often ask my wife in advance what she would like as a birthday present; I know that takes away some of the spontaneity and surprise, but if I have a true idea of what she's hoping for, I can select a gift that I know she really wants and can be pretty well assured that she'll be happy with it. This carries over into other aspects of our life as well; when we need emotional support, intimacy, or advice, we need to freely communicate our desires.

Communicating with openness and honesty means not making a guessing game out of our needs, not dropping hints and then assuming that because our partner loves us, he or she can read our minds. As an added bonus, I have found that invariably when couples communicate in an open, honest manner, their sense of closeness, understanding, mutual respect, and intimacy naturally improves.

Yes, Children Complicate the Process

Some couples simply give up on communicating with each other when kids enter the picture. It's difficult to have a conversation when a baby needs to be consoled, when homework is waiting, when school projects and ball games are demanding our attention. One mother told me she and her husband had actually considered learning sign language just so they could communicate over the din of their children!

Aside from the practical, everyday obstacles to communication when children are around, there are deeper obstacles. It's certainly a catch-22: Just when communication becomes so essential—when you're raising a family—the very presence of a baby and children creates big obstacles to communication. The first baby dramatically changes the dynamics of the family, two children alter the interactions even more, and so on. When a baby is born, communication can falter simply because parents are tired, emotions are soaring, and the whole family is going through a major adjustment. It's really after the "new babydom" settles down, after about six months to one year, that the couple has to turn its attention to developing a new communication style or, at the very least, modifying the style they had, one that works within the context of having a child or children in the picture.

Parent-to-Parent Meetings

I strongly recommend to parents that in order to improve their communication, they actually set a consistent time to talk one-on-one. I call these "parent-to-parent meetings." Think about it this way: Before your first child was born, every time you talked to your spouse it was one-on-one. After you have a baby, you actually have to make time for one-on-one. It's just a fact of raising a family. My wife and I set aside from nine to ten o'clock each night to sit down and talk. Although she likes to bring work home and sometimes tries to push back the hour, I gently remind her that we need this time together. Again, I encourage parents to get their kids to bed at a reasonable hour so that the children will get the sleep they need and the parents will get their time to talk and spend time together one-on-one. At the very least the kids should be in their beds and reading by that hour. If couples work split shifts or one parent can't be home at night, make sure to schedule another time (breakfast, lunch, or one evening out a week, for instance) to be together to talk on a regular basis. It's ideal that it be every day, but even a few times a week, or at an absolute minimum once a week, is a step in the right direction.

One of my clients, Nancy, came to me complaining that she was completely exhausted. Her three children were up until eleven o'clock every night, and the youngest often crawled into bed with them in the middle of the night. The kids were up and down the stairs each evening ten or twenty times, rummaging for snacks, watching TV, and generally running Nancy ragged. Her husband had given up on the situation and stayed late at the office or went down into the basement to putter while she dealt with the chaos upstairs.

Before any progress could be made, I needed to convince Nancy that her children should be in bed by eight o'clock. First, I asked her to talk to the kids, who were four, seven, and nine, and explain that the bedtime schedule needed to change for their health and so they could do better in school. Then we worked in small increments. The first few nights she put the youngest child to bed at 10:00 and the two older children at 10:15. This was fairly easy, and the children went along with it. After three nights on this timetable, she began putting her youngest to bed at 9:45 and the older two at 10:00. The kids didn't like this too much, but since it was only a fifteen-minute change, they went along with it. Over the course of several months we moved the bedtime forward by fifteen-minute intervals until the youngest child was asleep by 8:00 and the two older boys were in their beds reading, with lights out at 8:30. At the same time Nancy and her husband were to spend from 10:00 to 11:00 each night together. They could chat about the kids or work or personal thoughts, or they could just sit and cuddle. Nancy's husband was impressed that his wife had succeeded in getting the kids on a reasonable sleeping schedule, and by the end of the process he was participating in the nighttime rituals, helping the youngest child brush his teeth and reading him a story before lights out, so his wife could concentrate on the older boys.

Nancy was thrilled with the way things were going. Her kids were better behaved at home and in school, and had adjusted to their new schedule. I told Nancy that although they might never admit it, the kids were probably grateful to have some limits. (This seems to be especially true for boys. As Don and Jeanne Elium write in *Raising a Son*, boys like to know two things: What are the rules, and who's going to enforce them?) Nancy and her husband were spending time together again, and the father was drawn back into participating in daily routines.

Ships Passing in the Night

At times, of course, regular communication is nearly impossible because of our hectic schedules. But in order for parents to equally share in the care of their children, they need to communicate and exchange information even when time is limited.

Imagine what might happen if communication lines between two parents were down and one was handed the responsibility of caring for the baby, the three-year-old, and the six-year-old on a given afternoon. Let's suppose Mom, who usually cares for the kids three days a week while a sitter fills in the other two, needs to attend an important meeting, and Dad is required to take the helm.

At the very least he needs to know when the baby last ate, when the toddler went to the bathroom, and when the six-year-old's soccer game begins. If this vital information isn't communicated to him, the day is going to be quite confusing. The baby is soon going to be screaming for a bottle, the preschooler won't be asked until it's too late if he has to use the potty, and the six-year-old will miss his game. And this will just be the beginning, because bedtimes, dinnertimes, discipline problems, rules enforcement, and safety issues are going to arise when Mom walks out that door. Without good communication, Dad isn't going to be in the loop. Sure, he can wing it, but wouldn't it be better for all parties involved if he had an open, ongoing dialogue going with Mom about the children's schedules and care?

Lack of positive communication between parents is one reason that equal-balance parenting isn't yet a reality in so many families today. The balancing act truly begins when Mom and Dad sit down to talk.

Men and Women Communicate Differently

Let's look at some of the differences we bring to the discussion table from the get-go simply because we are men and women. Although there are always exceptions (some men are expressive and emotional, some women are reserved and analytical), women in general are encouraged from a very young age to form connections with other people through talking, to communicate feelings, and to seek advice and support through conversation. Men, on the other hand, have heard since they were little boys that they shouldn't cry or express sadness or fear. They aren't taught how to express anger with words. They are taught that they should be reserved and logical, and use conversation to inform and demand, thereby maintaining an image of male authority.

Both Parents Must be Active Communicators

While acknowledging that gender initially shapes our communication style and patterns, I also know that men and women who choose to make the effort can change habits that aren't productive or successful. One mother told me that she felt irritated when her husband sat silently at the dinner table. Becoming increasingly angered, this mother one day openly stated, "It really bothers me that you don't tell me anything. I'd just like to hear about your day and what happened at work. It doesn't have to be anything important, but I enjoy conversation and need you to talk to me."

The husband looked at his wife in surprise and said in a sincerely apologetic tone, "I had no idea! I just didn't want to bore you!"

This man began to make a concerted effort to relate the details of his day, and his wife was much happier because he was talking to her, although the subject of their conversation wasn't anything remarkable. The remarkable part was that they were talking after many years of the man's silence and the woman's resentment.

The Little Things Count

Parents should realize that the details of the day do matter and that no concern is really too small to bring up with your spouse. Have you ever noticed that when you go away on business for a few days, you actually have less to talk about when you get home from your trip than you would if you were just hanging around the house and taking care of the daily chores and responsibilities?

I've noticed that when I'm away on a business trip, I can pretty much sum up the happenings of the two or three days of my absence in five or ten minutes. But when I'm home with the family, involved in our everyday comings and goings, I find there's a lot that I need to discuss with my wife when we sit down to talk at 9 P.M. In a family the details really do matter. What your baby ate for breakfast and why your teen seems upset about her clothing are both significant to your family. Both fathers and mothers need to talk about the daily issues of family life as well as the larger, more philosophical issues we face as parents. Even if the father is not home to take his son to the dentist, he needs to be in on the decision about whether that molar really needs to be removed. If parents use a nanny, a family child care provider, or other day care provider, they need first to discuss and agree between them on their feelings about discipline, toilet training, time-out, early learning experiences, and other issues. The bottom line is, both parents need to be equally involved in the decisions, both large and small, that affect their children's daily lives. The opinions, actions, and aspirations of each parent matter equally. Fathers should be as intimately connected to the details of family life as mothers are.

Working on Minor Communication Problems Prepares You for the Big Ones

I used to get annoyed when my wife would come in from work and throw her coat down. For quite a few months I'd grimace as she flung down her coat, wondering to myself how much time it could possibly take her to hang that coat in the closet.

One day I realized that I intended to be married to my wife for a very long time, for the rest of our lives, in fact. Rather than be irritated permanently, I decided to bring it to her attention. Maybe she was a little annoyed that I mentioned the problem, but when I pointed out that it really bothered me, she agreed it would be easy to simply change the habit. Since then (most of the time), she has hung up her coat, and I don't have to worry about it anymore.

If something is bothering you, even if minor, it's best to bring it up rather than let it fester. Nagging and badgering aren't elements of good communication, but speaking to your mate directly about your concerns, without hinting or manipulating, is perfectly reasonable and healthier for the marriage in the long run. Talking about minor issues gives you and your spouse good practice to prepare for discussions about bigger issues.

Are You Listening?

This leads me to one of my favorite topics—listening, which is perhaps the most crucial element of positive communication. I like to ask the parents who come into my practice, and the parents I meet in my seminars, "Are you listening?" It's a loaded and important question that gets people thinking about the issues that matter. Active listeners are vital to the communication process in any arena; in the parenting arena this is especially true. If you aren't listening to your children and if you aren't listening to your spouse, chances are you're not getting anywhere.

Sometimes adults need to be "heard," just as children do. One day my wife came in the house complaining about some problem she'd had at work. My initial response was to offer her some solutions, to give her my opinion about how she could resolve her dilemma. When I started to offer my ideas, however, she said, "Please don't say anything. Just listen!" My wife just needed to "vent." She'd come up with her own solutions but wanted to use me as a sounding board for a while.

Noted psychologist John Gray, author of the runaway bestseller *Men Are from Mars, Women Are from Venus,* sums up the gender differences that create so many misunderstandings when males and females sit down to talk. Men are conditioned to use talking to articulate concrete solutions; women, more often than not, just need to be heard. It's a good rule of thumb for both sexes not to offer advice unless it's requested. A woman may be looking for a connection to her spouse, a sense that by listening to her feelings her partner has validated them. Men often believe that they should jump into action rather than simply listening to and accepting a woman's thoughts, feelings, and ideas.

Other times my wife really does want my input and will tell me straight out that she'd like my advice. In these cases we often have long discussions that involve lots of questioning and exchanges of ideas. It helps me to know what the parameters are. There's nothing wrong with saying, "Please listen to me. I just need to vent a little," or "Could you help me out here? I need some advice."

How to Be An Active Listener

Did your child ever stick his fingers in his ears and refuse to hear something you've told him? Some adults behave this way, too, but their refusal to listen is cloaked, unlike the easily visible tuning-out of a youngster.

Jeannette, one of my clients, told me that her husband, Sean, never "listened." He sat on the couch with his eyes focused on her, but even after she told him about all the issues that were bothering her—he never spent any time with the children, he didn't help with the laundry—he'd simply start with a counterattack, telling Jeannette that she was always talking about the office, that she kept forgetting to call her mom to babysit when she knew they had to go to his boss's wedding that was only two weeks away.

The problem was that each spouse was caught up with his or her own problems, and in plotting what he or she would say next, neither ever really took the time to listen. When I worked with Jeannette and Sean to develop their communication skills, the first skill we focused on was active listening.

Reflecting Back What Has Been Said

One important technique of active listening is to reflect back or paraphrase what your spouse has just said and to give your spouse the opportunity to say, "No, that's not what I meant," or "Yes, that's what I'm concerned about." Here's an example:

MOM: Everything is just too much. I have the baby all day, and then I pick up the twins at school and help them with their homework.

DAD: Okay, what I'm hearing is that the routine as it is right now is really taking a toll on you.

MOM: Yes, it is. It's just that the baby wants to be held all the time now that she's teething, and the twins need so much help with their math this year.

DAD: I understand. You're saying you'd feel less stressed if some part of the schedule could be taken off your shoulders. Do you want a sitter to come in more often?

MOM: No, that's not what I meant. What I want to know is if you would be willing to work with the twins on their homework twice a week.

DAD: Sure, I can do that. I didn't realize things were piling up so much.

Once you're clear on what the person is saying, you can respond appropriately. A good communicator is a good listener.

Train Yourself Not to Interrupt

Active listening also means avoiding interrupting the other person. Make sure that you concentrate on what your spouse is saying and that you don't interrupt. You aren't actively listening if you're spending the whole time thinking of what you're going to say next and then jumping in. Sometimes it's difficult to focus on what your partner is saying, especially if you vehemently disagree. But there's just no two ways about it: Good communication begins with receptive listening.

Give your partner a chance to express himself all the way to the end of his thought even if you disagree with his point of view. Resist the urge to finish his sentences. If you're angry with what your spouse is saying, that may be a good reason to listen even more closely. Sometimes we feel especially defensive about things that we know are true or partially true. If you still feel that the statements made were unfair or false, you might respond after your spouse is finished with something like "I don't agree with what you're saying right now, but I'll give it some thought and we can discuss it later." I'm the first to acknowledge how difficult it is to sit quietly when you disagree. But consider the alternative: If you want to make progress, interrupting will only slow things down. Remember, too, that your partner needs to listen to you as well. If you're talking and your spouse interrupts you, say, "Please let me finish my thought. It's important to me to say what's on my mind."

Nonverbal Cues Count, Too

Active listening also requires paying attention to the speaker's nonverbal cues. Sometimes called body language, these cues include tone of voice, eye contact, posture, and gestures, all of which contribute to the ways we communicate. If your spouse is avoiding eye contact, using a clipped tone, or folding his arms defensively across his chest, he may be telling you (in a nonverbal manner) that this is really not a good time to talk. Tune in to body language. If you detect something negative, say, "I can tell that this time isn't good for you. Can we schedule another time to talk when we're both feeling more relaxed?"

I tell my clients not to jump to conclusions about the nonverbal cues they pick up from their spouse. For example, a woman who turns away when her husband tries to embrace her may be harboring some unspoken resentment, she may be hiding information, or she may just be feeling unwell.

Also Watch for Indirect Messages

People send indirect messages with their behavior instead of with words when something is wrong and they don't know how to say it or are reluctant to say it for some reason. I have learned a lot about indirect messages from my kids. Recently, for example, my daughter wanted to spend some time with her mom. Instead of saying, "Mom, I need to be with you," A.J. began whining and acting sulky. I said to my wife, "A.J. is giving you a message. She needs to spend some time with you." Linda responded to the cue and planned an activity with our daughter, during which they had a chance to talk. Often, children will sulk, pick on siblings, or act out in some way to get a parent's attention. Children aren't always so good at saying, "Mom, I need to talk to you!" If you're paying attention, you'll get the message anyway.

A father who spends every evening glued to the TV might not be doing so because he's angry or bored with his family; he may actually be saying he doesn't feel needed. Not everyone always says what they mean even though that is a good goal to strive for. It's better to express to someone what you're perceiving and give the person the opportunity to confirm or disagree with you than to automatically assume a particular cue means one thing only and plan your next move based on that unconfirmed perception.

The Ground Rules: How to Communicate in a Positive Manner

Now that we've established how important it is to listen carefully, let's consider the best ways to express yourself clearly. When dealing with involvement issues (which all too often escalate into full-blown arguments), it really helps to step back a moment before you dive in. Anger and blame have no place in healthy communication, but there *are* skills couples can use to make discussions more meaningful and productive. Consider these basic guidelines, which I call the ground rules.

Know Your Intent

What is the outcome you're hoping to achieve? Often, spouses jump into a quarrel without thinking ahead to the desired result. They're angry and simply don't care or don't think about what they're about to say. If you're hoping that your husband will storm out of the house, slamming the door behind him and not returning for two or three hours, that's one thing. But if the outcome you have in mind is more along the lines of your spouse spending Saturday afternoons with the baby and making the kids' lunches on weekdays, then it pays to think ahead about communication tactics.

So before you begin to discuss an involvement issue (or any issue), make time to sit down for a quiet moment by yourself and focus on the desired outcome. Write down what you'd like the outcome of your conversation to be. (I know a working mom who routinely goes to a little park near her office with a bag lunch and jots down things she wants to talk to her husband about.) If you feel confused about what you want, try articulating just one desire or outcome. If you find that your list is endless, narrow it down to one or two objectives, or prioritize them in terms of the most "burning" ones, and then focus on them one at a time with your spouse over several months. So much time and energy is wasted when people don't know what they want. How can your spouse respond to your needs if you haven't really defined them yourself? In an emotional moment many couples lose sight of why they began talking in the first place. Pinpoint your destination before you take off.

State Your Intent Clearly and Directly

Don't keep your spouse guessing; be clear, direct, and honest about your desires. State your objectives clearly and in a straightforward manner. Hidden messages, sarcasm, exaggeration, and subtle or not-so-subtle hints have no place in a conversation between two adults who both want the best for each other and for their family. Women are notorious for being indirect. They think they're being polite, but they have to know that it's okay to just flat out say what they want or mean. The classic story goes that the woman says to her husband, "I'm thirsty, but we don't have any milk. I'm too tired, though, to go out right now." Her husband looks sideways at her and says, "Why don't you just say, 'Honey, would you be willing to go out and pick up a quart of milk?'" This applies to big issues, too. If what you really want to say is "I'm so beat at the end of the day, and I need you to be more involved in the bedtime routine with the kids," don't say, "This bedtime thing is really getting to me." Again, writing out your intent first and reading it over several times will help you choose the words to form the clearest message.

Show Respect at All Times, No Matter How Angry or Frustrated You Are

It amazes and saddens me to see how many adults are polite and courteous with their coworkers or people in the outside world and yet speak rudely—sometimes even cruelly—to a spouse. It's as if they know they won't be able to get away with antisocial behavior in the workplace—in one sense, they are being paid to be pleasant— but they somehow expect any behavior will be tolerated at home. Unconditional love is not a license to show disrespect. Kids are prone to this, too. Parents often find that children who behave appropriately in school, suddenly become loud and rude as soon as they enter their own homes.

Oftentimes, individuals "displace" anger that they feel toward a situation or person. Some people call this syndrome "kicking the cat." In this case, it's the spouse who gets dumped on. For instance, a woman comes home from work angry that her boss hasn't agreed with her publicity plan, and she snaps at her husband. The spouse is the focus of her displaced anger. In these situations I suggest that the woman either stop at the health club and work out before going home or take a walk to cool off. If that's not possible, she should simply say to her husband as soon as she gets in the door, "I'm really angry at my boss. She rejected all the ideas in my plan!"

Everyone kicks the cat once in a while. When displaced anger becomes an ongoing problem, however, it's time to look at the situation seriously. If an individual is really so angered by a situation outside the family and continually takes his or her frustration out on the family, it's time to make a change.

Monitor Your Tone of Voice and Language

Part of showing respect is to refrain from raising your voice or using a sarcastic or other negative tone. Both men and women have a tendency to use sharp or nasty tones when stressed or angry; some women use a high-pitched tone. Your intent will come across more clearly, and your partner will be more open to discussion, if you speak reasonably, respectfully, and in a calm manner. Furthermore, it goes without saying that screaming, yelling, and using abusive language are not options. They won't get you anywhere, will only annoy or hurt your spouse, and may actually delay progress. When you feel stressed or angry, try to step outside yourself and "listen" to how you're coming across.

Use "I Statements"

Rather than using accusatory language, try to use "I statements" whenever possible. The "I statement" is constructed of three parts: (1) I feel _____ (a particular emotion such as sad, angry, frustrated, disappointed) when you (2) _____ (a particular behavior or action such as forgetting to call, spending so much time on the phone, falling asleep right after dinner, paying more attention to friends than to me) because it (3) _____ (a particular effect such as makes me worry, takes away from our alone time together, or means you miss seeing the kids at bedtime). "I statements" focus on feelings rather than opinions; they focus on someone's specific behavior that is bothering you but don't attack the person as a whole.

Both women and men need practice with this communication skill. Many times during a counseling session when I hear a statement that I think can be rephrased, I wait until my client is finished speaking and then ask him or her to try rephrasing what was just said into an "I statement." To most people the language sounds fake at first, but once they get used to it, they realize that choosing the words for "I statements" makes them think more carefully before speaking, thus avoiding words that insult the other person or communicate disrespect.

Here are some more examples of rephrasing thoughts and feelings into "I statements."

Old statement: "You're so inconsiderate that you can't even pick up the phone when you're at work."

"I statement": "I feel frustrated when you'll be late at work but don't call because it is hard for me to plan dinner for the family."

Old statement: "You'd rather go outside after dinner and work on the yard than spend time with your children who haven't seen you all day. You don't consider the kids' needs at all."

"I statement": "I feel frustrated when you choose to do the yardwork after dinner because it would be a good time for you to spend time with the kids."

Avoid "Always" and "Never"

When you're angry with someone or want to bring up an issue that has frazzled your nerves or upset you, it's a natural inclination to begin your conversation with "You never . . ." or "You always . . ." These broad generalizations, however, only put your partner on the defensive and quite often aren't even true. Here is a suggestion for rephrasing to an "I statement":

Old statement: "You never help with the children's baths!"

"I statement": "I feel pressured when I have to make dinner and give the children their baths. I'd really like you to take on the bathing after dinner while I clear up the kitchen."

Timing Is Critical

When I was a child, my father used to sit at the kitchen table and pay the bills. Even at age seven I knew that this was not a good time to ask my father for my allowance or to urge him to come outside and play ball. Invariably he'd be cranky and irritable after those bills were paid; this, in fact, was an excellent time to steer clear of Dad.

Timing must be considered when we sit down to talk to each other as parents as well. Set a good time to talk about involvement issues—not in the heat of the moment (wait until you cool down) or when the kids are starving and dinner needs to be made or when your spouse is tired or preoccupied or watching a playoff game.

Some people hate to be hit with a big discussion first thing in the morning; if your spouse is like this and you wake up with a big issue on your mind, force yourself to hold your thoughts until a time that you know he or she will be more receptive. Think about the rhythms of your family and find a time to talk when both partners can give each other their full attention.

Set a Time Limit

I often hear the lament "We just don't have *time* to talk!" from frustrated parents. I've found, however, that most couples can find the time once they make up their minds to do so. As with making time to exercise or planning "alone time," making time to talk has to be a priority for married couples with children. One of the obstacles I see that prevents couples from doing so is the tendency to envision "time to talk" as an open-ended discussion. The reality is that in most families today we don't have the time to sit down to chat, chat, chat, or to debate for hours on end the way we used to before we had kids.

The solution is easy enough: Set a time limit and stick to it. It's easier to get your spouse to sit down and talk about becoming involved in bedtime routines if he knows the conversation is going to last twenty minutes instead of two hours. Some issues can be explored and potentially resolved in ten minutes or less, but for complicated matters you may need to set aside an hour or two, or two or three separate sessions.

If at the end of the allotted time you haven't reached a compromise or resolution, set another time to continue the discussion. Try to do it before you get up from the table. Resist the urge to keep pounding away at the subject; chances are you'll start bringing up unrelated issues that will cloud the matter.

Agree on the Topic to Be Discussed—and Stick to It

Make certain that you inform your spouse of the topic that you'd like to discuss. If the subject is to be your daughter's wish to have a sleepover party, keep the conversation limited to that topic. Try not to veer off into your son's upcoming band trip or your mother-in-law's tonsillectomy. This isn't to say that you can't discuss all these subjects at one point or another, but it's important to set some parameters. One of the main reasons couples fail to get anywhere in their communication efforts is that they can't stick to any one topic long enough to reach a resolution.

Another common scenario that derails couples during discussions is what I call Fight #67. This happens when the discussion wends its way into the same old fight even though the original topic is an unrelated issue. Whether Fight #67 is about money, sex, or the in-laws, no matter what the couple originally intended to discuss, the conversation always veers heatedly toward that ongoing argument. How do you stop this vicious pattern? It's the job of the spouse who requested or initiated the meeting to remind the other partner of the original purpose of the discussion. For instance, she might say, "I know that (money, sex, in-laws, or whatever) is a big issue for us, but right now we need to concentrate on whether we should let Debbie have her sleepover." In the therapy environment we call this "refocusing." When you sense the discussion taking a wrong turn, stop for a moment and gently, respectfully remind your partner that you need to "refocus." Assure your spouse that you can take up the other topic at another time—in fact, you might do well to schedule a separate meeting to really tackle the cause of Fight #67 once and for all. I know many couples that have done this successfully, and it improved their whole communication style with each other—permanently.

Be an Active Listener

I've made the point that listening is crucial, but I'll make it again since it's one of the best steps you can take toward achieving your goals and one of the core ground rules of positive communication. In order to express your own views clearly, you need to hear what's been expressed by your partner. Pay attention his or her statements before you respond with your own. Just to recap the most important aspects of active listening:

- Listen carefully.

- Do not interrupt.

- Reflect back what has been said.

- Maintain eye contact.

- Pay attention to nonverbal cues.

- Watch for indirect messages.

- Monitor your tone.

Reach a Conclusion

Once you've come to the end of your ten minutes (or two hours), resolve to conclude your discussion. (If you can't reach an agreement or conclusion, as noted above, reschedule another meeting to continue the dialogue.) Sum up the points and decide what you will do. Whenever possible, try to agree on a plan of specific action items (such as "Bob will arrange for a babysitter by next Wednesday," "I will talk to Kyle's teacher tomorrow morning").

Here's an example of a resolution to a parent-to-parent meeting. One of my clients, Adele, a woman with two school-age children, came to me expressing a great deal of frustration because she never knew where her husband was at a given moment during the day (Yoshi traveled locally as a salesman, was at the company headquarters only two days a week, and those two days changed every week). I suggested that she ask her husband to sit down with her at a mutually agreed upon time to discuss the situation, with the intent of resolving her frustration. At first Yoshi felt defensive and demanded to know why Adele needed to keep track of him. But after Adele listed several specific examples in the last month of when she had needed his advice or input for a decision that couldn't wait until the end of the day but didn't know where to reach him, Yoshi understood how important it was for his wife to know his whereabouts. He realized she wasn't keeping track of him but just wanted his involvement on key decisions that came up on a daily basis regarding family issues and schedules.

After a half hour of discussion, Yoshi came up with a solution on his own: He suggested that he would make his wife a weekly calendar, printed off his laptop datebook, with appropriate phone numbers next to blocks of time where he could be reached, including approximate times he would be in the car and his wife could use his cell phone number. He marked with an asterisk any meetings or appointments when he should be interrupted only in an emergency.

Communication Skills Can Make or Break Your Efforts

Now that we've covered some of the ground rules, let's look at some more instances in which good communication skills can result in a better balance of parenting responsibilities.

Abe, a public relations consultant, has just come in the door after a long, irritating day at work. Susanne, his wife, is waiting, having been thinking all day long about how angry she is. The school had called in the morning, and their son, Tomas, has been in trouble again. Susanne works as a dental hygienist three days a week, and this isn't the first time she has been called at home on her day off.

> **SUSANNE** (in an angry, agitated tone): The school called today. Guess what! Tomas is in trouble again, and it's all your fault. You never do anything with the kids, and I warned you this was going to happen. He's acting out again because he wants your attention.
>
> **ABE:** I've had a really rotten day, and I just got in the door. What did Tomas do that was so bad anyway?
>
> **SUSANNE:** You just don't care, do you! It's not what he did that's the point here, it's that you never spend any time with him.
>
> **ABE:** I'm not up for this now. I'm going to take a shower.

Abe seems like a pretty rotten guy, doesn't he? But the truth is, he may actually be quite concerned about his son and may want to be involved. Susanne might have initiated the dialogue differently to get a better response.

First of all, when your spouse walks in the door, remember

that he or she probably hasn't been thinking about the same things you've been contemplating all day. I know when I'm home with the kids an issue can come up, and I'll mull it over all day long. Then when Linda walks in, I sometimes forget that she hasn't had a chance to consider the problem, and I immediately bring it up—to her, seemingly out of left field. A better way to handle the situation is to give your spouse some downtime before presenting your thoughts. Let's say Susanne had handled the conversation this way:

SUSANNE: Hi, Abe. How did your presentation go? I was thinking about you.

ABE: It stank. The other group's was much better. I guess it's back to the drawing board.

SUSANNE: Oh, I'm sorry. Why don't you go upstairs, take a shower, and rest for a while? If you could give me about twenty minutes later this evening, I have some concerns about Tomas I'd like to talk with you about. Would seven be all right with you?

ABE: Seven's okay. What kind of concerns? Did something happen again?

SUSANNE: The school called, and the principal said Tomas had a fight with another boy at recess. We need to talk about what we can do to help him.

ABE: Okay. Let's sit down at seven on the patio while he's watching his TV show and have a talk.

This conversation went much better for several reasons. To open the dialogue, Susanne first asked a question about her husband, which showed that she'd been thinking about him and that she cared about him, and it helped her gauge his mood. She found out that he'd had a really bad day, a signal that she'd better schedule a discussion for later, after he'd had a chance to recover a little. Susanne then informed her husband that she needed to talk to him about a problem, and she stated specifically what the problem was. The couple then scheduled a time with a limit.

Conversation Is Not War

A common mistake couples make is to attack and counterattack. When one parent begins a conversation with an attack, the partner automatically gets defensive and blasts back by either denying the accusation or blurting out something that attacks back. For example, by beginning a dialogue with "Your attitude about the kids and child care is really uncalled for. Everything is an uphill battle with you," you're going to lose your mate's receptivity with the first line. His defenses are up, and you're off to the fights.

We all have defense mechanisms; these are natural and necessary. When you hear that someone has died, for instance, your first response is "I don't believe it!" or "No! That's not possible. I just saw her the other day!" We defend against this new knowledge because we haven't had time to prepare mentally, and we need to protect ourselves until we're ready to absorb the information. However, when it comes to communicating about parenting issues, most battles can be prevented by choosing language and timing carefully.

No Blame/No Fault Parenting

Instead of using accusations and blame as tools of the trade, try to approach discussions from what I call the no blame/no fault angle:

JEFF: I want to talk to you about Joey. He wants to spend more time with you. What does your schedule look like this week?

ELISE: This is a bad week. I'm really busy.

JEFF: How about next week?

ELISE: You know I have that big project next week.

JEFF: Is there something I could do to help you so that you could spend an afternoon with him or take him out some evening to the movies?

ELISE: Well, I guess if you could do the grocery shopping and a couple of other errands for me this Saturday, I could take Joey to the playground and out to lunch.

JEFF: It's a deal. Joey will really like that.

Jeff didn't accuse Elise of being a bad mom or blame her for being preoccupied with other commitments such as work. He simply stated his intent in a no blame/no fault manner.

When, Where, What, and How

When bringing up involvement issues, think about these four words: when, where, what, and how. Choose an appropriate time and place (not in the grocery store checkout line, for instance), express to your spouse clearly and directly what it is you want to discuss (don't hint or make sarcastic innuendos or cryptic remarks), and present your feelings in a nonaccusatory manner. Remember, of course, to listen.

My clients Martha and Bruce were very frustrated about the lack of communication in their family. Martha worked about thirty hours a week in a delicatessen, and Bruce sold insurance. He was out a lot but had flexible hours. Martha and Bruce were getting along okay on the surface, but they rarely talked about anything; they just coexisted. When Bruce had to go out of town, he rarely called home. Martha did most of the housework, set all the appointments, dealt with the children's school activities, and carted the three kids wherever they needed to go.

Before I could get any relief for Martha, I knew I had to help this couple learn to communicate. I asked them to switch roles. I then asked them to have a conversation in which each would play the part of the other.

We used this role-playing technique on a number of occasions. During the process, Martha learned that many of the things she'd been saying to Bruce were hurtful ("You're an irresponsible father" and "You're just like your dad was—never there when you needed him"). Bruce learned how frustrated and overwhelmed Martha felt when he stepped into her shoes ("I'm leaving town for three days, and while I'm gone, I want you to get the car fixed. I won't be able to call home because I'll be on the road").

Role-playing is an effective way to get to the bottom of a person's feelings. If you feel awkward actually role-playing, just try mentally to put yourself in the other person's shoes. Once Martha and Bruce began to see each other's side, they began talking on a regular basis, using the ground rules explained earlier. Bruce began helping Martha more at home and making himself more available. Martha became more sensitive to Bruce's feelings.

Don't Give In to Anger

Often there is so much pent-up anger and frustration revolving around involvement issues that attempts to communicate automatically start out on the wrong footing. When anger seems to be fueling your desire to talk, you need to step back and think about the guidelines above. Sit down and focus on or write down what you'd like to say. Remember, if you start your conversation with "I'm so angry at you! You're constantly on the golf course every spare minute, and you never spend any time with the kids!" your spouse will become defensive, and chances are progress won't be made. If you follow the ground rules for good communication, you'll have a much better chance of achieving positive change.

Nell, a physician, was always late coming home from the hospital. Her husband, Anthony, who cared for their two children while she worked the night shift, was always worried about her. When she came in the door, he'd invariably bark, "Where the heck have you been?" This made Nell feel as though she'd been doing something wrong when in fact she had been working very hard at her residency. Instead of directing anger at your spouse for behaviors that are upsetting, it's much more constructive to use a positive, no blame/no fault approach.

Start Small

Sometimes we're tempted to jump right in and talk out every aspect of our lives, hoping to change everything at once. But change comes slowly for most people, and if you throw too much at your spouse on one day, he or she may be stubborn about making even the slightest change. You can't just say to your partner, "Here's the changes I need. Make them tonight, and tomorrow everything will be different!'' You need to work slowly, one step at a time, moving toward your goals in realistic increments.

Colleen, one of my clients, complained a lot about her husband, Bret, who helped now and then with the kids but wouldn't do anything in the kitchen. The couple had four boys, and cooking was no small issue! With so many ravenous mouths to feed, Colleen, who was an accountant, felt that she was in the kitchen whenever she wasn't in her office.

Bret and Colleen got along well in spite of her complaints, but Bret was very set in his ways. His own father hadn't been involved in domestic tasks and didn't spend much time with his kids. So when Colleen asked her husband to pitch in with the cooking, he'd say he wasn't any good at it.

I encouraged Colleen to sit down and make a list of the things that were really bothering her. Since the cooking was number one, she decided that she'd concentrate on finding a creative method of dealing with it. That night she handed Bret a plate of hot dogs and hamburgers, and asked him to fire up the grill. Since barbecuing was "men's work" in Bret's opinion, he willingly complied.

The story might have ended there, but Colleen was now convinced that Bret could do more. So the next night she handed him some chicken to barbecue, along with some skewered vegetables. Again, since this was "men's work," Bret grilled the dinner.

For the next few nights Colleen kept adding to the list of items that could be made outside. On the last night of the week, as she prepared the salad and handed Bret a pot of beans to heat up on the grill next to the steak, Bret burst out laughing. He admitted that Colleen had finally made her point. Bret joined in on Colleen's solution to the dinner problem and got the kids involved in setting and clearing the table. Dinner was no longer a task delegated only to Mom; it was the responsibility of the entire family.

With persistence and creativity, Colleen showed her husband that he was perfectly capable of fixing dinner for the family, and in the weeks that followed, Bret became more involved in the planning and preparing of meals. She felt much better about the nights when she did cook dinner for the family because she wasn't the only one with the responsibility, and Bret came to the realization that feeding the family was not a gender-specific activity (but was a huge responsibility for one individual to shoulder alone). I like to recount this story because it shows that with positive thinking couples can often come to successful, creative solutions.

Children Learn Communication Styles from Their Parents

Good communication isn't only helpful to couples; it also sets the stage for how their children will communicate as they grow up. If children witness their parents engaged in bickering or name-calling, or if evenings are spent in stony silence, that's what they will learn. I'm reminded of a very negative man I once knew who came to dinner every evening with a complaint. His day was lousy, his job was rotten, his boss was a jerk, and so on. Yet this same parent seemed surprised when his own son began remarking that he hated school, his teachers were all idiots, and his friends were fools.

I encourage parents to work on good communication skills both for themselves and their own emotional health and sense of inner peace, and also for their children. It's much more beneficial for kids to see their parents discussing issues, exchanging ideas, and occasionally, when there has been a bad disagreement, hugging and making up. It's okay for children to know that their parents sometimes disagree; but it's also important for kids to see their parents coming together again. So often, misunderstandings between couples are resolved privately, after the children are asleep or when they're out playing. It's healthy for them to see that their parents can have differences and still love and care for each other.

Show Children That Talking Is Important

In our family we take turns at the dinner table discussing our day and telling about something we did. Other families may talk at bedtime (this is a good time to converse with children because they're wound down from the day) or over an early breakfast. The point is to show your kids that you value communication as a family and that these skills will serve your child well his entire life, from his own marriage to his future career. If a child has a mom who avoids confrontation or a dad who can't talk about his feelings or discourages communication about feelings, that child will have had only those poor role models when he enters his adult life. When good communication skills are modeled, however, kids learn early on how to communicate well and be active listeners. This sets a worthwhile precedent, too, for the teen years (the topic of chapter 9), offsetting the tendency that teens have to avoid talking to their parents.

Communication Breakthroughs Can Happen in Many Ways

Communication isn't always easy, but following the ground rules in this chapter will help you make real progress. I'm sure you'll find, however, that sometimes the lines of communication just can't seem to be pried open: the time isn't right, your spouse isn't receptive, the children are draining your energy, or you're so angry that you can't even begin. Occasionally, men and women don't know where to start. They may not even know what's troubling them. One of my clients, who was having panic attacks, seemed to have no clue regarding the roots of her anxiety.

Jean and Hank both worked; he was a building contractor, she was an engineer. Their two children, twelve and thirteen, were old enough to care for themselves after school. Both parents usually arrived home around the same time. Jean would make dinner and clean up, help the kids with their homework, and catch up on chores. Hank would basically take it easy or go into the garage to do some woodworking. Over the years, the family had fallen into this routine (both parents, in fact, had grown up with this pattern in their own childhood), and no one in the family—not even Jean— ever complained about it. Neither parent saw any need to make changes until, as is often the case, a crisis situation arose. Jean began to experience panic attacks and didn't know where they were coming from. She would suddenly be overcome by an inexplicable fear and was unable to get out of bed or go to work. One day she went so far as to ask her husband to call 911 because she thought she was having a heart attack. But there was nothing wrong with her heart, and no other medical problems were identified.

Jean came to see me, hoping I could help. In the course of talking to her, I soon realized that she rambled on and on about how much work she had to do. She was pressured on the job, and she gave me the rundown of what she did when she got home—cooking, cleaning, and paying a lot of attention to her two children. Never did she mention having a single moment to herself. I knew that Jean was stressed to the max; I decided to investigate further and asked her to bring her husband to the next session. Hank was very willing to do whatever he could to help the situation; he, too, was terrified that something he'd done had thrown Jean into this state. I explained to him that I felt Jean was sending an unconscious message to her family that she couldn't do it all anymore. Hank agreed to take on more of the domestic chores, and the kids were willing to pitch in, too. Because this family was willing to change, Jean's anxiety soon diminished, and life improved quickly for everyone.

What Upsets the Apple Cart:

The Nature of Change

W**E'RE CREATURES OF** habit. I get up very early each morning and drink two cups of coffee while I work in my home office. I work best in the morning, so I arrange my schedule accordingly. Although I'm busy with various activities on different days—Thursdays I teach classes, Wednesdays and Fridays I see clients—each week is set up in the same manner. Although my routine seems varied, it's really quite predictable.

As I sit thinking about the nature of change and how human beings grow attached to familiar rituals and routines, the paperboy rides by on his bike and throws the *Chicago Tribune* on my lawn. It lands in exactly the same spot next to the hedge every single morning. The carrier doesn't even notice that today the lawn sprinkler is on, and the paper will be drenched in a matter of moments. His paper-delivery pattern is set.

How Our Own Expectations Affect Our Thinking

Predictability brings order into the chaos of the big wide world, and it's part of human nature to like things to stay the same. We are comfortable with the familiar. In the 1950s, Erik Erikson asserted that from infancy, predictable routines—sets of activities that recur every day—create a sense of trust and comfort. A more recent psychological theory, called the information processing theory, echoes the same idea, asserting that people have a set of expectations that guides them through each day ("Today I'm carpooling with Joan . . . I have a meeting at 9:30 . . . I'm taking the kids to the movies tonight"). We don't generally even think about this set of expectancies until a monkey wrench is thrown in (Joan doesn't show up, the meeting is canceled, or the kids fight over which movie to see). All of a sudden our expectations are derailed, and we have to act differently.

An important life skill and parenting skill is to understand that these expectancies have a natural purpose: They bring predictability and familiarity and help us organize our thoughts and make decisions. It is also important, however, to be able to adjust our actions and reactions, to "flex," when the unexpected happens. Individuals who are not able to be flexible run into a number of obstacles as they make their way through life simply because life is characterized by constant change. As parents we understand that our children need schedules, limits, and boundaries, but we also have to be ready to go with the flow. A child may go to bed at 8 P.M., sleep soundly, and wake at 7 A.M., as he always does. Or just before bed he may lose a tooth, get a nosebleed, or start a fight with a sibling; or he may wake up in the night with a scary dream. Parents must face change constantly, and although sometimes it's hard to let go of old routines and habits as our children grow, we must learn to be flexible. When my son wanted to ride his bike alone across a busy street to play with friends, for instance, I said no because I was fearful that he might be hurt; but his request made me confront the reality that one day he *will* be old enough to cross that street without me and I will have to change my approach.

Everything in life is temporary. Having children certainly helps us become aware of that idea. As a baby grows and parents face each day's challenges, it's important to remember that change is really a healthy, normal part of life. We may feel afraid to make changes in the way we raise our children or in the way we are involved with them, but that shouldn't keep us from doing what we know is best in the long run.

Many of us have fallen into predictable parenting styles, and quite often we're comfortable with things just as they are—even when we suspect there might be a better way, for example, to get both parents more equally involved in our children's lives. Early in my training as a therapist I learned that the very fabric of human nature is designed to resist change. A few years after I started my practice, I had a female client who was very unhappy in her marriage. Her husband, who was emotionally distant, had no desire to have children and wasn't committed to the marriage. We spoke about ways she could improve her situation, and she admitted that she might be much better off without him. But at the end of our discussion the woman said she didn't want to stir up trouble; she was going home to her husband and intended to cope with things the way they were. Even in an unsatisfactory situation, some people may still resist change simply because the known is clearer to them than the unknown.

I call this my "climbing over the wall in therapy" story because it illustrates the point that when people come in for help and find it's not too difficult or stressful to make a change, they may do it. Many people can't climb all the way over the wall because it's just too darn hard—even with the support and encouragement of a therapist. They go halfway up and stop, deciding to keep things the way they are because it may be a whole lot easier than coping with permanent, never-look-back change. Here is an example of a father who felt this way:

Beau was a man who did everything according to plan. He took the 8:02 train to work each day, came home on the 5:17, had dinner at 6:00 (with one glass of red wine), and took a nap from 7:00 to 7:30. Beau had routines for everything he did, right down to the clothes he wore. If his wife didn't have the correct shirt back from the cleaner on time, Beau was annoyed. Beau had little to do with his two children, a boy and a girl, ages five and eight. His wife, Natalie, had raised the kids pretty much without his help. Now that the five-year-old was in school, Natalie wanted to get back to her career (she'd been a graphic artist), and she needed to take a computer course on Wednesday nights to polish up. Natalie loved Beau but felt he would never change, so she hired a babysitter to come on Wednesdays so she could pursue her goal. Beau didn't like the fact that Natalie had done this, but he figured it was better than having to watch the kids himself. Sadly, Beau was one of those guys who would probably never climb over the wall (or even halfway up). And although Natalie found a way to circumvent his obstinacy, she remained frustrated that she and her husband didn't connect better and more effectively, for themselves and for their kids.

Lenny and Margaret had been married for ten years; they had two small girls. Margaret's father had never been involved in her life when she was a child, but she wanted something different for her daughters. When she asked Lenny to take the girls to the park or play with them, however, Lenny always refused; he didn't feel comfortable in that role, he said. Instead he offered Margaret money and told her to hire a babysitter if she needed time off from the kids. He spent evenings out with his friends at a local bar and ignored his children and wife. Margaret was hurt and insulted; the marriage continued to deteriorate, and eventually the couple separated. Margaret told Lenny she had tried her best for ten years, and now she was through. Within a few months Lenny realized how lonely he was, and he began to miss his kids and Margaret. He was surprised to find out how much he really loved his daughters, and he began to see Margaret in a new light. He called and asked if she would give the marriage another chance; she said yes, but only if Lenny would try to be a more involved father and husband. Lenny went back home, determined to give the family more attention. He was poised to go over that "wall" to make permanent, positive changes in his life, but I don't know if he made it. I didn't hear from Lenny and Margaret again.

The Marriage Itself May Not Be the Issue

Very often when one parent or both parents come to see me with a problem such as anxiety, depression, or a child acting out, they automatically think something is wrong with the marriage. In therapy sessions, however, the couple learns quickly that the basic emotional structure of the marriage itself is not an issue; rather, balancing issues within the marriage are revealed. When I point out to clients that I don't perceive anything intrinsically wrong with the marriage as a whole but that I see balancing issues which I believe can be resolved, these couples are pretty much committed to making things work. Parents are often relieved to find that their problems can be solved by learning more effective communication skills and achieving better balance as a parenting team.

One Small Change Can Positively Affect the Whole Family System

Even a minor change alters the family system, and sometimes this can work to the benefit of everyone. Think of a thermostat and a furnace. If you make a small change in the thermostat setting, the furnace has to turn on. Similarly, if one parent makes a change, this will trigger a change in the behavior of that person's partner. This is why, even when a woman comes to my practice without her husband, we can work to identify logistical, behavioral, or attitudinal changes on her part that will help her reach her goals of having a husband who is more involved in the daily lives of the children. The changes a woman decides to make through her work in therapy or of her own accord automatically bring about change in her husband's behavior.

Let me quickly clarify that I'm not talking about secretly making changes that will somehow affect one's mate without his knowing. I encourage spouses to be open and honest about changes in their lives. However, when a mother (or father) chooses to change something about his or her life even when the other spouse isn't so willing to make a similar change, the family system will be affected. For example, a woman who makes a simple change in her schedule, such as working part-time on Saturdays, may find that her husband, who previously spent Saturday afternoons in his office, now comes home to be with the family, and the kids and the mom seem happier. If a man decides he will do something as simple as sit down with his son after dinner and read stories and play word and number games for an hour, he may find that now his wife seems more content and has some time to herself, and his son's grades are improving. There are many small, seemingly inconsequential changes that can be made on an everyday basis that will alter and enhance the quality of the equal-balance relationship.

Psychologist Uri Bronfenbrenner has studied how various influences affect the family. Work, church, school, health care, the neighborhood they live in—all have an impact. When change in these influencing factors occurs, from the micro to the macro, the family will be altered in some way. Emma was extremely worried because she hadn't been able to get pregnant. At thirty-seven she had been wanting a baby for several years, and her husband, Lou, was also anxious to become a father. The couple had discussed their desires on many occasions and had finally made the decision to go for fertility treatments. Emma scheduled an important battery of tests, and Lou agreed to accompany her, but a week before the appointment, Lou's boss told him he was required to attend a week-long conference on the West Coast. Lou told Emma he couldn't possibly make the appointment, but when she called to reschedule, she was told she'd have to wait another four months for the next opening. Since the couple had agreed on their commitment to having a baby, Emma pressed Lou to call his boss and ask to be excused from the trip or, at the very least, to be flown back for the appointment. Lou was hesitant but finally agreed to tell his boss the situation. To his surprise, his supervisor agreed to fly him back to New York even though it involved extra expense for the company. This was an example where Lou's decision to attend the week-long conference may have dramatically altered his chance to become a father but, happily, his employer agreed to go along with Lou's request. Emma, instead of backing down from something she really wanted, held firm in her conviction that Lou must remain committed and involved as they came closer to fulfilling their dream of a child.

Odette had been home with her kids for four years when she decided to return part-time to her job as an aerobics instructor. Her schedule changed in a way that affected the whole family, especially her husband who became more involved with the kids as a result of her decision. The children's schedules were also altered. Instead of coming home after school, Odette arranged for them to go to a friend's house until 5:00. Then Neill came home from work a half hour earlier than he used to, picked up the kids, and cared for them until 6:30. This meant he had to leave work on time and begin preparing dinner. The family adjusted because Neill was willing to support his wife's decision. What may seem like minor changes, however, were actually quite an adjustment for Neill and Odette and their children, who were faced with an entirely new after-school scenario. The family adjusted to the mother's schedule in a positive way, and the father became more involved in caring for his children as a result.

What Are the Obstacles That Stand in the Way of Change?

Beau illustrated that a lack of flexibility and an overdependency on routines can be taken to a disadvantageous extreme, but many other variables can stand in the way of change, some or all of which need to be examined before equal-balance parenting can occur. A mother or father's attitude can, for instance, stand in the way of progress and be very difficult to alter. Once some people develop a particular mind-set, they just want to stick with it. Other obstacles include negative comments from other family members, poor communication, criticism, unfinished business, and not allowing your spouse to perform child care activities different from the way you do.

Other Members of the Family Can Create an Obstacle to Change

Often I hear from couples who are discouraged about their attempts to change due to the negative influence of other family members.

Frequently, it's the husband's or wife's parents who can't under-stand why the father needs to be so involved in the children's lives since, in their day, things were different. It's important to remember that parents and in-laws who have raised their children in a different time and way have a right to their opinions, but in the long run, the choices we make about how we raise our kids are our own. We know so much more about the value of equal involvement from both parents than we did even a decade ago.

Joe had made the decision to stay home and take care of the baby; Amanda had the better-paying job and found her work as a TV producer very rewarding. Joe had adjusted well to being a stay-at-home dad. He took the baby to the park and for walks, did the grocery shopping and housework, and cooked most of the meals. He didn't intend to spend the rest of his life at home, but he wanted to be there for the first few years of his daughter Dawn's life. When Amanda's parents, who lived nearby, learned of Joe's decision to put his career as a copywriter on hold and stay home with his daughter, they were dismayed, and every time they came to visit, they criticized the couple's decision. Amanda's mother, in particular, felt that a little girl should be raised by her mother and was not supportive of her daughter's decision. She made incessant disparaging remarks about the way the baby was dressed and the way the house was kept. Joe, who was doing a great job taking care of Dawn, tried to ignore his mother-in-law's comments but found it difficult, and his feelings were hurt. Finally, Amanda sat down with her mother and explained that no matter what she thought, Joe and she had decided this was the way they were going to raise Dawn, and it worked well for them. Future "remarks" were not acceptable.

Poor Communication Can Create an Obstacle to Change

Change requires communication, and sometimes couples talk about change but, without using positive communication, fail to achieve progress. A mother may complain bitterly and constantly that her husband is always watching sports on TV and never pays any attention to the baby. But complaining isn't the same thing as communicating. A man may nag his wife to get home from work earlier, but unless he sits down with her and discusses the changes that need to be made so that she can arrive home on time, very little will happen. Couples may repeat the same complaints or demands time and time again, but without results. Change doesn't happen just by harping on the same subjects in the same old ways; communication requires active participation, as discussed in chapter 3.

Obstacles That Get in the Way of Meeting Your Goals

Because I believe that marriage and parenting should be a team effort, I expect neither mothers nor fathers to be responsible for all the work. I want to look at some of the more common obstacles for women that I see frequently in my practice. I will make suggestions about ways that the mother can make small but important changes in order to facilitate a better relationship with her husband and a richer understanding of parental roles. Then I will look at some complementary issues that I have found are common obstacles for men.

A Mother's Attitude Is a Strong Indicator of Change in the Father

Recent studies, reported in the *Journal of Marriage and the Family* and picked up by the national media, have revealed that a dad's involvement with his children is often contingent on the mother's attitude toward the father, her expectations and support, as well as on the extent of her involvement in the workforce. Researchers found that the mother's outlook actually had more impact on the level and quality of the father's involvement with the children than did the father's own parenting skills. This underscores, then, what I've believed all along: Women have a crucial role in determining the extent of their spouse's involvement. If a wife believes fathers should have more involvement, and she becomes comfortable and confident with that knowledge and communicates it effectively to her husband, even a man who has not gotten involved of his own accord is likely to respond well to her initiation of the subject. While I do not intend to undervalue a father's independent choices or overemphasize a mother's role in affecting her husband's behavior, I do want to stress how important it is for women to encourage their spouse's involvement.

It helps, I think, for women to keep in mind that parenting with an equal partner is a reasonable and fair expectation—not a prize granted only to certain winners. Though some women may feel that their spouses work hard already, we need to begin seeing involvement with children not as a manifestation of "work" but as a reciprocal relationship that benefits both child and parent. When women begin to view fatherhood as a rewarding experience for men and not part of their "job," they will feel greater validation, if they need it, for encouraging their husband's involvement.

Criticism is one obstacle some women unconsciously set up for themselves. Many of my male clients say, for instance, that their wife's criticism hurts and belittles them and discourages any desire they have to be equal partners. Criticism is an indirect form of hurt and disrespect, and it is also a negative communication pattern (as noted in chapter 3). Some of my female clients, for example, are not aware until I point it out to them that the one simple change of reining in critical behavior can elicit a positive response from a father. He is much more likely to pursue active involvement if he doesn't feel graded by the teacher. A woman recently phoned me and said she had attended one of my parenting seminars a few months back. While listening to my discussion of criticism, she said, it hit her like "a ton of bricks," and she vowed on the spot to curb the criticism that was spoiling her attempts to get her husband more involved. Happily, she reported, she got positive results almost immediately, and she was calling to thank me!

The following example illustrates that a woman's use of criticism is often completely unintentional. Melanie was a working mother whose husband, Steve, spent time with their two-year-old son, Ray, on Saturdays. Melanie used the day to do things for herself. She curled up with a good book, went shopping, visited friends, and walked by the lake near their house. Steve really looked forward to Saturdays with Ray, but his enthusiasm quickly waned when Melanie started to criticize every choice he made. "You can't take Ray to the playground. He's too young to play on that stuff. He'll fall off" or "You can't take him to run errands like going to the bank and the post office. He's a baby. He needs entertainment" or "Don't take him to the car wash. He'll get scared there." She ended up writing him a sort of prescription for every Saturday: what Ray should wear, what to do, where to go, what to feed him, and so on. Gradually, Steve became so turned off that he began staying at work later on weeknights and playing golf on weekend afternoons. He missed his son, but he hated the criticism.

When this couple started therapy, the friction between them was almost palpable. Melanie would say, "I feel as though I have two babies in the house," which further insulted Steve. He felt completely emasculated. This couple had many issues to address, but I felt it was important to start by helping Melanie realize that she wasn't the only woman who feels a crushing responsibility to raise good kids. Ever since Freud set forth his theory that it is neurotic women who make homes dysfunctional and children grow up marred, society has continued to put a tremendous amount of pressure on women to make their kids "come out right." On the flip side, this has taken pressure off the dads, who are more relaxed and say, "If I screw up, it doesn't really matter." The vicious cycle accelerates, and women feel additional pressure because they think, "If my husband messes up, it's my fault, too." Criticizing her husband was a mechanism Melanie used to make sure everything "came out right." But she admitted that she really didn't do it consciously.

One key part of our work was getting Melanie to focus on the fact that Ray, at the ripe old age of two, was learning from his mother how to be critical because she was criticizing Steve right in front of him. Ray was her first child, and she hadn't realized how quickly children absorb, process, and mimic the behaviors of their parents—the good and not so good.

The Replacement Process Can Be a Powerful Tool for Overcoming Obstacles

The other key part of our work was getting Melanie to replace her negative comments with some more positive tactic. In the therapy setting it is common for the therapist to encourage clients to look more deeply and analytically at a negative behavior pattern than they might on their own without a therapist. The therapist then helps them come to their own conclusions about how to replace the behavior with something healthier or more constructive. I encouraged Melanie to think about the negative outcomes of criticizing her husband (the unhealthy behavior pattern) and to focus on letting Steve have the opportunity to be a great dad (the positive replacement). Learning how to take yourself through this replacement process on your own is a great skill to have throughout life.

This process also underscored for Melanie that the opposite of criticism is, of course, praise. Everyone loves a compliment, especially if one is used to hearing criticism. If a dad gives the baby a bath and the water goes everywhere and the bath toys fly in every direction, but giggles (both dad's and baby's) are coming from the room, it's better to compliment the job than comment on the mess. If your toddler doesn't look picture perfect when your husband dresses her but she's wearing pants, a shirt, socks, and sneakers, say, "Thanks for dressing Angie. She looks great," and let your other thoughts go. Remember, too, that compliments beget compliments. My clients tell me that as soon as one partner starts complimenting the other, the reverse happens, too. Then both parents are getting the crucial positive reinforcement all parents need on a regular basis!

The Fact That Men Have a Different Way of Doing Things Is Good, Not Bad

Second to criticism, and related to it, is the idea that many parents resist when their partner attempts to perform a child care task in a way that is even slightly different from theirs. Many people—both men and women—believe that a mother instinctively knows how to care for children, while a man is less suited for the job. We now know that this is a myth. My research shows that most men learn "on the job" how to relate to and care for their children, just as women do, and that children learn flexibility when being cared for in more than one way.

Accept Your Spouse's Unfinished Business

Unfinished business refers to any major relationship or situation that one never addressed or put closure on before moving on with life. The turbulent or emotionally shallow relationship with a mother or father that was never resolved, or the disappointment or bruised self-esteem experienced with former boyfriends or girlfriends are just some examples. Unfinished business is a powerful obstacle to change. A common manifestation of unfinished business in men is unconsciously carrying over their own father's expectations of them to their own children. One example I see often in my practice is the father-son (or, increasingly, father-daughter) relationship involving sports.

Rick owned his own business, a print shop. He wanted his ten-year-old son, Greg, to play baseball and was determined that Greg would become a professional player even though Greg wasn't especially interested in baseball. When Greg didn't respond with the level of enthusiasm that he had hoped, Rick demanded that he play anyway: "Baseball is the great American sport. You'll love it once you get into it. And a baseball scholarship will pay for your college education. The World Series, here we come!" Rick had put Greg in a completely unfair position. Despite Greg's lack of interest in baseball, he knew what his father's expectations truly were and that he had disappointed him. Rick's wife, Sandy, didn't want to become involved in the issue. Whenever it came up at the dinner table, she'd leave the room. When Rick tried to talk to her about it after Greg went to bed at night, she'd invariably say, "I think you and Greg should work this out."

Rick, his wife, and I spent many sessions talking about Rick's relationship with his own father. It turned out that Rick's father had insisted Rick become a professional baseball player. When that didn't happen, Rick's father let it permanently poison the father-son relationship. Rick was never able to resolve these ill feelings with his father, and when he grew up, he unconsciously stepped into the same pattern that his own father had. I worked with Rick to help him see that whether or not he was able to resolve his feelings with his father directly, and even though he had not become a professional baseball player, he *was* a good person and a good father. Rick had a serious discussion with his father, saying essentially, "Dad, you pushed me, and I don't think it was right. But I'm over it." Rick was able to break the pattern that his dad had set.

Even though they had been married eleven years, Sandy never really understood how much pain her husband still carried around with him with respect to his relationship with his father. Once she learned more, Sandy made a stronger effort to understand her husband's approach to their son. Almost a year later, Rick found out that his son was interested in classical guitar. Rick nurtured Greg's interest through music lessons and attending concerts together. He began to find pleasure in a process-oriented, as opposed to a goal-oriented, activity. He also realized that learning to play the guitar was building Greg's self-esteem and confidence. Sandy found herself with a husband who was positively involved with their child.

Dads—Don't Go with the Status Quo

Now let's look at some of the obstacles that dads can overcome to increase their involvement; these are in addition to the practical tactics discussed in chapters 5 through 9, the "ages and stages" chapters of this book. First, I want to consider a father's mind-set, his basic attitude. How can fathers change the ways they view themselves and their role?

Oftentimes, fathers take a look around at what other dads are doing with their kids and say to themselves, "Hey, I'm doing a lot! I'm certainly a lot more involved than so-and-so." I've always found that when you compare yourself to others, you can end up looking really great or really pitiful, depending on whom you're looking at for comparison. If you judge your involvement based on your own family, your own children's needs, and your own definition of equal-balance parenting, you may find that you could be doing quite a bit more. Comparing yourself to other dads isn't constructive, and it isn't really what fair-share parenting is about. It's more about looking at your own marriage and adjusting your roles to better meet the needs of your unique family.

Remain Confident in Your Competence

Many fathers aren't confident in their child care capabilities and knowledge, or they're self-conscious about it, and this prevents them from greater participation. I understand that this lack of confidence comes from many places (society, gender roles, role models, and so on), but it can also be used as an excuse not to make that extra effort.

I believe that dads do know how to take care of their kids; they just may not know that they know it. For many people, even for many women, child rearing is on-the-job training. The notion that women are born with some innate knowledge of how to change a diaper is pure silliness. Fathers who stay home to care for their children are examples that prove the information is wrong; these guys just jump right in and learn on the job. Before long they're doing the cleaning, cooking, nurturing, soothing, and all the things that mothers do. Men need to let go of the notion that only moms are competent at caring for children. Plenty of women didn't babysit or take care of babies before they became moms. They had to learn, too, just like dads. Men may do some of these things differently from women, but they still get done.

Value Your Importance

Some men may feel—once again mainly due to outmoded attitudes from a previous era—that their involvement in their children's lives really isn't all that important. They hold on to the idea that a man's place is to be the breadwinner even when their wives, in many cases, are earning the same amount or more at their jobs. It's time for men to realize that the ways in which they are important to their children's healthy development are very complex. As discussed in chapter 2, fathers contribute to the social, emotional, and cognitive growth of their children in many different ways, and the more they are involved from infancy onward, the more positive the outcome for the child.

Children, I believe, show us more swiftly and plainly than research results or articles in the media that fathers are crucial influences. I'm reminded of a woman who grew up in the 1950s and sat at the living room window in the afternoons waiting for her father's car to pull in the driveway. She was especially anxious for him to get home from work during the summer when he got out by 4 P.M., which gave them plenty of time to play. This child and her father would go out to the backyard to swing on a homemade swing, talk, and sing, and after dinner they read together. During her school years it was her dad—not her mom—who helped with homework and encouraged her to pursue a career as a teacher. Whatever she wanted to learn or do, her father helped her with the positive reinforcement of "You can do it!" Early in her life there was no question in this woman's mind that her father was every bit as important to her growth and development as her mother.

If you pay attention to your children's signals and behaviors, they will show you how much they value your importance. Be cognizant of the messages they send and the ways in which they reach out to you.

Fathers Need to Check In—Not Out

Fathers sometimes feel they can afford to "check out" of child care and family involvement. They figure the mother will take care of that end of things. Only when fathers see and understand the worth of their involvement will they make the effort to remain active and present in their kids' lives. I am reminded of a dad who showed up on our summer camp family day, when the moms and dads play soccer against the kids. He was complaining that the whole afternoon was such a waste of time, and he'd rather be down at the country club. This was the man's attitude all throughout his son's life; not surprisingly, the child had many problems. The boy was involved with drugs and drinking in his preteens, and eventually was sent to military school.

It was a disturbing case, and although most children do not necessarily resort to negative behavior or peer pressure to do drugs and to drink when their fathers are not involved in their lives, it is not an uncommon outcome. I mention this story because it exemplifies how things can go wrong when dads check out emotionally.

Stan, a successful physician, was married to Lorraine, a stay-at-home mom. The couple had two children, Jake, two, and Mark, four. Stan's patients admired his medical skills, his compassion, and his ability to talk with and listen to them. Stan was very effective at communicating with his patients. He knew the best way to deliver both good and bad news to them, and he listened well as they described their symptoms. Stan's sensitivity was especially welcomed by his older patients, who were looking for a sympathetic ear, and his concern could be as effective as the medicine he prescribed. But at home it was a different story. "I think Stan is a different person when he walks in the door," Lorraine would say. "It feels as if he has used up all his warmth and people skills before he comes home at night, and he doesn't have anything left for the family."

Stan considered strong communication skills part of his job. Stan told me that it took a lot of effort and energy to do his job well, and when he came home, his mechanism for releasing frustration and anxiety and stress was to "zone out." He would stop listening or listen only halfheartedly when Lorraine discussed family issues. Lorraine felt left out, and after a whole day with the kids, she wanted to talk with her husband. She didn't understand, however, that demanding interaction from him as soon as he entered the door was not the best tactic for getting him to be receptive. At the time they came to see me, they were dealing with several issues, including that Lorraine wanted Stan to drive Mark to basketball practice three times a week at 5:30 P.M., watch his practice, and bring him home. That was just too much for Stan, and he was refusing to take Mark. Both Stan and Lorraine were frustrated and angry.

I told Stan that his people skills were needed just as badly at home as in the outside world. I encouraged Lorraine to respect Stan's need for downtime and to understand that it was because he loved his family and home so much that he felt safe to zone out for a while after work. We then worked on ways to meet their needs. Stan determined he could not take Mark to basketball practice or games during the week, but he could on weekends. On the weeknights Mark had practice, Lorraine took him, and Stan started going to the health club on his way home as an hour-and-a-half "pit stop" between work and home. After practice, Lorraine then fed the children and put them to bed. When Stan came home, he and Lorraine had a later dinner together, during which they had a chance to relax, enjoy each other's company, and talk about the day's issues and happenings. The fact that both Stan and Lorraine were willing to compromise was key to the plan's success.

Setting Goals for More Balanced Involvement

We are all familiar with setting goals for career or financial reasons, but setting goals for you as a couple and your family is also important. If told they had only six months to live, most people would cut out the nonessentials and focus on what really matters. But why wait for a personal crisis to do that?

Determine a time soon when you can sit down with your spouse and discuss your family's goals. Using the communication tactics discussed in chapter 3, talk about the changes or compromises you feel need to be made in order for the family to be together more. Make time for both you and your spouse to discuss the issues and obstacles that are bothering you. Then write down concrete goals that you want to reach. Make the wording specific:

- Chris wants to be with the kids at least two nights a week on his own.

- We both want to be with the kids together as a family one weekend day and at least two weekday evenings.

- For a couple with two children: We want to spend at least one evening or weekend day doing an activity with each child one-on-one.

- Helen needs two evenings a week to have time for her own activities.

Specific goals are easier to achieve than general statements like "Chris wants to spend more time with the kids" and "Helen wants more time to work out regularly." Think specifically about what you as a couple can do to make your partnership more equal and to get dad more involved with the family.

Make Goals Not Only Specific but Also Realistic

Sometimes mothers are tempted to dump everything on the father's shoulders; anger builds, and rather than moving slowly and taking small steps, one parent decides to unload the entire matter on the other partner in one fell swoop.

This strategy doesn't work. Instead, talk together to identify realistic ways you both can be involved in your children's lives. See how you might adjust the schedule on various days, but don't expect your entire parenting world to change at once. Be positive and talk through solutions. It's always better to discuss changes in schedules and policies together as a couple than for one person to plan it out and then spring it on the other. A slow, progressive approach to realistic change will be more effective and successful than expecting instant, sweeping change overnight.

Jane and Elio were bickering a lot. Jane, a stay-at-home mom, was unhappy that Elio spent so little time with their four children. Elio said they needed the very respectable income he made from a high hourly wage as an accountant for a large software company, and he didn't want to cut back on his hours or overtime. Jane said she would make a concerted effort to save money; she developed a spending plan and began shopping at cut-rate grocery clubs, clipped coupons, and kept to a strict budget. Elio saw that Jane was indeed saving money, but he still didn't want to cut back his hours. "Maybe this is our chance to invest some money," he told his wife. Jane kept talking to Elio about the benefits of involved fathers.

In the spring she began letting the kids play outside after school and do their homework after an early dinner, instead of in the afternoons as they did in the winter. Elio had always enjoyed dinner with the family, but now that Jane was serving dinner earlier, he'd have to leave the office earlier to join them. After a few weeks he began arriving home earlier, and at Jane's request he began to help the kids with their homework after they ate. Elio's forte—and his older two boys' weakness—was math, and before long he was staying home to help them with their math instead of going back to the office in the evening. Within weeks he realized that he was working fewer hours, and although he was making less money, Jane was continuing to be frugal and the family really wasn't suffering financially. Elio admitted he enjoyed being with the children, and they were thrilled to be spending more time with their dad and jumped all over him when he got home from work. He decided that the change was a good one, and he was proud that with his help they were making so much progress in their schoolwork. Elio could really see a difference in the whole family.

Jane and Elio had goals that brought them forward to meet changes. Jane wanted Elio to be more involved and Elio wanted to be more involved, but didn't want the family to suffer financially. Together they worked toward a viable solution.

One Important Goal for Everyone: Changing Our Definition of the On-Call Parent

When you sit down to discuss your family's goals, I recommend spending some time talking about who in your marriage is the on-call person for the kids. I introduced this term in chapter 1—it's the one parent who is "on call" most of the time, whether that person works or stays at home. In many families that person is the mom.

In my family I'm the on-call person because I'm the parent who stays home with the kids, and my wife works a good forty-five minutes from our home. I pack lunches, do the morning routine with the kids to get them on the school bus, and arrange after-school activities. Also, if one of our children gets sick at school and needs to be picked up or if a problem comes up during the day, I'm the parent who is contacted. This makes the most sense for our family because of my wife's workplace and also because I'm eager and willing to fill the role.

A lot of responsibility and a good deal of pressure go along with the role of the on-call parent. I am the first to admit that there have been days when I've thought to myself, "I just hope my daughter or son doesn't get sick today because I have so many things to do!" And invariably someone does get sick, and I get a call from the school—and, well, there goes my afternoon. The on-call role puts a tremendous amount of strain on an individual even if you never get that call to go to the school to pick someone up and even if your morning routine usually goes without a hitch. That sense of responsibility is always in the back of the on-call parent's mind even when it isn't beckoned to the forefront. Sometimes the psychological issues weigh most heavily: what's going on with peers at school, a child's upcoming test, or whether he'll be getting in trouble during lunch hour at the playground.

Just as was said in chapter 1, every family should have an on-call person. It's like driving defensively: You need to be thinking about what you will do if something comes up, and it makes sense in most cases for the parent who stays at home (if one does) to be that person. If both parents work, then it shouldn't be assumed that Mom will be on call. Couples should discuss the situation. Dad's office may be closer to the day care center, or it may be okay for him to get to work at ten instead of nine; it would then make sense for him to be the on-call person.

Sometimes one working parent has more flexible hours, which makes this person a likely candidate for the job. Francine and Mick were a good example of this. Francine was a school aide, and Mick was a broker. Mick's hours were pretty much his own. Francine, on the other hand, was a one-on-one aide for a handicapped child; her presence at school was needed every day. If Mick had to cancel on a client, he might potentially lose a lot more money than Francine, but usually his clients could be rescheduled. It made sense for him to be on call for the kids during the day and for Francine to be assured that she could be there to help the handicapped student.

How to Equalize or Alternate the On-Call Role

Instead of naming one parent as the on-call person, it is becoming increasingly common for couples to alternate or share this role. In one family I know, the dad works at night and is home during the day, so he's responsible for taking the kids to school, picking them up, taking them to activities and play dates, and so on, until the mom comes home and they switch roles. I know another couple, both trial lawyers, who worked out a good solution: Whoever was not in court on a particular day would be the on-call person. That person would pack the lunches, oversee the children in the morning, and so on, so the parent who had a court date was free to prepare and get to the courthouse. This was great for the husband, too, because he really became attuned to his children and their schedules and needs. Even though the on-call person changed from day to day or week to week, this solution worked best for them and the children.

Whether you work out a way to share the on-call role or you are both comfortable with one person taking on that role, I think it's important for each parent to get a taste of what it's like to be the parent who is on-call. For example, if one parent's workplace or schedule doesn't allow for him or her to be the on-call person, I think it's still crucial for the on-call parent to share his or her feelings about the role, to let the partner know what it's like to be responsible for the kids so much of the time. Many moms, I believe, just want their spouse to respect that being on call is a twenty-four-hour-a-day job that holds pressures and responsibilities not always perceived by others. If the parent who isn't on call can say to his or her partner, "Tell me what it was like for you today. What were you concerned about?" and show some empathy and appreciation, that will go far. If you and your spouse decide that one parent is always on call, it is very important that the parent who is *not* in that role take over the on-call responsibilities at least one whole day and evening a month. A weekend day is fine and makes the most sense for parents who work. It is important that it be *a whole day and evening* to get the full experience of being with the kids through all their daily activities and routines, from morning until lights out. I believe each spouse will see the other's role from a new and more appreciative perspective when this happens.

Benefits of the On-Call Role for Dads

My research on fatherhood indicates that many working dads don't know what their kids' schedules are during the day. Being on call is therefore an excellent opportunity for fathers to get in sync with their children's daily lives. It's also an excellent chance for dads to tap into their nurturing side; when a child is sick or falls down or feels unhappy, there's no reason that Dad can't be the one to dole out the chicken soup and love. The child will remember and appreciate it, and the father will feel good that he was there and able to do it. Bonds will be strengthened in this way, too. Instead of the dad saying, "How was your day?" an in-tune dad will ask open-ended questions (not yes or no questions) about specific activities and people in his child's life, such as "Tell me about tai kwan do class" or "What kind of questions were on your social studies quiz?" or "What were Isabella's new kittens doing today?" This kind of interaction also encourages kids to talk to their dads.

Katie and Ron had one child. Katie was home for the first three years with the baby, and then when she returned to work, she assumed the role of the on-call parent, never questioning the role even though Ron's office was much closer to the nursery school. Before long it became clear that the arrangement wasn't working; Lyla was often home sick with chronic ear infections, and there was a lot of pressure at Katie's newspaper office to be at her desk. Ron, an illustrator, had a very flexible work environment, and his boss didn't even mind if he brought work home. The couple switched the on-call role; Ron stayed home when Lyla was sick and really got to know her schedule. On the weekends Katie took over the on-call role, but arranged a standing date with herself to take her laptop to a nearby park for two hours every Sunday morning to work on her own writing. She returned home to share a late breakfast and the rest of the day with her husband and daughter.

Goal Setting Helps Couples Climb Over the ''Wall''

To get over that "wall" to reach real change, it helps to set goals. If we can see where we're going and have some expectation of what the result will be, change may not be so difficult after all. When our cognitive expectancies tell us that a particular scenario may lie ahead and we can begin to prepare mentally for what we will do when we get there, change can come about. Couples who think about, discuss, and envision what life might be like if parenting roles were shared more equally are one step ahead in their progress toward reaching that goal.

Right from the Start:

Pregnancy Through Infancy

THE VENERABLE NATURE-versus-nurture debate is seemingly never-ending. One moment scientists discover that some aspect of our behavior is "genetically wired," and the next they're finding that, given certain circumstances, wiring can somehow be altered or influenced. Certainly, genetics determine whether a baby has blue eyes or brown, but where you live, what you feed your baby, what you teach him, whether you read to him every night before bed, whether you play Mozart or folk songs for him each evening will all have an impact on the way that child learns and grows.

As a teacher I strongly believe that we can nurture our children in ways that will directly impact their lives. Involved fathering is one area in which the nature-versus-nurture debate points to the power of environmental factors. When dads maintain strong emotional bonds with their children and interact with them consistently and with love, children really bloom.

With this in mind, I encourage parents to approach pregnancy and infancy as a team, knowing that the contribution each parent makes to nurturing their baby will foster the infant's emotional, social, and intellectual growth. Much has been said and written about the mother's unique bond with her baby, and certainly the strength and importance of a mother's love is indisputable. But more and more we're seeing how influential a father's involved presence can be, not only as a child grows older but in the very first days and months of a baby's life. While I recognize the singularity of the mother-child bond—a woman carries her baby for nine months and is intimately connected in ways unfathomable to all but herself and her child—I also know the circle of love and attachment needs to include the father as well.

Some fathers are afraid to pick up their newborns. They fear that their hands are too large and rough, their shoulders too bulky, their voices too gruff. I hear about fathers who don't really want much to do with their infants until the baby is larger and stronger. I've seen fathers who will not change a newborn's diapers—not because they're adverse to changing diapers (although some men are) but because they're intimidated by the fragility and vulnerability of their baby. To these men I say that caring for infants is on-the-job training. Do it and you will learn.

Stop Thinking of Dad as the "Helper"

If a couple assumes that the mom will be the nurturing caregiver, then she will probably fall into that role. But if a couple decides it's the responsibility of both parents, then from conception forward they will follow a road of involved, active fathering. Although it's never too late for dads to become involved, the best way to establish an equal parenting connection is at the very beginning.

With this in mind I'd like to point out that lots of times dads are encouraged to "help" or "pitch in" with their baby. It's tempting to use these terms, but in reality, dads shouldn't look at what they do as "helping," as if child rearing is the mom's real job and the father is just the assistant. When two parents approach child rearing equally, they ask themselves and each other: What is my role? How best can I contribute to this child's growth and development? How can I support and nurture my family and my partner in our parenting endeavor? This isn't a question of "helping out," and though I may sometimes use the word "help" to get my point across, the message of this book is to equalize the parenting partnership. Women have for centuries made plenty of changes in their lifestyles and work habits when children entered the picture. To create a balanced parenting partnership, change is required by *both* parents, so men, too, need to make some changes in their lifestyle and work habits, and even before the baby is born.

Begin Before the Baby Is Born: Talk About Your Dreams

Talk candidly with your partner about your dreams for your unborn child. It's healthy and positive to discuss and explore those ideas rather than brush them aside; they're bound to resurface someday anyway. Discussing the dreams of what you'd like your child to be is less harmful than one day pushing your child to be something he or she is not. When we think and talk about the way we'd like things to be, we put our dreams on the table. If the reality is something different, we'll need to deal with that then.

My wife and I had a dream of a boy and a girl. Luckily, it was fulfilled since I had already painted Kevin's blue nursery pink when A.J. was born! I wanted A.J. to be the epitome of a girl, with pierced ears and long hair and a closet full of dresses. I encourage parents to get beyond just saying, "I want a healthy baby; I don't care what the gender is." Allow yourself to have a preference—for the sake of discussion—and then talk openly with your spouse about how you feel and how you think you'll be with a baby. If you really don't have a gender preference, then talk about both scenarios—a boy or a girl. Get in touch with your realities and expectations, how you and your spouse want your child to turn out, and increase your own awareness of how your expectations will play out as you make decisions about raising your child. To get started, each spouse can ask the other such questions as:

- What would your gender preference be and why? How will you feel if you get the other gender? What specific fears or concerns do you have about having the other gender? (As you'll read in chapter 7, a parent who really wanted a boy and gets a girl, for example, may unconsciously impose too many "boy" expectations on that girl.)

- What are your dreams for the child? Do you want her to be pretty or cute? Do you want the child to love sports? The arts? Do you want the child to have a strong sense of family? Do you want him or her to have certain personality characteristics? Generosity of spirit? Patience? Friendliness? Concern for others? Good manners? What else?

- Is it important if you have a girl that she be strong and independent as well as feminine? If you have a boy, is it important that he be sensitive and caring as well as masculine? What gender stereotypes do you agree and disagree with?

- In what ways do you feel your parents pushed you to become a certain way or a certain type of person? How are these feelings and experiences going to translate into your child rearing goals and decisions?

This "dreams" discussion makes an early connection between the parents and the unborn child, and it is meaningful for both men and women. When couples discuss their dreams, they begin their bonding in the context of parenthood, which in turn prepares them for the attachment they will soon make with their baby.

Jared had no involvement right from the start; he refused even to discuss a name for the baby, and each suggestion his wife Irene made was rejected. When Irene came up with a series of boy's names, even one that was a family name on Jared's side, he said, "Absolutely not." Irene's suggestions for girl's names were also met with negative remarks. When she asked Jared for his suggestions, he shrugged his shoulders and said he didn't have time to think about it. Irene had come to see me several years before about an unrelated problem, so she called me when she suspected that something was troubling Jared. After meeting with Jared on several occasions, he revealed that there had been a number of deaths in his family when he was a boy, and he was afraid to become attached to his newborn for fear that something might happen to the baby. We discussed the fact that experiencing loss in one's life can help us to love even more in the future. I encouraged Jared to look at his reaction to the baby names not as an indication that he didn't want to attach to his baby but, rather, that he had a huge well of love he was preparing to tap into fully once his child was born. I thought a man with so much love and concern would be a wonderful father.

Face the Unknown as a Couple: What Will You Do If Something Goes Wrong?

As well as dreams and aspirations, couples should talk about what might happen if something goes wrong. How do you as a couple feel about abortion? Or about raising a child who is disabled or developmentally delayed or challenged in some way? Though it's healthy and normal to prepare for the best possible pregnancy outcome, it's also useful to talk about what might happen if things don't proceed normally. The cognitive expectations theory points to the fact that we can better deal with the unexpected if we have some notion of a backup plan.

Eliana and her husband, Tim, were having their first baby. Eliana was thirty-eight, and her obstetrician informed her that women of her age are advised to have amniocentesis, a procedure in which a small portion of amniotic fluid is removed to test for genetic abnormalities. Eliana went home that day and told Tim she'd have to have the test, but she was feeling very uncomfortable about it since she knew it involved a very small chance of miscarriage. As they talked, they realized they weren't comfortable with the idea of abortion, and both agreed they would be willing to raise a handicapped child. Tim went with Eliana to her next appointment, and together they told her obstetrician that they had talked it over and decided not to have amnio. Eliana signed a waiver and was not required to have the test. She was relieved and happy to know that had the baby been handicapped, her husband would have been supportive and involved. They had faced their fears and made a very important decision together, and the knowledge that they agreed on this issue strengthened their partnership.

Talk to Your Baby *in Utero*

One way fathers can begin to forge an early bond is by talking to the baby *in utero*. Babies become "habituated" to familiar sounds; studies confirm that when they emerge into the world, babies are already very familiar with the sound of their mother's voice. Well-known pediatrician T. Berry Brazelton recounts how a newborn baby turns her head to her mother's voice and sometimes to her father's voice, but not to the voice of the pediatrician. Nature makes sure that babies know well ahead of time who their primary caregivers are.

One dad told how he used to hum to his baby *in utero*, and later, when the baby was born, that same humming seemed to comfort the infant. From the very start babies recognize familiar sounds; dads as well as moms can begin to connect with their unborn child in this way.

Take a Hard Look at Your Own Health and Lifestyle as a Couple

The first four weeks of gestation is a critical time for the development of the baby's central nervous system, but many women who might not be aware they are pregnant may still be engaging in habits that can be potentially harmful to their unborn baby, such as smoking or drinking alcohol. I advise couples to begin making healthy lifestyle changes long before they plan to have a baby, and I also recommend that fathers be as involved in these changes as the moms are. Yes, the onus is certainly on the mom since she'll be carrying the fetus for nine months. But once that baby is born, a father is going to need the energy that comes from adequate sleep, proper nutrition, and a lifestyle that values good health habits.

My clients Raul and Selena had been trying to conceive a child for some time. They both wanted to be in good health, so they began waking early and going for brisk, thirty-minute walks before work. They had eaten a lot of junk food on the run and take-out in the past, but now they made an effort to shop together for the ingredients to make healthy meals. They were committed to changing because they felt it would be a strong factor in their ability to conceive and carry a healthy baby to term. Raul had been a light smoker for many years, and when he decided to become a father, he quit completely; it was easy for him because he'd never really been "hooked." Selena, however, had been a pack-a-day smoker for several years, and quitting required a concerted effort on her part. Raul's support was unwavering: He threw away all her cigarettes and ashtrays, and the couple banned smoking from their home entirely. Every time Selena craved a cigarette, Raul came up with a distraction—going to the movies, going for a walk. He even got a beeper so Selena could call him whenever she got a craving, and he talked her out of it! They also joined an infertility support group and met another couple who was trying to quit smoking, too. They made a friendly competition of it. The plan worked, and once she conceived, Selena was so motivated to be healthy for the baby that she knew she had kicked the habit forever.

The story of quitting smoking is one of my favorites, but I have gathered lots of stories of great things dads-to-be have done for their wives while pregnant, including:

- making meal plans and shopping for food together to help Mom get all the nutrients she needs while pregnant

- inventing creative ways to get milk and greens into the diet (I know one dad who was so determined to get his wife to increase her intake of dairy and fresh produce that he taught himself how to cook and in the process discovered he was really a closet gourmet)

- changing language use (stopping swearing)

- thinking about the loss of certain aspects of your "freedom" once the baby is born (any parent will tell you to see a lot of movies before your baby is born!)

Read Books on Pregnancy and Childbirth

Many women read extensively about childbirth and child rearing during their pregnancies. One mom I know headed straight to the bookstore on the way home from her obstetrician when she first learned she was pregnant. She had picked up several titles on pregnancy even before she told her husband they were expecting.

Fathers-to-be can be equally involved in gaining knowledge during this time period. Many men and women attend natural childbirth classes together, and this is great because it gets men thinking right away about what their role will be during the birth. Classes in infant child care and infant CPR, often offered or publicized by OB-GYNs or local YWCAs, are also excellent for couples to attend together.

Some books that make good reading for expectant parents are listed in the bibliography, but I'd like to stress the point that dads need to know and prepare for what's coming on down the pike just as moms do. Mothers and fathers need to educate themselves as best they can ahead of time, in addition to the on-the-job training that will come later.

Here's the rub: Most men don't exhibit much of an interest in reading books about child rearing, child care, or pregnancy. If that's the case, the mother-to-be may want to share interesting sections of a book she's reading, for example, by reading them aloud over dinner in a did-you-know kind of fashion. Or she might hand her husband a book and ask him to skim one particular short section, telling him what it is about; it might be a subject that will be coming up at childbirth class or a topic he seems nervous about, such as bathing or feeding. Set aside time to talk about issues on a consistent basis, as discussed in chapter 3. Pregnancy is a good time to begin scheduling periodic parent-to-parent meetings. I know one mom who got her husband to read parenting magazines and baby books, marked with bookmarks at the pertinent pages, by leaving them in the bathroom!

Preparing for the Baby's Arrival

One dad I know bought about two dozen stuffed animals when his wife became pregnant. This father revealed early on that he was excited about and committed to creating his baby's environment. He wasn't going to leave it all up to Mom.

This is an important step that many fathers fail to take, and in relinquishing the preparation for the baby's arrival to their wives, men give the message that this newborn phase really isn't for them. Some men may have little or no inherent interest in choosing nursery decor or baby clothing, but I believe it's important for dads to make an effort to get involved in some way because an interest in making the baby's environment safe, attractive, and comfortable establishes an emotional investment. Preparing a nursery is an excellent way of expressing right from the start that you are going to be involved in your baby's life. Even if the dad isn't interested in paint color, he might do the painting and hang the blinds or curtains; even if he isn't interested in choosing baby furniture, he can assemble the crib or stain/paint an unfinished wood or second-hand bureau; even if he doesn't care about deciding between the Winnie-the-Pooh or the Beatrix Potter lampshade, he can install a dimmer switch.

Virginia pored over pictures of nurseries in magazines. She knew the furniture was expensive, but she showed her husband Ernie all her favorites anyway. He made disparaging remarks like "Honey, I don't think much of that" and "Who's that nursery for—the king of France?" Disheartened and frustrated, Virginia's enthusiasm waned. Then one day she was talking to a coworker about the situation, and the woman shed some important light on the issue. "Maybe he's intimidated by the cost and thinks he's disappointing you because you can't spend a lot of money on the nursery. Ernie's a talented carpenter. Why don't you take advantage of that and ask him to design and build a changing table with drawers underneath and maybe some shelves for the baby's toys?" Virginia talked to Ernie that same night, saying, "You know, I don't really think we need all these different pieces of furniture. I love the shelves you built for Mom and Dad last year. What if you came up with something like that for the baby's room?" Ernie agreed it was a good idea, and the couple collaborated every step of the way. Throughout the rest of her pregnancy, Virginia never felt that she was facing the experience alone, nor did she doubt that her husband was every bit as excited as she was that they were having a baby. Virginia's coworker's comment underscores an important concept: If you want to get someone involved, "invite them in" by asking them to do something they really like to do and enjoy or are good at, not just something you want.

Rethink Rituals That Shut Dads Out

I respect traditions and rituals, but we need to take a second look at how they fit into contemporary life. In the past, the baby shower was a time for women to get together and talk about pregnancy and childbirth, an opportunity to give gifts to prepare for the baby and to connect as women and mothers. I'm not suggesting that we throw out all the old traditions, but I do see that involved fathering has made some inroads in some of the rituals that previously were labeled "for mothers only."

In my parenting seminars I often recommend ways to give a coed shower without the men rolling their eyes. Here's just a few ideas that couples I know have enjoyed:

- Whatever the theme, avoid too-cute decorations and focus instead on celebrating the couple. Barriers are broken when the rules change, and that's what is happening when fathers are invited early on to participate in the rituals and preparations for childbirth. How you handle a shower may at first seem like a pretty unimportant concern, but when men are excluded, what is the message?

■ Make it a family affair. Invite all the relatives—grandparents, kids, aunts, uncles, cousins for a potluck dinner or a Sunday afternoon picnic in the park. Let the parents-to-be enjoy opening presents galore.

■ Invite just friends of the parents-to-be to a real Saturday night dinner party, so it feels like a special night out, not a stereotypical shower. If you play "baby games," make sure to have a male winner and a female winner for each. Give prizes, keeping them inexpensive and unisex, such as small picture frames, mugs, or movie gift certificates.

■ Here's a fun game for the men only (women are the cheerleaders). Fill up the foyer by the front door with baby gear—car seat, diaper bag, suitcase, bag of toys, portable crib, and baby doll to put in the car seat. Park a car in the driveway or curbside. With a stopwatch, first have a real "experienced" dad load the car and put in the car seat and the "baby." Then have the dad-to-be do it! The results are always hilarious.

■ Here's another great way to include men and tap into the knowledge of the moms *and* dads present. Ask everyone who is a parent to fill in a short questionnaire (anonymously if they wish) with questions like: What's the best piece of advice you can give the parents-to-be? What special things did you do with your baby that made you feel connected during the first weeks? What's your best tip for calming a crying baby?

Make Prenatal Visits Together When Possible

I advise dads to accompany their wives to prenatal OB-GYN or midwife visits whenever possible. For one thing, it strengthens the bond between father and mother; together they're charting the unborn baby's progress and the expectant mother's health while strengthening ties that will soon be tested when a new member enters the family.

I clearly remember visiting the obstetrician with my wife and the excitement I felt when our doctor took a small calendar from his desk and used a special circular-shaped dial card to predict our baby's due date. I can envision that calendar, the placement of the chairs in the office, how the sun hit the doctor's desk through the drapes. I can feel the sense of excitement my wife and I shared as if it were yesterday.

A pregnant woman tries on maternity clothes and is aware of the weight of the baby in her womb; at night she shifts and turns in her sleep and feels the baby's movements. Dads, on the other hand, don't have these constant physical reminders. Being included in the prenatal visits helps a father-to-be stay physically connected to a process that is happening in his wife's body. These visits can also keep him cognizant of the baby's development and will put him on equal footing with the mother during the learning process. In addition, he'll establish a rapport with the obstetrician and can participate in asking questions and making important decisions along the way.

Develop a Financial Plan

Before your baby arrives is a good time to sit down as a couple and work out a financial plan. You may want to budget a certain amount of your income for new baby-related expenses. These may include planning ahead for child care, getting extra help with cleaning, saving to put that extra room on the house, moving to a bigger apartment, or buying life insurance. (Both my brother and my dad sell life insurance, and it seems as if every Thanksgiving I walk away with another insurance policy they have convinced me I need; I think I'm insured for hundreds of thousands of dollars!)

Both parents should participate in financial discussions and consider ways to contribute financially or to cut back in certain areas. Though college seems a long way off when preparing to welcome a newborn, it's never too early to start setting aside a portion of your income for the baby's future. Also important is readjusting your budget if one parent who is now working plans to stay home with the baby and not return to work. As another example, if a working mom plans to stay home without pay for any length of time past the classic six weeks, it is better for the couple to save ahead to make up for that lost income instead of racking up debt until she returns to work.

Maternity and Paternity Leave

Most women who work outside the home find out what's available in terms of maternity leave as soon as they become pregnant, if not before. But many men aren't aware of the options available to them, or they opt not to take advantage of paternity leave for fear of reprisal by employer or colleagues.

I encourage fathers to take as much time as they can to be with their newborns. If their job allows for paternity leave, then my advice is to take as much time as possible. If sick days, personal days, or vacation days can be utilized, use as many as is reasonable. If flextime, working from home part-time (telecommuting), or even night shifts are possible, fathers should consider them. Even if such options are not available, I encourage men to research and ask for these privileges. There is always a first in every company. Explain to your employer how you plan to manage your workload, make up for lost hours, and so on, to show your allegiance to your job as well as your new family. (As stated in chapter 2, research shows that employees whose bosses let them take time off or arrange work schedules to accommodate family needs are better, happier, more loyal employees.) When dads miss out on this crucial period of infancy, which is often the case, they not only relinquish the magic and excitement of the first three months of life, but they also jeopardize their chance to learn how to care for their own child right from the start.

Tina, a working mom, had taken a three month maternity leave from her job as a production editor at a magazine. She worked until three days before her delivery and then found herself, after a two-day stay in the hospital, at home with a newborn infant. Tina had never cared for a baby before, but she'd read many books during her pregnancy and had found an excellent pediatrician to guide her. However, her husband, Geno, a photographer, didn't take any time off; in fact, he took even more assignments than usual because he knew with a new baby they'd need the money. Within a few weeks Tina grew angry and felt trapped in the apartment with the baby. Although she adored the infant and was enjoying her time at home, she was also confused and alone; the nearly overnight transition from the full-time work world to full-time motherhood was disorienting, and the lack of sleep and constant care of the baby was draining. To make matters worse, Geno was constantly rushing out of the house or setting up shoots on the phone; even when he was home, he wasn't really there.

Too often new mothers are forced to make the transition to parenthood all alone. Tina had no relatives nearby, and her closest friends were all single or newly married without children. Parenthood is a wonderful experience, but it's also a stressful, demanding, twenty-four-hour-a-day job. Fathers need to look at paternity leave as a high priority. Because our society has focused in the past on fathers as breadwinners, we need to shift our thinking to consider other ways in which men can participate in the newborn phase.

What Fathers Can Do While Mom Is in the Hospital

Along with the father's role as labor partner, sometimes called a labor coach, it's important that he be empathetic and ready and willing to do whatever his partner requires. There is no point in pretending that men can ever understand the pain of childbirth, but they can make an effort to understand their own role of supporting their wives during the process of childbirth.

After the actual birth, in addition to the traditional job of calling friends and family, there are many ways fathers can contribute to make the mother's hospital or birthing center stay go easier:

- If this is not the parent's first child, the father can plan the arrangements for the care of the first child or children while the couple goes to the hospital for the birth and for when he visits the mom at the hospital afterward.

- He can spend some extra one-on-one time with the first child to assure him or her that there is still plenty of love to go around.

- He can talk to physicians and nurses and take part in classes the hospital offers on infant care. Some hospitals now have nursery nurses who go to the new mom's room for one-on-one sessions, usually in the evenings. Make sure Dad can be available, too.

- If finances allow, the father can arrange for a professional house cleaner while mom's away (or he can clean the house himself if time allows, though I feel in general that this time is best spent with the newborn or the anxious sibling). Drop a hint that a gift certificate for one or more visits from a cleaning service would be a welcome shower present.

- The father can tap into what will really please his wife: a bouquet of her favorite flowers, a special shampoo to remind her of home, or a sandwich or salad from her favorite deli if the hospital food isn't exactly gourmet fare. One mom I know remembers being thrilled when her husband returned from a trip "to check on things at home" with a fresh fruit salad and her favorite bottled water. Another mom recalls waking in the middle of the night to nurse her baby and finding that her husband had placed a basket of fresh muffins by her bed.

Coming Home: Establish Attachment Right from the Start

A recent survey by Prudential Healthcare and the National Center for Fathering revealed that although 71 percent of fathers today say they feel more capable of being involved in child care, two-thirds still agree that once the baby is born, mothers have the greatest responsibility. I still believe that men are conditioned to think this way. And those men who want to be involved in the bonding process during those first days and weeks with a newborn baby may feel that those wishes are inappropriate or secretly discouraged, so they hold back.

This is an emotionally charged and very physically demanding period in the lives of parents, and the more time a father spends with his infant, the more he will understand the baby's needs and signals and be able to take an active part in his care. And when his spouse needs to rest, he can take over with confidence. When each of our children was born, my wife and I spent many an hour cuddling, talking to, singing to, and generally trying to amuse and entertain the newborn. I recall that period as one of the best and most precious times of my life.

Fathers Should Spend Time Alone with Their Newborn

I also recommend that fathers spend time alone with their newborn, to learn how to care for and nurture the baby and read his cues. Mothers need their own time to take a backseat and will probably be thankful for the chance to rest or get out and resume some normal activities, and at the same time the dad can take some responsibility on his own.

Spending time alone with the newborn is an entirely different experience for a father than spending time with his wife and newborn as a threesome. It is an essential experience of discovery during which dads come up with their own unique way of doing the very same child care "tasks" moms do, including bathing, feeding, rocking, taking the baby to the pediatrician, and more.

Amy asked her husband, Warren, to take their new baby for hours at a time during the first weeks of life. An artist, Amy was completing several paintings and needed time alone. Often in the evenings Warren would place the new baby in the Snugli and go out for a walk. The breeze was soft in the spring, and although there was sometimes a gentle rain, the baby was safe and warm in the Snugli, tucked into his father's jacket, with an umbrella overhead. Sometimes the moon was so bright it cast a shadow of their figure on the sidewalk. As he walked with his newborn son in the warm rain or breeze, alone with his child, Warren began to feel that the baby was really his; he began to feel that the bond they forged in the first days of the baby's life was enduring.

From Duo to Trio: A New Baby Changes the Family Dynamics

Prior to having kids, my wife and I were much more spontaneous. We might have decided to go out to dinner at a moment's notice or to pack up and leave for the weekend on a whim. After the children were born, and especially after the first baby, the change was enormous. With marriage an individual changes from "I" to "we." With the first child the couple changes from "we" to "all of us." The duo becomes a trio. Keep adding kids, and "we" just keeps expanding.

The effects of this overwhelming change can be minimized somewhat by couples striving to stay connected as a couple while meeting the needs of their baby—this new, dependent life. Lots of issues can arise, not the least of which is that the husband may suddenly feel like the odd man out. Literally overnight, his wife's attention and energy are centered on the infant. Add to this the fact that sexual relations are often put on hold, sometimes for weeks or months before as well as after the baby is born, and men can end up feeling excluded or ignored. On the other side of the table, the wife feels thrown into the deep end, what with a baby that needs constant care and attention, coupled with the physical demands of breastfeeding and lack of sleep.

I always try to reassure couples that there are ways to ease this monumental transition to a threesome. One, as mentioned earlier, is to be certain that the dad gets some private time with the baby, not only to take pressure off the mom but also to establish his own bond with the baby and to become competent and confident in caring for the infant. Second, parents should spend time together caring for their infant and getting used to the idea of "three."

A third and equally important way to ease the transition from duo to trio is to consistently schedule some time to be alone together as a couple. This may mean setting a time to share a cup of tea while the baby is napping or getting a relative or trusted friend to entertain the baby while you take a walk or go to a nearby restaurant. One mom remembers her first outing with her husband about a month after their baby was born. She was nervous about leaving the baby with a sitter and didn't have any close relatives nearby, but her best friend offered to come over one morning so the couple could go out for breakfast. Just one hour out as a couple (granted, they talked mostly about the baby!) helped them begin a regular schedule of spending time alone.

How Fathers Can Play a Role in Breastfeeding or Bottle Feeding

Fathers and mothers need to talk about how to support each other in that all-important goal of feeding the baby. If the choice is the bottle, fathers can certainly share in the feeding. Giving a bottle is an opportunity for fathers to hold, make eye contact with, and spend time with their baby. Feeding the baby is an opportunity to cuddle and enjoy the infant, and it's also the key caregiving activity for both parents during the first weeks and months of life. I noticed a dad feeding his baby at the park recently. He was sitting in a low lawn chair with his infant daughter propped on his knees facing him. He helped her hold the bottle and looked directly into her eyes, smiling and in loving tones encouraging her to drink. What a wonderful sight this was!

If breastfeeding is the choice (and it is recommended by the American Academy of Pediatrics for the first year of life), the father can still be involved. Many women express milk for their babies while they are at work. (In my study of stay-at-home dads I found that 45 percent of the working moms expressed milk.) Even mothers who stay at home or moms who are on maternity leave should consider expressing milk during the day so that the father can do one nighttime feeding—and mom can sleep! Or if the mom prefers not to pump, the couple may use formula for dad's feeding.

Experts recommend that couples introduce the bottle to the baby at approximately four to five weeks of age even if for just one feeding a day. Also, if possible, the father should be the person to introduce the bottle; the mom shouldn't even be in the room at first, so the baby doesn't get confused by the smell of the mother and cry for the breast. Perseverance is key, especially if the baby doesn't take to the nipple right away. You may need to try different nipples, different bottles, different settings and times of day. See the bibliography for suggested readings on breastfeeding and bottle feeding.

Even if initially the mother feels no strong inclination to express milk or use formula, I strongly recommend that couples include at least one or two bottles a day, both to nurture the father-baby bond and to make life easier later on when Mom and Dad want to go out as a couple. Someone else can then care for and feed the baby. I've known so many couples who complain they feel chained to their homes because the mom is breastfeeding and the baby won't take a bottle.

Nursing mothers benefit from a supportive partner in other ways, too. The father can bring the baby to the mother in bed during the night and return the baby to the crib or bassinet when nursing is over, or he can sit with the mother and baby during this time. There is no reason for dads to be banished because the mother is breastfeeding. Occasionally an older baby may be distracted from nursing if her dad is looking on, but if that's not the case, it's perfectly fine for fathers to assist the nursing mom and baby by fluffing up the pillows, bringing the mother a glass of water or milk, or dimming the lights and playing some soft music.

First-time mothers may need extra support from their spouse during the initial weeks of breastfeeding. A positive attitude from a supportive husband can make all the difference when a first-time mom and her baby are making the adjustment to nursing, especially if other relatives have made negative remarks or if the mother is frustrated by engorged breasts, low milk production, or a baby who has trouble latching on. Fathers can be a strong, positive influence on the establishment of successful breastfeeding.

Learning to Eat Solid Foods

Somewhere during the period of four to six months, depending on the baby's weight and needs, most pediatricians recommend starting solids—usually some infant cereal mixed with breast milk or formula or mashed bananas to start. Most parents experience the introduction of solid foods as both an exciting and perplexing process. Here's a story I like to tell at my parenting seminars about a dad who really took an initiative with feeding his baby.

When Maureen, a home health care aide, and Vern, a bus driver, went to see their pediatrician with their five-month-old son, the doctor advised them to start introducing solids. Maureen told him they were interested in making their own baby food and asked for some suggestions on how to do that. The pediatrician rolled his eyes and said, "Do yourself a favor and just buy jarred baby food." Maureen was annoyed. She and Vern decided to go to a bookstore on the way home and buy a baby food cookbook and teach themselves. Vern said he thought the doctor's suggestion was pretty outrageous, and he offered to become the food "masher" for the baby. Each morning before he left for work, or sometimes the evening before, Vern would mash bananas or steam and mash various vegetables or fruit with a fork or spoon. Then, he would place the baby's food for the day in small covered containers in the refrigerator. It was an easy job, but it made him feel connected to the baby while he was away all day. His wife appreciated it, and she called him "the masher." They even joked about writing their own cookbook, and Maureen bought him a mini food processor to make his "mashing" easier.

Share the Visits to the Pediatrician

If feasible, I encourage parents to bring their baby to the pediatrician together. This may be difficult when couples work outside the home; however, many doctors provide evening or weekend hours, and it's well worth the effort to attend these visits together. (When you interview pediatricians before the baby is born, you might ask whether evening or weekend hours are available.) You will learn much about your newborn baby together, and you'll be able to ask questions and address concerns. At the very least, alternate the visits so that the father will get to know the pediatrician and will be familiar with the child's growth and health. When this critical, informative experience is left up to the mom, it usually just serves to put a knowledge chasm between the parents and "justifies" fathers who say, "I don't know anything about that. My wife knows all that stuff."

If the mother is always the one who takes the baby to the doctor and then suddenly a situation occurs where the baby needs to be taken, the mother is unavailable, and the father has to take the baby, he will be at a disadvantage and will not have a rapport with the doctor. Further, when problems arise with a baby's health or the baby is ill or not progressing well, the visits to the pediatrician are likely to be stressful—all the more reason parents should make an attempt to attend together, to share and support each other during the visit.

When our babies were born, my wife made a point of taking time off from work or requesting appointments we could both attend. This was no small effort! Our pediatrician was an hour from our home, and the visits, traveling time included, took a good three hours of our day. We felt it was important to make this effort. At the office I could hold Kevin while he got a shot, and Linda could ask questions, or vice versa. We worked as a team, and if one of us forgot to ask whether vitamins were needed or whether a rash was of concern, the other would remember.

Learning to Sleep Through the Night and Establishing a Napping Routine

Good sleep habits can be learned, and during their first year of life, most babies adjust to a schedule of napping and sleeping. Many parents just don't realize that this is much more challenging for the parents than for the baby. Time and again I meet couples who "give up" on trying to get their infant to sleep through the night, let alone nap regularly in the morning and afternoon. There are many theories about the best strategy to take to teach your baby night and day, and how and when to stay out of the nursery after putting the baby to bed and she cries and cries. What I have discovered in my fifteen years as a family therapist is that whether parents let the baby "cry it out" and learn to soothe themselves, as noted pediatrician Richard Ferber proposes in *Solve Your Child's Sleep Problems,* or focus on taking the baby outside often during the day and keeping nighttime visits or feedings short and uneventful, what matters most is that the couple discusses and agrees on the method to be used. Whether these parents succeed in their efforts because the baby senses that the parents are "sure" about what they're doing or because parents who make such important decisions mutually motivate each other to stick with it, I don't know, but I do know that a united front is the way to go.

Jake was the on-call parent at night. Marleen took care of the newborn during the day, but she had developed diabetes during her pregnancy and needed to take good care of herself. Jake agreed that Marleen needed a full night's rest each night, so he rose with the baby in the night. He worked as a cable installer and arranged with his company to work the 7 A.M. to 3 P.M. shift, and napped when he got home. Unfortunately, baby Jesse was awake every hour looking for a bottle and would scream, waking up Marleen and their two older children. Jake knew he had to get Jesse to sleep through the night; he began by putting the older kids to bed at a reasonable hour, and Marleen did the last evening feeding just before 11 P.M. Jake darkened the room with a dimmer switch and placed the baby in the crib with his teddy bear and soft blanket, while he was still drowsy so that his last "memory" of being awake was seeing his crib around him. (This helps babies recognize their environment if they awaken in the night.) When Jesse would awaken in the night, Jake wouldn't pick him up but would rub his back softly and briefly, and leave the room. Although the first few nights were rough, Jesse eventually learned to soothe himself, and he felt secure in his own crib with his familiar objects and surroundings. Soon the whole family was sleeping through the night, and Marleen gradually moved up the last evening feeding until the baby was going to bed at ten, then nine. She also kept Jesse active during the day (except, of course, during his naps), so that he was ready for a good night's sleep when Jake took over.

The Working Life: Who Will Stay Home with the Baby?

The decision of who will stay home to care for the baby looms large with most parents, especially first-timers. I cannot overemphasize the importance of making this a joint decision and of considering each and every option. If the caregiver is not going to be the mother, father, or relative but rather a nanny, au pair, day care center, or family day care provider, weigh your options carefully. Don't give up until you find what you want.

Current research shows that steady, loving care makes a significant difference in the development of healthy emotions and attachments. Isabelle Fox, Ph.D., author of *Being There*, argues in favor of one parent staying home to care for the baby for the first three years of life. Fox contends that during this time of critical attachment it's imperative for a child to have a consistent, devoted caregiver. I like this option, but I realize it is not an option in every family, so I recommend that whatever option a couple chooses, they make consistency and a nurturing approach a high priority. Choose your caregiver carefully and do your homework in order to minimize your chances of having to change caregivers, which can be disruptive to the child. Let's look at some of the many options a couple might choose and how both parents can be involved in a balanced manner.

The Stay-at-Home Mother

A mother who chooses to stay home with her baby is entitled to an equal parenting partner. Just as research confirms that working moms jump into action when they get home from work, working fathers should be actively involved in home life. The stay-at-home parent needs a break at the end of the day, and even something as simple as picking up take-out food or offering to prepare dinner on some weekdays can represent the most welcome support. When fathers arrive home, I encourage them to be as involved as they can, enabling their wives to take this break.

One of the biggest mistakes couples make when one parent stays at home is that the working parent automatically assumes the stay-at-home parent is going to do it all. Every parent—stay-at-home, working, married, single, or divorced—needs to create a support system in order to raise babies to become healthy, happy kids.

Sue, a high school teacher, wanted to be home with her baby girl. Though Sue was dedicated to teaching, she was prepared to make some sacrifices. She took two years off, unpaid, and lost her seniority in the school district. Her husband, Cal, worked as a supervisor in an electronics company. He didn't make a great deal of money, but it was enough for the family to live on if they were frugal. While Sue was pregnant, she and Cal sat down together and devised a budget, each promising to stick to it. Rather than spend money on child care, they decided that Sue could return to her career later (which she successfully did) and be home for the baby during the first two years. The plan worked well, and since Sue was a teacher she still had summers off to be with her child after she returned to work. To share in the parenting responsibilities, Cal gave the baby a bath and put her to bed each evening, spent all day Sundays with the baby (sometimes Sue joined them, and sometimes she took the time for herself), and did the dinner dishes on weeknights.

When Dads Stay Home

As stated in earlier chapters, in my family I was the natural choice to stay home with the kids; my wife had a full-time job she enjoyed, and I had the more flexible schedule. Throughout my years of finishing my Ph.D., opening a private practice, and teaching, my job as a full-time father has been my first priority. I've molded my other work commitments to fit our family's needs.

Obviously, this choice is neither practical nor necessarily desirable for every father, but an increasing number of couples are seeing the stay-at-home dad as a viable option. There are more than two million stay-at-home dads in this country who care for their children, many of whom are infants and preschoolers, and they have proven that fathers are every bit as capable of caring for children as are mothers. For interested couples, the *At-Home Dad Handbook* is an excellent resource that covers a range of topics from finances to starting play groups to beating prejudice in the grocery store and playground. (See the bibliography for more recommended readings, and I also recommend the website www.slowlane.com.)

Irv, a social worker in his early forties, had been married before, when he was in his twenties, and had been an uninvolved father. The second time around, Irv wanted to do things differently. His second wife, who was in her late thirties, had a lucrative career as an architect. When she became pregnant, she and Irv agreed they were comfortable with the idea of Irv staying home. Irv absolutely adored his baby daughter; he took her to the park, fed her, totally immersed himself in her well-being and care. He hooked up with other stay-at-home dads through the Internet and became an active proponent of the stay-at-home dad "movement." His older son, from his first marriage, was now in his early twenties, and Irv regretted that he had missed so much of the boy's childhood. While reconnecting with his older son, Irv delved into fatherhood with his newborn. He put his "working life" on hold, as many women do, while he devoted himself to his child. Irv made taking care of his baby his passion for the years he was a stay-at-home dad.

When Both Parents Work

When parents become a dual-career couple again, it's important to discuss ahead of time the needs that must be met, especially during the transition time. Even if an outside caregiver is coming to the home or the baby is being brought to day care, working fathers play a substantial role when their wives return to work. It's important to sit down several months before the mother returns to work to discuss how both parents can contribute to make the transition go smoothly.

Nina, an advertising executive, was preparing to go back to work. She was frantic, not knowing how she would ever manage to get the baby fed, dressed, and to day care in time to make a 7:20

bus each morning. Her husband, Roger, worked near their home and didn't need to leave quite so early. About four months into her six-month maternity leave, Nina had lunch with a girlfriend, and the topic of her return to work came up. Nina's friend asked quite matter-of-factly, "So what is Roger going to do to help you every day?" Nina realized she had not even talked to her husband about his participating in the morning routine. She spent some time organizing her thoughts and then sat down with Roger. Nina's confidence in what she was going to request was buoyed by the fact that Roger really supported her career and work life. They agreed that every morning Nina would nurse the baby, and then Roger would dress him while Nina showered. Roger would drop the baby at family day care on his way to his office, and Nina would pick him up on her way home since she usually arrived home earlier. After Nina stopped nursing when her son was about eight months old, Roger gave the baby his morning bottle, and then when he started on solid foods, Roger gave him breakfast. Making these plans in advance relieved Nina of a great deal of worry and pressure.

Another point I wanted to make on the subject of dual-working couples is that increasingly the father's workplace and not the mother's may present the best option for day care. Martin's company had a small, on-site day care facility with just ten children and two caregivers, which seemed a happy medium between family day care and a day care center. Also, the cost was subsidized by Martin's company, so it was very affordable. The company that his wife, Jocelyn, worked for, which was nearby, did not offer day care. Jocelyn could drive over each day to the day care at Martin's office to spend an hour with her baby, and sometimes Martin joined them. It was also easy for either parent to drop off or pick up the baby.

Jorge worked for a major pharmaceutical company, and his wife, Caroline, worked out of their home as a human resources consultant. When Caroline became pregnant, she and Jorge decided that she would take five months off from work, and then they would put the baby in Jorge's company day care facility three days a week to start. Jorge could drop off and pick up the baby, and Caroline could get her work and phone calls done and be available for client meetings. Of course, these kinds of options depend on the father's workplace, but I relay these examples to underscore the importance of couples exploring every possible option together to maximize both parents' involvement and to address the individual logistics of each family.

Both Parents Need to Establish Rapport with the Caregiver

Whatever working parents decide concerning who will care for the new baby, it is very important that the dad be involved in the decision-making process. I recommend that fathers and mothers interview prospective caregivers together, and if the couple is looking for day care outside the home, they should visit day care centers or family day care providers' homes.

Gary was a human relations consultant; it was his job to hire employees for a Fortune 500 company. When it came time to hire a family day care provider for his new daughter, Gary got right on the case. Helene, his wife, was shy and soft-spoken; she sat in on the discussions but wasn't too good at asking pointed questions. Gary interviewed at least a dozen caregivers until he found one who held similar values and beliefs about child rearing. During the interviews, while Helene seemed to react to prospective caregivers on an instinctual, gut level, saying things like "Sorry, but I just couldn't warm up to her," Gary was ruthless albeit polite about presenting important concerns. He even had a prepared list of questions (which could be addressed to a nanny or day care director as well):

- What is a typical day like for a ____ year (or month) old?

- How are activities selected?

- Do you smoke, or does anyone in the household smoke?

- When do you do your housecleaning?

- May I drop in anytime during the day?

- What activities are encouraged, or what stimulation will my child receive?

- What is your policy about outdoor play?

- What do you do if you're outside with the children and one needs to go in to use the potty?

- How do you handle feeding times?

- May I see where she will sleep?

- What do you do when a child misbehaves?

These are probing questions, but they need to be asked, and quality day care directors and family day care providers expect to address them. Gary was comfortable asking these questions, but Helene was not, so he took the responsibility. Once the caregiver had been hired, he maintained an ongoing dialogue with her, and when concerns or questions arose, he wasn't hesitant to ask. It was even his idea that the caregiver keep a log each day so that he and Helene would know when the baby napped and ate, and whether any problems occurred in their absence.

The Toddler Years:

Twelve to Thirty-Six Months

A FEW WEEKS BACK I spent the morning with my two-year-old nephew—or, I should say, running around with him and after him. With my kids now in school, I had forgotten just how exhausting it is to keep up with a toddler. Thank goodness A.J., my ten-year-old daughter, took over. I needed a nap!

The toddler years, ages twelve to thirty-six months, are demanding and exhilarating for parents. Parents of toddlers will be challenged by their insatiable curiosity and tested by their newly emerging quest for independence. It is important to remember that the toddler's mind is developing faster than his motor and verbal skills. Feelings of frustration at not always being able to control his own environment lead to the inevitable tantrums that characterize "the terrible twos." Toddlers experiment with learning to control their environment by using the word "no," sometimes dozens of times a day, and are prone to changing their minds at a whim.

This is the period when what I call tag-team parenting is especially valuable. Make it a priority to continue to find ways to give yourself and your spouse breaks in your caregiving responsibilities. It is helpful to learn first about the developmental issues characteristic of this period and then make decisions in the context of these issues. I find that too many parents of young children not only jump to conclusions about what certain behaviors mean but also make decisions by regarding only their own needs. This chapter is designed to give the "why" behind some of the behavioral issues that are the mark of toddlerhood so that you and your spouse will be able to relax and understand that your toddler is not purposefully trying to make you sprout gray hairs.

This is a crucial time for mothers and fathers to work together on building the child's sense of security while encouraging independent play and exploration. I tell parents of toddlers to continue parent-to-parent meetings, to reinforce their commitment to a "unified front" and to tailor ways to share parenting responsibilities that meet the needs of their individual family.

One of my clients, a mother of a toddler, was finally making progress on her husband's becoming more involved in the daily life of their son. She announced proudly, "The other day when I picked up my son, he looked at me and said, 'I want my other mommy!' I asked, 'What is her name?' And my son said, "Daddy!' I thought to myself, 'Yes!' "

Physical Development: Toddlers on the Move

Arlene, a stay-at-home mother, and Fritz, a mechanic at a car dealership, had a two-year-old son, Randolph. Fritz spent as much time as he could with the family. He was a very likable, talkative guy who loved to meet people and hold lengthy conversations. Arlene admired this aspect of her husband's personality, but she became increasingly frustrated because even when the family was on an outing together, Fritz was always running into people he knew and chatting or even striking up conversations with people he didn't know, leaving Arlene to chase Randolph. Fritz was unaware that his outgoing personality was causing Arlene to feel resentful.

Arlene had decided to talk to me about Fritz. Summer was just beginning, and she was worried that since they would be spending lots of time in the park, the problems she was experiencing would just escalate. I suggested that she talk to Fritz at a quiet time when they were relaxed and alone, and communicate her need for him to pay closer attention to Randolph. I also suggested that she ask Fritz to take Randolph to the park on some summer evenings and on weekends so that she could get some time to herself.

Arlene chose to speak to Fritz after Randolph went to bed; the house was quiet, and Fritz was more relaxed. In a nonaccusatory tone, Arlene broached the issue: "I know you like to talk with everyone when we go out on errands together or to the park, and I know that's your way. But did you know that sometimes I feel you're not paying attention to me and Randolph, and when I'm the only one watching him, it's draining?" Fritz admitted that he hadn't even noticed his conversations with others were causing Arlene distress. Like many men who aren't involved in the daily, ongoing care of a toddler, he hadn't realized how demanding and energy-draining it can be.

Arlene had learned from previous conversations with her husband that it was counterproductive to tell him to change instantly. It worked best if she just expressed her thoughts and feelings. Then Fritz would think about things for a few days and bring it up again when he was ready to talk more. Fritz was a little hurt at first at Arlene's remarks, but after thinking about it, he agreed to her request that he sometimes take Randolph to the park by himself. He also made a concerted effort when they went out as a family, to introduce Arlene and Randolph to the person he was speaking with and include them in the conversation. I also gave her these ideas to share with Fritz:

- Invest in a baby seat for your bike.

- Invite another dad and his toddler over for the afternoon.

- Go to the park and bring bubbles! This is a little secret of stay-at-home dads. Bringing bubbles—and extra bubble wands—is a surefire magnet for other children.

Incorporate Quiet Time for Your Child and You

Just as toddlers need to be active and to explore, they also need quiet time to reflect and relax and to process the amazing amounts of information they're soaking up. Make naptime, storytime, and quiet time part of your daily routine with a toddler. Between the ages of two and three, many toddlers give up their morning nap and begin taking one afternoon nap. It's still important to offset the toddler's hectic pace with quiet periods during the day.

Bethann, who worked full-time as a human resources manager for a bank, expressed a lot of frustration because her husband, George, never played with their eighteen-month-old son, Nathaniel, while she made dinner. She said to me, "We're both tired when we get home, and Nathaniel just gets underfoot if he's in the kitchen while I'm making dinner. I've asked George lots of times to do something with Nathaniel, but he just groans and says he's so worn out."

The toddler years can be so exhausting for some parents that sometimes one spouse may directly or indirectly avoid having to watch the child for extended periods of time. I reminded Bethann about quiet time and how it's a great way to spend meaningful time with a child without having to expend a lot of physical energy. I suggested that she ask George to try to find nonstrenuous ways to unwind after a day of work that also included Nathaniel. I encouraged her to start small and assure George that a half hour curled up with new books from the library, a magnetic puzzle board, Duplos, or blocks would be fine.

When moms and dads "tag-team," they need to agree that quiet time will be included during each parent's one-on-one time with the child. It's not a good idea for one parent to do constant high-energy activity with the child while the other always makes room for quiet time.

Cognitive Development: How Toddlers Learn

Two theories about how children learn are especially compelling. In the realm of cognitive, or intellectual, development, I lean toward the work of French psychologist Jean Piaget, who believed that certain developmental milestones occur at certain predictable points. A child won't learn to read, write, or understand shapes and sizes until he is developmentally primed. Here is an example. If you give your five-year-old son two cookies and your two-and-a-half-year-old daughter one cookie, and she says she wants two like her brother, you need only break her cookie in half and she'll be pleased. Before long, however, she'll understand that she still doesn't have what her brother has. While Piagetian theory holds that no amount of prodding or cajoling will get children to do something they're not "maturationally" ready to do, I believe it is still important for parents and caregivers to expose children to intellectual concepts such as opposites (big-little, tall-short) and cause and effect (when we pour a bucket of ocean water on the sand castle, it crumbles), and practice them. Then when children hit their own maturation points, those areas of development will kick in with gusto.

Len Vygotsky, a Russian psychoanalyst who was "rediscovered" in the 1960s, asserted that children learn by observing: if they see you pick up a ball and throw it one hundred times, they will intellectually process that information and begin to figure out how to do it. At some point the concept will click, and the child will pick up a ball and throw it. Vygotsky believed that children learn from what they see in their culture and their environment.

While I lean toward Piaget's approach on most things, I think that when dealing with children it is valuable for parents to use a combination of the two. Of course, your toddler is not going to learn the concept of cause and effect until he is developmentally mature enough to do so, but if you want to teach him not to scamper into the street, I recommend a strategy based on Vygotsky's method: Hold the toddler's hand at the curb, point to the curb and then the pavement, and explain to him firmly and repeatedly that he shouldn't run out into the street. Do this over several consecutive days. The child may not be old enough to intellectualize about the dangers of crossing the street, but he *is* old enough to begin to learn that when he goes near the street, he must stop and take Mom's or Dad's hand. (Holding hands while crossing the street is an early rule that also sets and reinforces a precedent for the parent as both authority figure and protector.)

Nurturing a Toddler's "I Can Do It Myself" Attitude

Fostering the toddler's natural desire to do as many tasks as possible by himself is invaluable for building the foundation of independence and positive self-esteem. At my parenting seminars I always talk about the psychologist Eleanor Gibson's theory of affordances, which in a nutshell means making available to the child as many learning experiences as possible. Anything you do to enhance the child's learning and to give her opportunities to help and participate in everyday activities is an "affordance," such as going to the farmer's market and picking out ripe tomatoes, and noticing a ladybug on the inside of the screen door and helping your child put it back outside.

I have found that talking about the theory of affordances is helpful with parents, especially dads, who tell me they are hesitant to be with their toddler because they don't feel confident about how to spend the time. They somehow think that toddlers need elaborate activities. Once you understand the value of the theory of affordances, however, you quickly realize that you can go pretty much wherever you want to with your toddler, and just by explaining what she sees along the way and answering her questions in a simple, matter-of-fact way, you are doing just fine. Remember, you may have been to the hardware store or the bank or the gas station a hundred times, but to the toddler this is a vast new territory, and she is filled with awe and curiosity.

My son, Kevin, was insatiably curious as a toddler; he was one of those kids who needs to touch and hold everything. No matter what we were doing, Kevin would follow me around the house. While doing the laundry I'd tell Kevin all about the washing machine and how it worked, and then I'd place him right in the basket with the clean clothes and carry him up the stairs. What might have been considered drudgery was lots of fun for Kevin—and made it more fun for me, too.

In addition to getting a free ride in the laundry basket, Kevin and his sister, A.J., helped me with a number of other household chores. Toddlers are not too young to tag along and "help." They can put away toys, water outdoor plants, pick clothes up off the floor, and help place the spoons around the table for breakfast. By participating in these everyday tasks the toddler not only absorbs vast amounts of information about the way things work but more quickly develops the "I can do it myself!" attitude. Don't pay any attention to the fact that the dust on the floor your child just "swept" with his toy broom merely got moved to the other side of the room. The more the child learns to do on her own, the better she will feel about her own capabilities, and her self-esteem will reflect that sense of confidence.

The Toddler's Work Is Play

Maria Montessori, the founder of the Montessori preschool method, coined the phrase that play is child's work. Children learn many concepts such as cause and effect, big and small, and basic physics such as volume and speed, as they sift sand, build with blocks, or pour water from container to container. It's hard for some parents to accept that real learning is taking place while kids are "just playing." When you take your child to the park, he's using his gross motor skills to climb up the stairs to the slide; he's using social skills to interact with other children; and he's building and constructing in the sandbox. All of these activities are important for the development of the toddler's cognitive, physical, social, and emotional skills. The parent doesn't need to be "teaching" all the time; play is the primary way that children learn.

During a session with a working mother, she told me that while she wanted to enjoy the evening time she had with her two-and-a-half year old son, she found herself increasingly stressed by a nagging feeling that her son had to work on "mastering" some skill each day, such as getting out of the car seat on his own after she had unlatched the shoulder strap. She felt that every evening should include another "lesson." After all, she said, she wasn't with her son all day, so wasn't it her responsibility to make the most of every evening? I told her that while this was a natural assumption of many working parents, it actually was not the healthiest way to look at that time spent together.

I asked her, "What would you do with your son if you had more time in the evenings and didn't have to worry so much about dinner or working on a puzzle to learn shapes?" She said, "Oh, lots of things! First of all, I wouldn't always take him straight home from work. I would take him to the orchard near our house. I would take him to the beach, which is only twenty minutes away, and make sand castles until the sun set." So I said, "Okay, do it! Do those things! Once a week, twice a week, whenever the idea grabs you. Pack two extra sandwiches and some healthy snacks in a bag and take them to work. Then pick up your son and do those things. Let him eat an apple at the orchard, and he can eat something else when you get home." By placing value on just spending time with her son, this mom was able to let go of much of her stress.

Another way toddlers learn, of course, is by spending time with both parents together. Parents learn to be receptive simultaneously to their children and to their spouse, and kids learn to view themselves as an integral part of a family. One couple I know rented a room at a very nice historic hotel at the seashore. When the dad made their reservation, he explained that he and his wife wanted to bring their toddler with them. The manager happily offered to set up a crib in the room and to provide a high chair in the dining room. Instead of shying away from new experiences with their toddler, this couple brought their son everywhere; as long as he was well fed, well rested, and with his parents, he seemed quite content.

What Is Emotional Intelligence?

In his book *Emotional Intelligence,* Daniel Goleman sets forth the idea that there is another, often neglected side of intelligence—that of emotional intelligence. Sometimes referred to as EQ, emotional intelligence involves your ability to respond to situations in an emotionally mature manner; to raise your awareness of your own emotions in order to increase your ability to problem-solve, handle change, and make good decisions; and to look past your own issues and listen well in order to successfully view situations from another person's point of view. For kids the benefits include developing longer attention spans and positive interpersonal skills.

Goleman believes, and I agree, that emotional intelligence can be taught to children, and the earlier we begin, the better. We can start by helping our children verbalize feelings and by validating their emotions in connection with problem-solving and looking at options, developing self-control, and considering the ethical and moral implications of simple actions and decisions.

Here's an example: If the toddler wants to bang on a drum while his mom is taking a nap, his dad can say, "Mommy is sleeping now, and it wouldn't be nice to wake her up. Your drum will be too loud. You can play your drum later, or if you like, we can go outside together and you can play your drum." Many parents probably don't realize it, but as they work on the typical toddler developmental issues—teaching toddlers to be kind to others, explaining that we don't hit or bite or push, introducing the concepts of sharing and learning the names of different basic emotions such as mad, sad, and happy—they are fostering emotional intelligence.

I have found that dads are especially adept at this kind of thing—mostly without realizing it. They challenge their children to think, to experiment, and to explore in the course of regular play and day-to-day goings-on. For example, when dads roughhouse with their kids, the kids are automatically presented with a problem-solving scenario: "What's going on here? How should I react? How can I get him before he gets me? How much is too much?"

Handling the Terrible Twos as a Parenting Team

Toddlers are notorious for saying "no!" This can drive parents crazy, but there are ways to get around the natural tendency of the toddler to be almost maniacally independent and uncooperative. It's important for parents to understand from a developmental point of view that the toddler's quest for control and independence is necessary and natural, and that it's perfectly normal for him to be egocentric at this stage. Rather than becoming angry with a toddler, parents need to respect the toddler's developmental "place" and learn ways to deal effectively with it.

The following two ideas are key to understanding the mind of the toddler (and to maintaining one's cool in the thick of it):

1. By saying "no," toddlers are helping define their own "separateness" from others. This identity development is an important step toward independent behavior and thinking.

2. Toddlers spend most of their time being told what to do: "Please get in the car now. We're going to the store," "Time to clean up now, we have to eat dinner," and so on. They quickly learn that while they can't control the big world, they can start by trying to "control" their parents.

Moms and dads need to realize that by giving the toddler options—and when I say that, I mean *limited* options—the toddler's "no" response can sometimes be minimized because he will feel some control. For instance, instead of asking a yes-no question like "Do you want to wear this blue sunhat to the beach?" (believe me, he'll say no) you might ask the toddler, "Which sunhat would you like to wear today? The blue one or the red?"

Tantrums often go hand in hand with the "no" stage. The two- or three-year-old definitely has his own ideas about how he wants things to go, and if things don't go his way, the normally charming toddler may appear possessed, literally throwing himself on the floor and beating his arms and legs. The number one technique for countering tantrums is to stay calm, no matter what. By using a straightforward, matter-of-fact tone, you send the message to the child that screaming is not going to be successful. Likewise, a parent who is screaming will only exacerbate the situation; kids pick up on their parents' feelings, and if a child feels that mom or dad has "lost it," he'll only act worse. The toddler isn't saying "no" just to irritate you; it's part of his quest for independence and his growing awareness that he can control his environment and that his actions affect others.

Remember, too, that if there is no audience, there is no party. If your child is throwing a tantrum about not wanting to go to bed, stay calm and in a normal tone say something like "I'm going into the living room now. You can come to get me when you're ready to go to bed." Chances are the tantrum will dissipate.

Roy was the father of a twenty-six-month-old boy named Charlie. Roy's wife, Marietta, was home with Charlie all day and found his temper tantrums difficult to tolerate. By the time Roy, a school janitor, walked in the door at night, Marietta was often in tears. She was beginning to take Charlie's behavior personally and feeling that she wasn't a "good mother." Fortunately, Roy had a flair for figuring out how to calm his son. When Charlie clamored for cookies before dinner, Roy would scoop him up, carry him into the backyard with a book, sit in the hammock, and read a story. If Charlie demanded to go outside when it was time to stay in, Roy would bring him into the basement and pull out some toys that Charlie hadn't played with in a while. Changing the location, replacing the toy, or refocusing the child when he becomes demanding beats engaging in a power struggle.

Of course, Marietta was with Charlie all day long, and her energies were pretty well drained by the time Roy got home at night. It was a relief to her that her husband was easily able to "read" Charlie's needs and respond in a positive way. He never lost his temper with his son, and when he noticed that Marietta was becoming frustrated, he'd step right in and resolve the situation. Soon, Roy and Marietta were exchanging "distraction" techniques and ideas.

Marietta's end-of-the-day fatigue and frustration were perfectly normal, I assured her, and in families like hers where both parents are involved, the parent who is not "always there" can sometimes provide a fresh perspective while giving the spouse a much-needed break. I applauded the fact that Marietta was not threatened or annoyed by her husband's tantrum-thwarting abilities. Parenting is not a competition.

When their child throws a tantrum, I encourage parents to step back, breathe, and count to ten before uttering a word. Although they may not see the humor in it at the moment, it is hoped that days or weeks later they'll laugh about how their toddler mortified them in the department store. I am adamantly opposed to spanking in any discipline or behavior management situation, and I talk about this more in the next chapter (as well as alternatives to spanking).

Another characteristic of the terrible twos is what some parents call the Dr. Jekyll and Mr. Hyde syndrome: The toddler may say yes and the very next moment say no. Very often the toddler isn't really sure *what* he wants. He may want to take his toy dinosaurs to the playground, and two seconds later decide that he definitely doesn't want to. After another two seconds he may decide again that of course he will bring them, as if he had never thought otherwise. This may be frustrating for parents, but it's all part of the toddler's growing need to assert himself and to explore his new-found independence. Don't let your toddler see that his mind-changing is having any effect on you. Let him change his mind as many times as he needs. Remember, this decision-making stuff is new to him.

Scrap the Agenda

In my practice I have encountered a number of couples in which the mom presents the dad with an agenda for the day when he goes off with the toddler. I recommend just saying, "Have fun. See you at six o'clock!" Fathers are perfectly capable of thinking independently about how they will manage their time with their children. Many times, however, when the dad looks to the mom for suggestions and then she gives them, a bad pattern is set because the father doesn't think for himself. I suggest to moms that if their spouse asks for suggestions of what to do with the child, she should say, "Hey, do whatever you want. You'll figure something out." (After all, moms have to do the same thing. They don't have all the answers.)

To dads I say that the great thing about toddlers is, as I wrote earlier, they'll be so pleased to spend time with you, it really doesn't matter what you do with them. Take them on your errands or go splash around barefoot in a big puddle. One dad I know sometimes took his toddler out for pancakes on Saturday mornings and then to his office. The dad caught up on some paperwork, and the child enjoyed drawing on scrap computer paper. When the dad was finished, they played silly games such as sending funny e-mails to mom at home. Whatever you do, remember that the very simple act of spending time with your toddler gives your child a sense of well-being and makes him feel important and loved.

Pay Attention to Gender Roles

Young children need to see their parents in various roles—to see Dad making dinner and Mom playing ball. Research shows that a child's gender identity is set by age three, so pretty much from the time your child is born, it's important to be aware of and to give your child messages about what you and your spouse consider acceptable gender-related activities. Some of this research shows, for example, that if a boy in a playroom wanders between a truck and a play kitchen, his parent may unconsciously ease the child toward the truck. Make an effort to pay attention to the gender-related examples you set for your child early on.

As always, assumptions about gender may be complicated and not always accurate. I receive a number of calls from parents (usually dads) who are concerned when their boys play with dolls or gravitate toward the doll or play kitchen areas at day care. Is this a problem? Not from my perspective. A boy needs to develop his nurturing, caring side, and it's perfectly natural for toddlers of either gender to be interested in dolls, stuffed animals, or play utensils and food.

The concern on the part of some parents seems to be that a

child who engages in nontraditional play roles may become a homosexual when he or she grows up. There's simply no evidence to support this. Some girls prefer to play with trucks. Some boys love to cook in a play kitchen. Neither activity is cause for concern. My experience in private practice has confirmed that parents who expect their children to engage only in certain types of gender-specific play tend to have more difficulty not only in sharing gender roles in their marriage but also in achieving an equally balanced parenting relationship. Sometimes I suggest a specific change in the family's routine to broaden their perspective.

Hal was reluctant when his wife, Jessica, a stay-at-home mom, suggested he join a "mommy or daddy and me" class with his two-and-a-half-year-old daughter, Nicole, but he admitted it would be a good way to spend some consistent time with her. Hal was a successful scientist who spent a lot of time at his lab. He took his daughter every week, and although he was one of only two fathers in a class of twelve, he felt very comfortable with the moms and instructor, who gladly welcomed him. Hal found it fascinating to watch Nicole as she played in the sandbox, painted, and began to relate to other children. The commitment he made to this regular class enhanced his relationship with his daughter, and Jessica noticed that he seemed much more willing to read to and play with Nicole before bedtime.

My wife, Linda, belonged to a "daddy and me" group that met on Saturday mornings and was run by our town parks department. At first the guys in the group thought it was a little weird that she had signed up for the class in the first place, but as soon as she explained that she worked all week and was the wife of a stay-at-home dad, they readily welcomed her and Kevin.

Many stay-at-home dads tell me that the traditional "mommy and me" classes have welcomed them, and some organizations have even changed their name to "parent and child" classes or "mommy or daddy and me" classes. One mom told me that when she joined her first "mommy and me" class with her son, one of the most helpful participants was the father of a little girl. In fact, when the teacher was absent for one reason or another, this dad led the class. Several years later when this child entered school, the father took on the care of a second baby girl. (The mom worked as a school principal.) Eventually the girls entered grade school, and the dad returned to an at-home business he had been running part-time at night while the children were in his care. And a note to dads who work on weekends: Many communities offer weekday classes.

I have often found that these structured classes encourage an increase in the time shared by the dad and child. The downside may occur when a father feels he has done "his share" because he has shown up for an hour-long class once a week. Obviously, that's not true. As long as the "daddy and me" class is viewed as a fun *supplemental* activity, then I'm all for it. If a mother perceives that her husband is using the class as a way to shirk greater involvement, then chapters 3 and 4 can help define what equal-balance parenting means to you as a couple and how best to communicate those needs and concerns for ongoing father involvement.

I really like the idea of these classes because they provide a consistent, organized block of time for dads to plan to be with their toddler, and they play an indirect role in shaking up gender-identity assumptions. I also recommend these classes to dads who don't have a lot of child care experience or who are just becoming more involved in their children's daily lives. They create a natural forum for dads to see other toddlers in action and to learn firsthand how kids this age behave. Yet another benefit is that fathers meet other dads in these classes and may develop friendships that include the children as well. Just the other day my wife was commenting that a ten-year-old boy she had first met in a "daddy and me" class when Kevin was three was still one of his good pals, and we're still friends with the family. Relationships are cultivated in these classes, and some dads feel especially committed to a structured time when they have signed up—and probably paid money!—to do so.

In addition to, or instead of, parent and child classes, many stay-at-home dads and working dads who are with their toddlers primarily on weekends have formed play groups for their toddlers, just as many stay-at-home moms do. All it takes is one or two other fathers with toddlers to begin a group. (Interested dads can hook up with play groups in their area through the website www.slowlane.com.)

Eating Habits and Introducing New Foods

Food is a source of fascination for toddlers, and as the baby continues to grow, more and more types of foods are gradually introduced. During this period the toddler begins to eat with his fingers, then with a child-sized spoon or fork, and can be introduced straight to the cup or to a sippy cup (sometimes called a tippy cup). Parents need to communicate about and to agree on what the toddler will eat; they need to compare notes as new foods are introduced and to monitor whether the child is allergic to a particular item. Make sure you and your spouse agree on items such as how treats will be handled, how much sugar the child is allowed to have, what the child's eating schedule will be, and what snacks are acceptable.

Food, like money, is often fodder for arguments among parents. Don't argue over how much your child should eat. Forcing a young child to clean her plate is not a good idea and can lead to food-related problems later in life. It's much more important to acclimate your child to the whole idea of sitting down for meals, using utensils, trying new foods, and eating a variety of foods. Back each other up on the decisions you make as a couple.

I always remind parents who are worried about how much their toddler is eating that children at this age don't eat very much at one sitting; many experts say that if your toddler eats one good meal a day, he's doing fine. Healthy children do not purposefully starve themselves; they will eat when they're hungry. "Grazing," or nibbling on finger foods throughout the day, even if they are healthy foods, instead of sit-down meals is generally not recommended. Remember that toddler-size servings are quite small; one tablespoon per year of age is the accepted recommendation for a serving. That means two tablespoons of peas, two tablespoons of mashed potatoes, and two tablespoons of cut-up chicken is a realistic meal for a two-year-old.

Since I was the primary caregiver at home with my children, I was very involved in deciding how, when, and what they would eat. Even fathers who work outside the home and are not present for all the meals can take an active interest in their toddler's diet and help their baby learn to eat. One dad I know regularly does the family's grocery shopping on Tuesday nights, and one of his favorite tasks is choosing healthy snacks and fruits for his children. While the mother in this family is more adept at thinking of meals and what is needed to prepare them, the dad always comes home from shopping with interesting snacks such as pizza bagels, Italian breadsticks, kiwis, mangoes, or figs.

Recently, my family and I were out at a restaurant when I noticed a young couple entering with a baby in a stroller. The baby looked to be about one or so, and I watched the couple with interest, since dining out with little ones is always tricky. I was disappointed to see that the couple placed the baby's stroller at the mother's side, and the father sat across the table; needless to say, he couldn't possibly participate in the baby's feeding. It would have been feasible for the couple to place the baby near the father or in between them. While the mother's meal cooled, the father happily ate, drank a glass of wine, and ordered dessert and coffee. Had the parents placed the baby in another position, the dad certainly could have assisted in her meal, and the mom could have enjoyed her dinner.

When my wife and I dined out when our kids were young, we always placed our babies in a position where we both could assist. We also often took turns eating; Linda would have her main course while I walked the baby around the restaurant to look at pictures or check out the fountain in the foyer, and then we'd switch. Sometimes we'd actually both be sitting for coffee; but more often than not, I'd go outside with the baby while Linda enjoyed her dessert "shift," and then I'd go back in and have mine while Linda strolled the baby outside. This was teamwork, and it's a method I'd advise all couples to try. Just because parents have a baby, they needn't always hire a babysitter if they want to go out to eat, nor should they always assume one parent (usually Mom) will attend to the baby during mealtimes. This goes for eating at home, too.

Stimulating Language Development

Most parents are familiar with the term "motherese," a lilting, melodic, repetitive method of speaking to babies. Motherese is characterized by short words or sentences, slow tempo, repetitive words, and simple questions, and is usually presented in a high pitch. It's a simplified way of speaking to a baby that stimulates his language skills. Both moms and dads often speak to their babies and toddlers in this manner, so I prefer to use the term "parentese." I know from my own experience that I've had many a sentimental, soft, intimate conversation with my babies.

Parentese has its place, but the toddler is also ready for more. By the time your child reaches her first birthday, you can drop the parentese completely and just speak in your normal voice. Your child will actually begin to respond more positively and attentively to normal tones of voice.

A couple I know kept a constant and quite sophisticated dialogue going as their baby grew from infant to toddler. At every occasion the parents explained to their daughter, Sarah, what they were doing, where they were going, what they were buying, and so on, in a very normal pitch and matter-of-fact tone. They verbalized everything in a natural, conversational way. "This is a pitcher, and I'm going to put some lemonade in it. I'm mixing juice from real lemons with water and a little sugar, and in a minute I'll put in some ice cubes." After opening the freezer door: "Oooh, it's very cold in there! Now I'll let you mix it up with this big wooden spoon, and then we can taste it," the mom or dad might say. Call it coincidence or call it the influence of a nurturing environment, but Sarah turned out to be an intellectually gifted girl with a huge vocabulary who became an avid reader and a talented writer at an early age.

Reading and being read to is a positive experience that should begin early. Reading is crucial for stimulating language and brain development, and there are many other benefits, too. As the parent reads, the child and parent bond, the child becomes familiar with the ebb and flow of his parent's voice, and he receives his parent's undivided attention. Reading together also provides a comforting routine, lengthens the child's attention span, and expands his vocabulary. Though picture books and "easy readers" are great, you can also read your children short passages of more sophisticated books; eventually they will mimic the words and learn them. I know one dad who favored Beatrix Potter books because the language this beloved British writer used was full of elegant words, phrasings, and perfect grammar. From a very young age this dad wanted to expose his child to the beauty, poetry, and scope of the English language.

Language development is one area where it's very easy for parents to share the responsibility. There are an almost infinite number of ways to share words and language with your toddler. In one family I know, the mom, who studied children's literature in college, was fascinated with choosing the most engaging picture books for her daughter; they took weekly trips to the library and read at least one story before bed each night. The father, on the other hand, preferred to spend some time each day curled up with his daughter looking at the pictures and words in the newspaper and news magazines. The dad would point out buildings and people and name them, saying, "This is the White House. That's where the president lives." The daughter would point to a picture and say, "Who are those guys?" and the dad would say, "Those guys are professional baseball players." The daughter delighted in these "reading sessions," and even though the dad knew she couldn't fully understand what he was talking about, they were sharing a valuable experience. Indeed, as the daughter grew older, she learned to appreciate the importance of keeping up with and discussing current events and news.

Agree on a TV Policy

Interestingly, I have found that many couples disagree on the amount and kind of television their child should be allowed to watch. Yet instead of coming to a compromise, one spouse usually gives in to the other's wishes. I have always advocated strictly limiting television watching early on.

In *The Read-Aloud Handbook,* Jim Trelease provides compelling evidence about the negative effects of television watching on young children, and the positive effects of reading aloud. Trelease provides a convincing discussion of studies that reveal the more television children watch, the lower their test scores in school. I know it is easy to use the television as a babysitter or to pop a tape in the VCR when we have chores or work to do, but the consistent use of the television in this way sets sedentary behavior patterns and stunts imagination and social skills. Watching television is the exact opposite of an interactive social experience. Research confirms the social learning theory, also known as the "you watch it, you learn it" theory: By watching violence on television, children learn that violence is an "acceptable" way to resolve conflict and frustration.

Even if you allow your children to watch only educational TV and videos, the bottom line is that you should limit and monitor your children's TV watching. It's hard to put a time frame on it. I go by this rule of thumb: If you think your child is in front of the TV too much, she probably is. Also, if your kid doesn't bother you or come "bug" you often, she's probably watching too much TV and needs to be engaged in other activities.

Both Parents Need to Be Involved in the Child's Potty Training

Somewhere between ages two and three, most kids (though not all) are ready to begin potty training. Both parents need to be involved in this important process; there is no reason to leave potty training up to the mom. Even dads who work full-time can stick close to home on weeknights and weekends and help their toddler practice potty skills. Successful potty training will occur more quickly if both parents are involved. If the child feels equally comfortable saying he has to go to the potty to both father and mother, there will be fewer accidents and the child will be trained faster. For boys, of course, a male role model is great. The main thing is to remember not to force the issue or to be angry, or to shame the child when accidents happen, as they inevitably will.

Potty readiness is an individual process. Most parents are able to tell when their child is ready to potty train—when the child knows the language of the potty or begins to show interest in it. You don't get extra credit for starting early. Toilet training is bound to be a faster and more successful experience if you wait for cues from your child. For about three months before even attempting toilet training, it's a good idea for both parents, in general conversation with the child, to talk about all the different things big boys and girls can do: eat by themselves at the table instead of a high chair, drink out of a cup, and so forth. Big boys and girls also help Mommy and Daddy (water the garden, pick up toys, make supper), sleep in a bed, and don't have to wear diapers anymore. ("Dry pants feel good!") This approach helps the child form a strong, well-rounded concept of what it means to be "big" and all the privileges and feelings of independence that go along with it.

Support and encouragement from both parents is essential, as is a unified approach. Discuss together how you will begin training. A number of books and videos are available to help parents negotiate the potty training process. As discussed in chapter 5 about how to help your child learn to sleep through the night, there are certainly different tacks to take, but the most important thing is unity between the parents and an agreement of what language to use.

Annie and Dave, a dual working couple, were concerned about potty training their son, Liam, because they knew they wouldn't be able to be with him constantly. He was in family day care with a woman named Margaret who had been watching children for twenty years and had raised five children of her own. Annie and Dave trusted Margaret's instincts completely, and when she said she thought Liam was ready at two years and ten months, they agreed on a plan.

Annie bought the video *Once Upon a Potty*, and she and Dave watched it with Liam once or twice every evening for a week before they began potty training. Liam loved the video and asked to watch it again and again. The weekend before they started watching the video, Annie took Liam on a shopping trip and made a big deal out of buying lots of big boy underpants, which she let Liam pick out, and a small potty. Dave and Annie agreed they would let Liam have the option of either the big potty or the little one at home. Dave let Liam help him snap together the parts of the potty and pick a place in the bathroom for it.

On Saturday morning of the next weekend, Annie made a big show of letting Liam open a package of big boy underwear and helped him put on a pair. He immediately peed in them. Annie didn't make a fuss; she just reiterated to Liam that when he needed to pee, he should tell Mommy or Daddy. She took him into the bathroom and pointed to the potty. "See. That's where you'll go pee and poop. Big boys have dry pants. Don't dry pants feel good?" Annie or Dave also asked Liam about every thirty minutes if he had to use the potty. (Remember to use a normal, matter-of-fact tone, not a cute singsong voice, and if the child says no, he doesn't have to go, trust him. Don't ask five times, "Are you sure?") When Annie had to go out for a couple of hours on Saturday afternoon and to the gym Sunday morning, Dave took over, using exactly the same phrases and approach. By the end of that first Saturday, Liam had gone through ten pairs of underpants, but by Sunday afternoon he had peed in the potty twice in a row.

When Annie dropped Liam off at Margaret's on Monday morning, she gave her an account of the whole weekend. Margaret did the same during the week, giving an account of each day, and on the weeknights, Annie and Dave stuck close to home so Liam could be near the potty. By Thursday, Liam was having only one or two accidents a day. Liam felt comfortable telling the three most important adults in his life—Mommy, Daddy, and Margaret—when he had to use the potty. By the end of month two, Liam was waking up from naps and during the night to use the potty. What ensured success for this family and caregiver was that they worked as a team and were consistent and communicative, with Liam and with one another.

I'm often asked how to handle outings at restaurants or other public places with little girls who are potty training, and this seems to be an issue of consternation for some fathers. My advice is to take your daughter—whether she is two, three, four, or even older—into the men's room and supervise her. You can go straight into a stall with your daughter, where your privacy will be maintained, or if she is old enough, you can wait directly outside the booth. I do not recommend sending a little girl into the ladies' room by herself or with a stranger.

Encouraging Dads to Stay Involved in Child Care Issues

Unless a parent is the primary caregiver, by age one the infant who was cared for by a grandmother or other family member may need to go to day care or another arrangement. Fathers should be involved in deciding who will care for their toddler, and as discussed in chapter 5, both parents need to visit and observe day care facilities and get to know the caregivers.

Grayson, a pastry chef, was the father of a fourteen-month-old girl, Tanya. His wife, Phoebe, worked as an architect. Grayson had irregular hours, but he often went in early to the restaurant where he worked and came home in the late afternoon. Although he often arrived home well before his wife, Grayson didn't pick Tanya up at day care. Instead, he drove straight home, showered, took a short nap, read the paper, and started dinner. Phoebe, who often worked past five, would pick up Tanya on her way home. When this couple came to see me, one of the first things I suggested was that Grayson pick up Tanya on the way home from the restaurant—or, if he was feeling really tired, to run home, take a short nap, and then get her. Grayson was hesitant to do this at first and presented a number of excuses: He needed time to unwind after work (but his wife didn't? I asked); he didn't know Tanya's likes and dislikes; she would be happier with her friends at day care; he didn't want to disrupt her schedule. And he did, after all, make dinner. Wasn't that enough?

While I reinforced that it was great that he made dinner for the family, I encouraged Grayson to look at the situation from Tanya's perspective: She needed time with her father as much as she needed time with peers. I also told him that he might enjoy their time together and that it would be a natural opportunity for him to get to know his daughter better (and her "likes and dislikes"), and vice versa. I suggested that they could devise a new schedule and that Grayson could be an integral part of Tanya's day. Even if he picked up his daughter by 4:00 or 4:30, he would have a good hour or two with her, one-on-one.

Pay Attention to Your Toddler

I was at the park recently when I noticed a father pushing his toddler in the swing. One hand was on his daughter's back, the other was on his cell phone. He was having a heated conversation about something that sounded very much like business. Perhaps he was closing an important deal, but I left the park wondering what message his daughter was getting.

This is an ongoing problem for parents of both genders, and I'll address it in forthcoming chapters as well. I would like to make the point, however, that when you're with your child, it's very important to focus on your child. (This is especially crucial during the toddler years because children this age can get into a great deal of mischief or even danger within seconds.) Sure, we all have busy lives and other things to do besides push a toddler in a swing. But the message we give our kids when our attention is always elsewhere is that we don't really think they're important.

Claude was a dad I met at that same local park a few years back since we often seemed to be there at the same time. He didn't pay that much attention to his son, who was two, except when the child whined, cried, or threw a tantrum, which he did quite often. He approached me where my older kids were in-line skating and asked if I had a newspaper he could read. I said I didn't, and he sat down to chat. "I'm here with my kid," he announced almost with embarrassment, "and I forgot to bring the paper. Oh, well." I'd often see Claude at the park in the coming weeks, and he usually had his nose buried in his newspaper. His son, whose name I learned was

Brandon, would play on the swings and slide until he got bored, while his dad sat silently by, reading the paper. I felt sorry for Claude and for Brandon; though this dad was making an effort to be with his son, he was getting little out of the time they spent together.

Unlike Claude, my friend Juan was very involved with his two-and-a-half-year-old son. One day as I sat chatting with a group of adults at a barbecue, one of the women present commented, "Oh, poor Juan! He's still stuck outside in front, playing ball with the children." Juan's wife, Samantha, spoke right up and said, "Oh, he's not stuck out there. He loves it. There's no place he'd rather be than with Christopher and the other kids."

And that was the truth about Juan. He traveled during the week for his job, and on weekends he devoted himself exclusively to his son. Although the quantity of their time together wasn't as great as the time Christopher spent with his mother, when Juan and Christopher were together, they were totally focused on each other. They planted the garden together, rode Juan's bike (with Christopher in a seat on the back), took walks, played games, and read stories. There was really no one (except his wife) whom Juan would rather be with than Christopher.

Males aren't always expressive about their feelings, but most dads do deeply love their kids. What was sad about Claude was that he didn't enjoy being with his son; he hadn't really taken the time to get "hooked" on his child. Fathers need to be with and interact with their toddlers to begin to understand the unique joy this phase of a child's life has to offer. At the barbecue, when I watched Christopher raise his arms to be lifted up high by his father, I was convinced that this little boy and his father shared a deep and rewarding love.

Maintain Your Relationship as a Couple

A toddler can pretty much dominate a family. Remember, he is probably not being demanding to aggravate you, he's just being himself. He needs his food cut up, his cup of milk replenished, his shoes tied; he needs to be bathed, helped with the potty, and accompanied wherever he goes.

Again, creativity leads to the best solutions. I have recommended to many couples that they explore the opportunity of creating a babysitting co-op with friends or neighbors. Since babysitters (even teens) can be very expensive, and many parents feel more comfortable leaving their baby with an adult they know well, they join together with friends to create a swap system. One Saturday night the couple drops their toddler at their friends' house while they go out to dinner, and the next Saturday night or Sunday afternoon they reciprocate by watching the friends' baby while that couple goes out. This can work quite well, especially if the toddlers are playmates or if the family structures are similar. Things may get a little more complicated if one family has three children under the age of six, and the other just has a baby, so it's best to work out this type of arrangement with a family similar to your own.

The Early Childhood Years:

Ages Three to Six

ONE EVENING I was taking a walk after dinner when I noticed a dad and his four-year-old daughter playing ball in their front yard. At first I thought how nice it was to see this father outside with his child in the early evening, but as I passed, I couldn't help but notice the way the father was speaking. Instead of encouraging his daughter with words of praise, he was pressuring her to hit the ball harder and farther with her bat; and he was sounding annoyed and disappointed when she didn't succeed. Instead of enjoying the time spent together and giving his daughter positive feedback, he was giving her the message that she just wasn't good enough at baseball. This father may have had good intentions, but his expectations weren't in line with his young child's capabilities.

Early childhood—ages three to six—is a time when children really look to their parents to set standards, limits, and examples, and to give consistent words of love and encouragement in all areas of their daily activities and routines. This is the time, before they enter the world of grade school and peer groups, when kids eagerly absorb all they can from their parents. The challenge for both mothers and fathers during this stage is to focus on establishing rules and limits, and giving the messages and lessons that they truly want their children to learn and remember. While issues of discipline may jump to your mind, I'm also talking about giving positive messages, such as parents letting their children see them being affectionate with and nurturing to each other. I know in my family, for example, I never leave the house without kissing my wife good-bye, and she always gives me a hello and a hug and kiss whenever she comes home. This physical connection that says "I love you" is as important to your children as setting rules about where they play outside or teaching table manners.

Also, we'll look at the issues that typically surface as dads and moms work as a team to nurture and teach their three- to six-year-olds, and several ways that real families have worked to meet their children's developmental needs.

Fostering the Ability to Make Friends

Your three-year-old will gradually make the transition from "parallel" play (playing side by side but basically ignoring his playmate) to engaging in one-on-one friendships with other children of his age. To encourage friendships I advise parents to get their child together for play dates with other couples and their children. When a dad is involved in helping his child make new friends and encouraging the child to share and relate to other kids, he becomes intimately connected to fostering the child's social development. In addition to play dates, good places for dads to take kids are the park, indoor play areas, and library or bookstore story hours where the children can meet and play with others their age.

It's important that both parents learn the names of the child's friends. (Men are notorious for not learning and remembering others' names and for leaving that "job" up to their wives.) In my house I help both myself and Linda remember the names of our kids' friends by putting two lists—one for A.J. and one for Kevin—on the fridge. They include each friend's name, one or both of the parents' names, and their phone number. Then when either Linda or I is arranging a play date, we have got all the information in a handy place. I also update it—even at the ripe old age of eight or nine, friends come and go. Plenty of fathers have come over to our house, seen the lists, and said, "Wow, I wish my wife would do something like that for me." And I love saying, "Well, actually, I did that."

Another simple way fathers can be involved in their children's friendships is to ask specific questions. Instead of "Did you have a nice time?" the involved father can ask, "What did you and Tim like best about your trip to the zoo?" I always tell parents to think ahead: When you begin showing interest in your child's socializing at an early age, your older child won't be so surprised when you want to know where he's going and whom he'll be with!

When children have difficulty making friends, parents can step in to offer support. Parents can't change the inborn temperament of the shy child, but they can help the child adjust more easily to new situations. Matt, an outgoing dad who was a newspaper reporter, was frustrated with the temperament of his shy five-year-old son, Andy, who was in his third month of kindergarten. While he was clearly very smart, he didn't seem to be "clicking" socially with any of his classmates. Matt's wife was concerned that her husband was intimidating the son and making things worse. In counseling and role-playing sessions, I helped Matt learn how to teach Andy "social etiquette." I would play a game or do a puzzle for a while with Andy and then say, "Now you say, 'That was fun. Let's play again!'" I also taught Andy that it is a good idea when you meet another kid to say things like "Hi. You look nice. I like your shirt." Gradually, Matt took over the role-modeling, so when he and his son finished an activity together, Matt said things like "I had a really good time. Thanks for playing with me." It's kind of like learning the art of small talk, which translates to: I like you.

I encouraged both Matt and his wife to be patient and comfortable with this process, not to have unrealistic expectations, and, most of all, to take it slowly. In my practice I've found that it can take a year or more of therapy for a shy child to learn social etiquette. Other suggestions I gave them included inviting just one friend over to play rather than always expecting Andy to interact with a large group of children, letting him know that one or both parents would be nearby when he enters into a social situation such as the playground or a party, reading books about friendships (friendships between animals seem to be the most universally engaging), and talking about experiences with their own friends. In this way Andy would begin to get a broader picture of what friendship means and how people interact with each other.

The aggressive child presents an entirely different set of needs. For obvious reasons aggressive children often have trouble making friends. I had a client family with two children, a boy named Doug, age six, and a girl named JoEllen, age five, who were both hyperactive and very aggressive. The family came to me because teachers, school counselors, and parents of other children were complaining about their behavior. Unlike most doctors, I still make house calls. What I saw when I visited their home was sheer havoc. The whole household was extremely disorganized: The dog ran inside and outside constantly, barking at an outrageous pitch, sniffing everyone, tracking mud, and getting the kids completely wound up; the kids had no set mealtime or bedtime; the TV and the stereo were blaring; the mom was yelling a lot, and the dad had basically just given up on trying to get control of the situation. Also, the parents went out five or six nights a week, so having a sitter further upset the kids' routine.

I worked with the family to restructure the household completely. It took some time, but the most important factor in the successful turnaround was the involvement and commitment of both parents. I explained to them how the physical environment of the home and their own lack of communication and limits with their children were exacerbating the kids' aggression, which in turn was making their school and social lives unsuccessful. My plan included simple organizational tactics: getting on a schedule, including regular meals and a bedtime routine with bath and quiet play or reading; limiting TV and allowing only nonaggressive programs;

leaving the phone ringer on in only one room the rest of the day; penning the dog up during meals; and getting the parents to commit to fewer nights out so they could spend more time with their children. This dramatic shift took several months, but ultimately it paid off. The children became more relaxed and friendly, and other children started to become friends with them. I sometimes use this story in my parenting seminars or with other clients to drive home the message that parents working in tandem can make or break their child's tendency to be aggressive and, therefore, their ability to make and keep friends.

Birthday Parties

A key aspect of social development during the early childhood years is the birthday party—loathed and feared by many parents but mostly by moms who feel pressured to outdo the kid next door who had two ponies, a professional magician, and a mom who made a cake from scratch and hand-decorated it with a 3-D scene from *The Tale of Peter Rabbit*—in marzipan! Invariably, once the child becomes part of a larger peer group—through nursery school, kindergarten, or other play settings—the demand for larger and better parties seems to increase yearly.

My advice is to keep parties modest; it's not necessary to have twenty children (and their parents) over for a three-year-old's party. (The child will undoubtedly become overstimulated and is just that much more likely to have a meltdown or to misbehave.) The general rule of one guest per each year of the child's age seems quite reasonable—three guests for three-year-olds, four guests for four-year-olds, and so on.

Planning a party of any size can be stressful for the party-giver, who is usually the mother, so I suggest that fathers participate in the planning and facilitating of the birthday party from start to finish, whether that means ordering the cake, buying goodies for the loot bags, designing invitations on the computer, or cleaning up the deck. The thing with a reluctant dad is that he doesn't know what to do, but you can help him choose a role for before and during the party so he has something to do. In our family everyone gets assigned a task; if a person doesn't do his task, it messes up everyone else.

I recommend that parents sit down together about six weeks in advance to establish parameters: how many children can be invited, where the party will be held, how much they want to spend, and so on. Then discuss the party with your child. Let your child make some choices; for example, "Which five friends would you like to invite?" or "Do you want ice cream cake or cupcakes?" But also be clear about the limits you've set as a couple: "Mommy and I are not going to rent out the entire roller rink."

Once you've made these decisions, divvy up the work for each parent—and the child if she's old enough. Moms, you should operate under the assumption that your husband will be involved. Here is how one couple I know approached their child's party: The dad appointed himself the "entertainment" man when his wife admitted she had no idea what to do with a group of three-year-olds but said she felt quite comfortable handling the food and decorations. While sitting in the doctor's waiting room one day, he happened to pick up a parenting magazine with a cover story on birthday parties. He learned that it's helpful to pick a theme for the party; to set a time limit on the party, such as from 12:00 to 1:30, and write it on the invitation; and to break up activities into twenty-minute intervals.

He chose a beach theme. His "icebreaker" activity for when the children arrived was making sand trays: out on the deck, each child got a plastic tray filled with sand and could choose from buckets of different shells to create patterns and pictures. Then he staged a "beach" parade with musical instruments and colorful Hawaiian lei necklaces for the kids, and he videotaped them as they paraded around the yard. The next step was lunch, followed by cake and ice cream. Then the dad turned on four sprinklers in the backyard (having borrowed three from neighbors) and let the kids go wild in their swimsuits. The party wrapped up with each child getting his or her own beach towel (purchased on sale at a local discount store) and a beach pail with party favors. Rather than assuming that his wife would handle the whole party, he took an active role from start to finish.

When a child's father is involved in the birthday parties, it sends the message to the child that the father is an integral part of important events within the family.

Addressing the Common Fears of Early Childhood

Young children can be afraid of many things. Monsters are a very common fear, as are thunder and lightning, the dark, loud noises, the wind, dogs or other animals, or riding the school bus for the first time. Such fears are perfectly normal and natural at this age and are best calmed with patience and kindness rather than scolding. If, for example, your little one is afraid of monsters under the bed or in the closet, it's important to tell him that there are no monsters, but you'll check nevertheless. Go with your child and look under the bed or in the closet. Let him look, too. If your child wants to play monsters, let him; he's just working things out for himself. If your child charges at you with "claws" outstretched and yells, "I'm a very scary monster. I'm going to get you!" it's a good idea to let him experience that power. I recommend that you act scared or horrified for a brief moment, then grab him and tickle him or burst out laughing to make it all funny and to give him the message that he is safe. Never admonish the child: "Big boys aren't afraid!"

If your child is afraid of something that can be explained scientifically, such as thunder, go to the library together and take out a children's book on the subject, read it together, and discuss why thunder occurs and what is the safest thing to do in a lightning storm. Information and honesty are needed; the parent should also validate and acknowledge the child's feelings. Children at this age need cuddling and encouragement from their mothers *and* their fathers to calm their fears. Actually, hugs are important every day, not just when your child is scared. Remember to hold your child on a daily basis.

Lynn, a Ph.D. candidate, and Jordan, a sound technician for a recording studio, had a three-and-a-half-year-old boy named Jake.

Lynn's friend had a free pass to a traveling circus coming to town one weekend, but because she was single and had no children, she thought Lynn, Jordan, and Jake would enjoy the show. Lynn accepted the pass because she didn't want to hurt her friend's feelings, but deep down she had a suspicion that Jake was too young for the circus and would be afraid of the clowns. She broached the subject with her husband, and he thought Jake was definitely not old enough and would be scared. Lynn ended up taking Jake to the circus, with the promise to Jordan that she would leave immediately if Jake got scared.

About twenty minutes into the performance, Jake got very upset and announced, "Those clowns are scary. I want to go home." On the way home, awash in guilt, Lynn tried to explain to her son that the clowns were just men in costume and weren't real. For literally weeks afterward Jake would be in the middle of something such as eating breakfast or playing with his race cars, and out of the blue he would announce, "Those clowns are too scary for me." One day when Lynn and Jake were in the car, an ambulance passed with a loud siren. Jake said, "There must be clowns in there." Lynn was amazed that even after so much time had passed, her son was still processing the experience. She told Jordan at dinner that night, and he got very angry. "I told you not to take him. Now he'll probably be frightened of clowns for the rest of his life. What were you thinking?"

If I had had the opportunity to speak with this couple beforehand, I would still have had to let the parents make their own decision about whether to take Jake to the circus. However, had they opted to take Jake, I would have recommended that they first prepare him by laying a foundation of understanding—by reading books or renting videos about clowns. Children make transitions more easily when they are prepared for new experiences in advance.

Stress and the Young Child

I've saved a more in-depth discussion of stress and the "hurried child" for the next chapter, but I mention it here, too, because I have found that many parents are not aware that stress can have negative effects on the very young. Just because a child can't talk about her stress doesn't mean she can't feel it. I see these young children frequently in my family practice; the causes are many, including divorce, an undiagnosed learning disability, too much pressure from parents, lack of parent-child communication, parents who fight a lot, and too much stimulation (as we saw with Doug and JoEllen, mentioned earlier in the chapter).

I once had a client whose child, a five-year-old named Petros, was extremely nervous. Whenever he came to me for a session, he would suck on his whole hand, not just the typical thumb or two fingers. He was showing signs of depression, including being a little slow and lethargic, being whiny, and not getting enough sleep. As at Doug and JoEllen's home, I discovered during a home visit that little Petros's house was constantly filled with activity—phones and doorbells ringing, people slamming doors as they went in and out, neighbors revving their cars and motorcycles. While some adults thrive on excitement, most children are adversely affected by constant noise and activity. (One of my greatest pet peeves is parents who leave the TV on for background noise. Try no noise or classical music.)

When parents wonder why their children are overexcited, having meltdowns all the time, or are unable to wind down and go to sleep, the first place I suggest they look for clues is their home environment. Many children in this age group still need a nap or a "quiet" time in the afternoon. And as I said earlier, it's a good idea to alternate outdoor or active play with low-key, quiet activities. I like to suggest that parents discuss their child's scheduled activities from time to time and determine together whether changes need to be made. A cranky, irritable child or an overly quiet child may be giving his parents the unheeded message that he's overstimulated and needs more quiet time.

Gender and Play Issues

Our culture teaches boys and girls how to behave in gender-specific ways, and if anything it's the parents' job to counteract some of the false messages kids receive from peers and the media—television, music, videos, and so forth. When children enter school, they begin to receive the broad message that boys are more "rough and tumble" and girls are "pretty and delicate."

In this age group I have two primary recommendations for mothers and fathers for counteracting the development of gender stereotypes: be good role models and encourage choices. As long as we give our children the message that we believe in them, that we love them unconditionally, and that they do have choices, I think we'll continue to move in the right direction. Girls can sign up for soccer, T-ball, tai kwon do, and ballet; boys can act and dance in the school play, learn gymnastics or karate, or take music lessons *if they express a desire to do so.* The important thing is to find out what your child is interested in. I encourage parents to think before they speak, lest the message "You can't do that because you're a girl (or boy)!" comes out.

Hands-On Learning Through the Five Senses

When my son, Kevin, was three and four, he liked to touch and feel and hold everything; he learned best by using his senses. He loved to take a big deep sniff of an orange or a new bar of soap. One day at an indoor ice-skating rink, I introduced him to a friend of mine who was wearing a fake fur coat; she was a large woman, and in her fur she looked like a bear. Kevin stood stroking her coat, getting to know my friend and learning about the fur's texture.

Exploring new sights, sounds, textures, tastes, and smells is a natural area where dads can really get involved. One dad I know who lives in the city loves to take his kids to children's museums and other hands-on exhibits that focus on science or art. Another finds that camping and canoeing expeditions allow him to educate his children about the sights, sounds, and beauty in the natural world. Find ways to create opportunities for your children to learn by using their five senses.

Derrick, a web page designer who had attended a prestigious art school, and Eileen, a stay-at-home mom, had a four-year-old daughter, Christy, who had just entered preschool. Eileen was a client of mine who was struggling with trying to get Derrick more involved in Christy's activities and routines. At one point I asked her how Christy was getting along in preschool, and she said fine, but Derrick didn't seem to be showing any interest in it. When she mentioned that parents' night was only two weeks away, I encouraged her to have Derrick attend with her and suggested that she tell him it would be good for Christy to get validation of her early school experiences from her dad. Derrick agreed to go.

At the open house, the teacher explained the curriculum, focusing on how weekly themes were explored through the five senses and in the different areas of the room. For example, to explore the theme of family, the children brought in photographs of their family and made a giant classroom collage; the pretend play area was set up like a family room; other activities focused on the concepts of big (parents) and little (infants and children) and having the children tell what they liked best about their families. The plans also included creating a basic family tree on the computer and hosting a "family" of hamsters. Derrick was impressed not only with how much thought the teacher had put into her classroom activities but also how the computer was being integrated into this multifaceted learning process. He started showing much more interest in Christy's day and always asked her lots of questions at dinnertime. He ended up designing a web page for the school's marketing director and volunteering once a week to do special art and computer projects with the kids.

The Value of Pretend Play

Fantasy play is another way young children process the vast amounts of information they are absorbing; it helps them practice mastery of the real world and nurtures their imagination. Children may want to play superheroes or house or dolls or any number of pretend games, and they may want to play by themselves, among peers, or with a parent. One of the best ways a dad can contribute to pretend play is by following his child's lead. I once watched a father follow his child all around the park one day, pretending to be whatever animal the child desired. Pretend play is a great bonding and attachment experience for the father and child, a time when a child learns that she deserves her father's full attention and that her imagination is important and valued.

Some dads are really good at making "props" for their child's pretend play. I once suggested to a father who was a client of mine, and very adept at making things, that a great way he could be more involved with his kids was to make props for pretend play instead of buying them. Over the course of just one year he made a combination stovetop/counter/refrigerator, a platform to put chairs on to make a plane or train, and a long table with a mock conveyor belt to play supermarket checkout.

I also suggest to dads—and moms, too—that they keep their eye out at work for things to bring home from the office that kids can use in pretend play. Depending on where you work, you might uncover boxes, office forms, junk mail, old magazines, scrap paper, notebooks, hospital robes, sample products (child-safe only), used unbreakable kitchenware, expired credit cards, and old name tags.

Establish Discipline Methods as a Team

Anne Lamott is a wonderful writer who is perhaps best known for her very funny, insightful book *Operating Instructions,* which chronicles her son's first year and her experiences as a single mother. In another book, *Bird by Bird,* which is actually about writing, she includes some stories about her son and writes: "Every day kids need discipline. And every day kids need a break." I think this is so true. Kids need both. One of the toughest concepts I have to work on with parents in counseling is convincing them that their children do require boundaries in order to feel loved. If you let them do whatever they please whenever they want, they'll soon feel out of control, and they could begin to lose their self-esteem and feel as if nobody really cares about them. Parents need to work together as a team to give their children the message that there are boundaries, rules, and limits in their lives that will be taught and enforced.

It is common for moms and dads to run into some disagreements in this area, but with effective communication these issues can usually be resolved. Quite often one parent is more lenient than the other, and kids soon pick up on the fact that they can "get away with" something when mom (or dad) is around but not when the other parent is in charge.

Ryan, a carpenter, let his daughters, age four and six, pretty much run the show. They would play dress up and strew clothing all around the house, color and draw and not pick up after themselves, eat snacks in their bedrooms, and generally do whatever they pleased while Ryan was in charge. When his wife, Sheila, a teacher, came home from work, she'd be irritated and angry; the house would be a mess, and she'd have to work overtime to get the girls to clean up and behave. Sheila felt that Ryan needed to tighten the reins; the kids were getting mixed messages from their parents.

Ryan disagreed. He was convinced that the girls were simply creative and fun-loving, and he didn't want to spoil their childhood. One night Ryan invited his boss and family over for dinner, and that really turned things around. When he saw how politely the boss's children behaved at dinner, how they cleared their own plates and conversed nicely, he began to wonder. His own girls had poor table manners, came to dinner late, didn't excuse themselves when they were through, and ran off to the next-door neighbor's house to play with some other friends after the meal, ignoring the boss and his family. It wasn't until Ryan was directly affected by his daughters' behavior that he began to admit the girls needed rules and limits. The very next evening after the girls were in bed, he and Sheila sat down and discussed ways in which to implement changes.

Discipline Methods for Three- to Six-Year-Olds

Time-out is perhaps the most common discipline method with children this age. It involves removing the child to a part of the room or yard where there are no toys, children, or other interesting diversions, and requiring him to sit there for several minutes as a direct "effect" of a specific episode of misbehavior. Personally, I'm against sending kids to their room for time-out for two reasons: (1) I think kids should enjoy spending time in their room, and it shouldn't be relegated to a punishment area; (2) the parent or caregiver can keep on eye on the child if she's in the same room. But sometimes—for example, in a small apartment—it's the only choice.

If a home has stairs, I sometimes recommend using the lowest stair as a time-out spot. The rule of thumb is to give the child a time-out that is about one minute per year of age, so a three-year-old should have a three-minute time-out. When you place her in time-out it's important to explain to the child what she did that was inappropriate and to give her an opportunity to think about it.

If they agree to use time-out as a discipline method, it's also important for both parents to be consistent and to follow through. Moms especially are famous for threatening time-out (as in "If you don't stop running through the living room, you'll get a time-out") and stalling or, worse, never following through at all; if the dad in such a family *does* follow through when he's watching the kids, the kids are not going to understand. Further, if you're trying to nip in the bud a really serious behavior problem like hitting, you must both be consistent about following through. I recommend that parents agree ahead of time on what behaviors will require the discipline of a time-out (for example, biting, hitting, throwing toys), act consistently and swiftly when they occur, and *stick with it.* Also keep the lines of communication open: Make sure to tell your partner when he or she comes home whether your child had any time-outs and what happened.

Denying privileges or favorite activities is a more effective form of discipline when children have outgrown time-out, at about age four or five. For example, if a child is being fussy and squirmy about letting you put on sunscreen before going to the community pool, you can simply say, "No sunscreen, no pool."

Another technique that helps prevent discipline problems

before they arise is the two-minute warning. This can be particularly useful for fathers who are just getting the hang of caring for young children. Simply say to the child, "In two minutes we're going to leave the playground and go home for lunch." That gives the child the chance to prepare mentally for the change and to finish up what he's doing.

Along the same lines as the two-minute warning is ending the activity before it ends itself. If a game goes on too long, your child will likely become bored and may start to misbehave; he likely only needs to be redirected (a nice way of saying distracted) into another activity. Dads may be especially susceptible to making the mistake of thinking "Great! Frankie's been coloring for an hour; might as well keep on with it." But parents usually learn that it's better to end the activity before the novelty wears off.

My position on spanking is an unqualified no. Hitting and spanking teach kids that physical aggression is an acceptable means of conflict resolution; to me that doesn't make sense. I've yet to see the research revealing that spanking does any good in terms of effective behavior control, and I've seen plenty of research revealing that it may have damaging consequences and side effects, including lying (children will lie in order not to get spanked) and aggression. I counsel parents who do spank to stop right away and switch to time-out, focusing more on verbal communication.

Are Rewards Worth It?

Psychologists and parents alike have long debated the issue of whether rewards or incentives should be used to motivate children to do what you want them to, or to provide positive reinforcement when they do something well. My opinion is that parents should use rewards moderately and intermittently; mothers and fathers run into problems when rewards or bribes are used on a consistent basis. (For example, when we were toilet training A.J., we kept a basket of gift-wrapped toys and trinkets like new barrettes and little troll dolls above the toilet; when she went successfully, she got to choose and open a "present." When she was fully trained, we slowly phased out the reward.) If children behave as expected only in order to get a reward, they lose any sense of intrinsic motivation and won't attempt to tie their own sneakers in the morning without expecting a treat. If the child isn't sure when he's going to get the reward, he will keep trying. If it's too often or too soon, the reward loses its effect.

Intrinsic motivation is the goal, and it comes from finding the experience itself of value rather than seeking value in the form of a reward when the experience is over. To encourage intrinsic motivation in children, you have to stimulate interest in good behavior. The theory of affordances—creating interesting experiences—was introduced in chapter 6. By giving your child affordances, you can begin to foster intrinsic motivation. Discuss, question, and help your child find enjoyment, interest, or intrigue in everyday tasks and experiences. For example, in conjunction with house rules about chores, make a game out of doing the dishes or picking up. And again, don't communicate drudgery as you do your own chores or household tasks; figure out ways to make things fun and to keep kids included.

In *Punished by Rewards,* author Alfie Kohn provides a fascinating discussion of the ways in which we use and abuse the reward system with our children and in our society. Kohn believes that we've gone overboard in our use of the reward system. In many ways I agree. Some kids, such as those with attention deficit hyperactivity disorder (ADHD), respond very well to star charts, for example, but other kids, when given the option of a reward, can't do anything without a carrot dangling in front of their noses. I'd save the chart for really difficult issues because we don't get star charts in the real world. Also be careful not to use food as a reward because that can cause problems with food later on. Lastly, decide with your spouse what activity does or does not merit a reward; for example, children should not be rewarded for picking up toys at the end of playtime, but they may be rewarded for not hitting. If you do use a reward, the goal should be to phase it out after a reasonable amount of time.

Establish Family Routines

Family routines help children feel secure and learn what behavior is expected. By age three, children are ready to learn and understand them. When your child asks, "Why do I have to say please and thank you/brush my teeth/put my clothes away?" you simply answer, "That's our family routine" or "That's our family rule." As children get older and start saying things like "Well, Mary's mom and dad let her do such and such," you can respond, "Other families may do that. This is what our family does." Patterns and predictability give kids comfort, security, and a sense that life has some measure of logic. This isn't to say that you can't ever be flexible and spontaneous—cereal for supper once in a while or a spur-of-the-moment campout in the living room are allowed—but rules, routines, and predictability do help young children know how they are expected to behave.

The Messages We Send

When juggling all our work and parenting responsibilities, it is easy to overlook the fact that we can be sending our children negative nonverbal messages when we least realize it. At the summer sports camp I direct, one father always arrived late to pick up his daughter. His child was always the last one sitting on the step. Her dad was a busy man with an important position at work, but he had agreed to accept the responsibility of picking up his daughter at the end of the day. Because he was so busy, he didn't think it would matter if he was ten, fifteen, or even twenty minutes late each day to pick up Jenny. But the truth was, even though the camp counselors didn't mind, Jenny was beginning to feel abandoned and sad at the end of each afternoon, and before long she told her parents she didn't want to go to camp anymore.

Any working parent, fathers and mothers, can understandably be caught up in work and delayed on occasion by meetings or traffic. But when this lateness occurs frequently, the message to the child is that she or he isn't as important as work. I try to emphasize to working fathers, who seem a bit more prone to being late when it's their turn to pick up the kids than working moms, that the spouse who is the on-call or pick-up parent needs to take the role seriously because the unspoken message will be taken seriously by the child. It may seem very minor in importance to the parent, but to the child it is big.

When my daughter, A.J., was five or six, I promised to "watch" when I brought her to ballet class instead of reading a book. She let me know that it was important for her to have my full attention during her lesson and that I shouldn't be spending the half-hour chatting or catching up on reading. Naturally, there are times when kids have to be told, "No, I can't watch you now, I have work to do." But there should be just as many, if not more, occasions when we say to our children, in our actions as well as our words, "Yes! You are important to me, and I will watch you and listen to you and be there just for you." At about age three, as the child begins to master more difficult skills, attention from parents becomes even more important.

Honesty

There are many good traits and habits that parents can begin to demonstrate as role models during this time, but I'd like to focus on honesty for a moment. If we speed down the highway and lie when the policeman stops the car, or we find a wallet and don't report it found, or if a cashier hands us too much change and we pocket it anyway, how can we then look into our child's eyes and expect her to tell the truth?

One mom called my office specifically to tell me that she was leaving for a trip for five days and was planning not to tell her four-year-old daughter because she didn't want to upset her (the live-in housekeeper was going to watch the child). I advised the woman to go immediately to her daughter and begin preparing her child for the reality of her departure. Not only does this give the child the message that the parent is honest and trustworthy, but it lets the child begin to prepare—through pretend play and conversation—

for the separation. The child may pack her doll's suitcase and say, "It's time for you to go on an important trip!" Also, don't interrupt your child's private conversation so that she can process that information in her own way, in her own time frame. I give the same advice when a mom or dad asks if it's necessary to tell a child he's going to receive a shot from the pediatrician or needs to have a tooth pulled at the dentist's office. I'm not saying you should frighten the child with excessive detail or overdramatize the event, but a simple, honest explanation of the upcoming event given in a calm and reassuring manner is best.

Sports and Extracurricular Activities

Early childhood is the time when many children become actively engaged in sports. Leaders and trainers often warn that if a parent wants his child to excel, it's necessary to take sports seriously and sign up for the extra hours, the traveling teams, and so on.

Although I'm an avid sports fan and I believe in keeping an active lifestyle, I do not believe it's necessary to teach the "fundamentals" of the game to the three- or four-year-old. This is a time to learn to throw a ball or jump high in the air for the sake of throwing and jumping, not for the sake of making a point or scoring. Fathers often think they need to teach their children to be competitive, but this isn't the case. Competition will develop naturally and gradually as a child matures and grows.

In the sports camp, we teach young kids the basics by having them engage in running games; they don't even realize that they're learning to play soccer because they're having so much fun. Dads often stop by the camp and say, "What has my child learned about soccer today?" I have to remind these dads that the children are so young, they really are learning how to play together and have fun, and that's what they're there for.

Shawn was a man who had taken sports seriously all his life; he played basketball as a youth, and now, as the director of a YMCA sports program, he was passing his knowledge on to kids of all ages. Having grown up in the inner city, Shawn had seen plenty of boys who had gone down the wrong path, and he wanted to lead as many youths as he could away from failure, including his own five-year-old, Marquis (pronounced Mar-kus). Marquis had loved basketball ever since he received his first plastic hoop for Christmas one year, and whenever Shawn went to the gym to play basketball with some other men in a league three evenings a week, he took Marquis along. Soon the other guys began bringing their young sons and daughters, who would play ball in an adjacent court with kid-sized hoops while the fathers played in theirs.

During the summer, when he ran a sports camp at the Y, he signed his son up and brought him to work with him every day. Marquis could choose to play soccer, basketball, or kickball, or to do arts and crafts projects. Shawn was giving his young son the message that playing sports is a fun, active, healthy pastime that should be enjoyed and learned from but isn't the only important thing in life. Shawn's expectations were in line with Marquis's developmental stage; he never placed pressure on Marquis when he didn't play well.

Stay Involved in School Issues

As in my previous discussion about choosing day care, fathers should be active in choosing a preschool for their child. With his wife and child, a father can visit prospective schools, interview school directors, and ask questions about the school's curriculum philosophy, discipline techniques, special programs, and so on. One dad I know helped his wife track down a cooperative preschool where both parents could volunteer each month. When you're aware of what goes on at your child's preschool and get to know the teachers, you'll be able to ask specific questions about your child's day and his school experience.

The first day of preschool or kindergarten can be exciting but also emotionally draining, especially for children who aren't used to being away from their primary caregivers. One working couple I know discovered that it was best for the father to drop their three-year-old at preschool on his way to work because the child was less likely to cling and cry when the dad dropped him off than when the mother did.

I advise dads to take a day off, if possible, or at least the morning off, on the first day of preschool and the first day of kindergarten. Seeing your child off to school on the first day can be a rewarding experience, and it makes a significant impact on the child to see that both parents are equally interested in this momentous occasion. Many mothers also feel overburdened at this time of year between buying new school clothes and school supplies, preparing the child for the separation, and getting adjusted to a new schedule. This is an excellent time to sit down and engage in a parent-to-parent meeting and decide which parent is going to do what. Again, I suggest to moms that the dad do something related to what he enjoys. One mom I know was willing to get all the clothes and supplies for her son's first day of kindergarten, and she knew all the relatives would be demanding pictures of his "first day." Her husband was an avid amateur photographer, and by asking him to take pictures and develop them, she not only got to strike one item off her to-do list but she ensured that her husband would come the first day.

Research proves that school involvement is changing for fathers. A recent Department of Education study of seventeen thousand families found that when a father is consistently involved in at least three areas, such as parent-teacher conferences, attending school events, and volunteering at the school, his child is more likely to enjoy school, do well academically, and participate in extracurricular activities.

After that very important first day, here are just a few of the many ways you and your spouse can be involved in kindergarten and elementary school:

- Join the school's PTA or PTO. If possible, become a "class parent." If the school uses the antiquated term "room mother," ask that the term be updated to include fathers.

- Attend Back to School Nights, teacher conferences, special events such as holiday shows, and preschool orientation day—

usually a portion of a day for parents and their children to attend the facility together before the child formally begins to attend.

- Volunteer to read books to your child's preschool or kindergarten class.

- Volunteer to do a demonstration of something related to your occupation or hobby. Some dads have demonstrated musical instruments, simple science experiments or carpentry projects, computers, construction, or cooking. Keep your demonstration simple and short for this age group. Your young child will be infinitely proud that his or her dad has come to visit the class.

- Don't shy away from school because of your work schedule. Take a personal day and visit the school now and then. Some dads can't be present during the week, but at school events such as a weekend holiday bazaar they are out in full force, running the games and the snack bar. Some schools have after-school programs or evening events that you will surely be able to attend.

- Serve on your local school board or volunteer for a parent committee such as a technology committee or a committee to improve the school playground.

Give the message to your child early on that school is very important to both parents. Let your child know that both her mom and dad are going to be supportive and involved in her academic progress.

Take Your Child to Work

Just as you want to visit the child's environment, you can bring your three- to six-year-old into yours. This gives the young child a visual picture of where Mom or Dad is during the day (or evening) and may help with separation issues. Whether it's an office, a store, a school, a hospital, or a fire station, your child can visit it. One mom told me her employer, a single man, had no objection to her or her colleagues, both male and female, bringing babies or children to the Manhattan magazine office where she worked. As long as the work got done and the kids behaved, the man didn't mind. Babies occasionally sat in strollers or on blankets in this mom's office, and the older children brought books to occupy them while their parents worked. The art department was more than happy to contribute scrap paper and markers. No one in the office brought kids in to work too often, but it made the editors and writers feel much less pressured when a babysitter called in sick or an older child had a school snow day or teachers in-service training day. This same mother recalls visiting her dad's office when she was a child. She would sit at his secretary's desk and pretend to type while her dad worked; then he would take her on the elevator to visit the luncheonette in the lobby. Knowing where her father worked and where he was going each day was comforting to her.

I think it's a really nice idea for a father or mother to take an occasional afternoon off or a whole day, if possible, and tell his daughter, for instance, "This is Melissa's Day." They can go out to lunch and to a movie—or to whatever activity his daughter would like. Particularly when there's another sibling, I recommend that, on occasion, each parent (if they both work) take a half or whole day off and devote it to one child. The other sibling will have his or her turn on another day.

Finding Other Couples with Common Interests

Not only is this an important time to maintain your relationship as a couple, but it's also a good time to branch out and socialize with other families who have kids. Because I was home with our children and got to know a lot of the moms from being with the kids at the park and at school, I'd often mention something one mom or another had said. My wife would look at me blankly and wonder who in the world I was talking about. One weekend I suggested we invite one of Kevin's friends and his whole family over for a barbecue. The kids played, my wife got to know the mom and her children, and we both got to know the father. This made arranging play dates and outings easier in the future since my wife now felt comfortable calling and so did I.

Usually, it's the dad who doesn't know the family or the children, and so he is virtually left out of arranging play dates or social outings. I suggest inviting the family of one of your child's friends over, getting to know each other, and opening the relationship so it's not exclusively a mom-to-mom thing. Naturally, you're not going to enjoy socializing with the family of each and every child with whom your child plays, but on occasion, when your child has a close peer, it's nice to get to know his siblings and parents, too. Some of our best friends are people we've met through our children; mothers have always enjoyed friendships made this way, and fathers can also benefit. If the dads get to know one another, they, too, can make plans to do things with the children, whether it's a morning hike or a Saturday afternoon lunch at a family-style restaurant.

Dads Enjoy Talking About Their Kids, Too

It used to be that when men got together, they talked about sports or business. I know plenty of Monday morning quarterbacks, and I enjoy that sort of banter, too. But we also talk about our kids when we're together, and I believe that once the subject is opened, many men are relieved to be able to talk about it. At a convention of stay-at-home dads I help arrange each year, I'm always heartened by the conversations fathers have when they talk about their kids. Fathers are just as concerned about their children's health, their school problems, and their peer relationships as are moms, but in the past, men haven't been encouraged to trade information on the subject.

Recently, a man I know who is a classical musician told me that he almost missed his cue during a rehearsal because he was talking to the bassoonist behind him about what kind of fishing lure to use when he took his six-year-old fishing the next day. The bassoonist was excited to hear that the oboist was taking the boy fishing because he, too, had taken his son fishing for many years and found that catching a big fish was a great self-esteem booster for his child. I think this indicates a real change for the better when two professional men nearly miss the downbeat because they're talking about their kids! Indeed, this shows that men are beginning to realize how important they are to their children and how important their children are to them.

The Middle Childhood Years:

Ages Seven to Twelve

A s your children advance toward the teen years, you may perceive that they begin to "ignore" you; however, they really do still need a strong emotional, physical, and verbal connection to both their mom and dad. Just the other day, for example, A.J.'s retainer broke at school. She called and left a message for me to come and pick it up. When I got the message around 2:00 P.M., I still went, even though school would be over at 2:30. These little incidents, seemingly minor to the parent, are quite important to the preteen. And, furthermore, the minimal effort that it took for me to do it reinforced it for A.J. that her parents are there for her whenever she needs them. When I arrived at A.J.'s class, all her classmates greeted me heartily and shouted, "A.J.! Your dad's here!" A.J. took great pride in telling me all about a project she was working on, and I chatted with her teacher for a while. A.J. also likes to whisper in my ear, "Dad, you're my best friend. Don't tell Mom," but I know she also does the same to Linda. It's just her way of connecting with us and making sure we stay close.

Like any worthwhile effort, achieving equal-balance parenting doesn't necessarily get easier with time. Yet most couples who lay the groundwork in the early years find that the key is to continually reassess their "game plan" according to their children's developmental needs and the needs of each parent. In other families, mothers still take responsibility for the far greater proportion of involvement in the various aspects of their children's daily lives. Here are a few scenarios that illustrate the involvement of fathers during the middle childhood years:

- Brian, who is seven, is marking off the days on his calendar until the big baseball playoff game. He's so excited that he's going with his dad and that he'll be able to buy a cap from his favorite team, sit in the stands, and get some soda and popcorn. Brian may not really understand or pay that much attention to the game; he's just thrilled that he'll be with his dad doing something special—just the two of them. Brian's father is looking forward to it as much as he is. On the same day, Brian's mom is going into the city to meet a college friend who is in town for a conference, and they're going to the ballet.

- Nine-year-old Janelle started fourth grade six weeks ago. She does her homework when she gets home from school, then plays with her girlfriends. On the weekend she may beg her parents to have a sleepover, and she's happy when all her new friends can come. Still, Janelle adores spending time with her parents; she likes to play soccer with her dad in the backyard or play board games with her mom on rainy weekends. She's excited to be entering a more independent social life, but she still looks to her parents for friendship and love. Janelle will hold her father's hand on their weekly walk to the supermarket, and she eagerly ask him lots of questions and chatters about school.

- Kurt, who is eleven, is embarrassed when his dad picks him up at school, but usually he's happy to toss a football with him after dinner or shoot hoops or go to the bookstore to get a spy novel by his favorite author. Kurt admires his dad and enjoys his company. They banter about sports, teachers, and plans for a camping trip. Yet, on the cusp of adolescence, the lure of the peer group tugs at Kurt, and sometimes he would rather be with his friends than spend time with his family. Other times, when his father suggests they get up the next day for Dad's specialty—homemade buttermilk pancakes—and an early morning hike, Kurt reluctantly agrees but then has the time of his life looking for snakes and bugs and collecting colorful autumn leaves with his dad.

- Donnie, an eight-year-old, plays on the basketball team. He has two brothers, ten and twelve, who also play, and on weekends his mom runs herself ragged taking the boys to their various games. Donnie has joined a traveling team, which complicates matters even further. His mom has to drive him to the games at other schools or arrange with another parent to get him there. While Donnie loves basketball, he also misses time with his dad who isn't interested in sports at all. Donnie's father considers the children's activities his wife's responsibility and reserves weekends for puttering in the garage, washing the cars, and relaxing.

- Katie, who just turned eleven, spends every day after school alone. Both her parents work, and because she is very mature, they've decided to let Katie keep herself busy at home in the afternoons. Katie never gets into any trouble, but she often struggles with her homework alone. She's not doing very well in English or math and often wishes she had someone to help her or someone to talk to while she's working. When her mom gets home around six, Katie cheers up, and the two make dinner together. Then they eat and clean up the dishes, and Katie's mom spends the rest of the evening with her daughter, going over her homework. Katie's two younger siblings, who have arrived home from day care with her mother, demand a lot of attention, too. She wishes her father were able to help, but when he gets home from work at seven, he eats dinner alone, leaving the homework and bedtime rituals to his wife.

The challenge for parents during the middle childhood years is for them to continually redefine how each one will be involved in their child's day-to-day activities, one-on-one and as a family. If your husband picked up the baby from the sitter and now your child is in school, his involvement has to take a different tack. You may need to look at new ways for both of you to connect with your children. If curling up with your toddler and reading a bedtime story was the high point of your day, now that she's reading on her own, your involvement needs redefining.

The balanced involvement of both parents continues to be crucial during this period. In too many families, mothers still shoulder most of the responsibilities—helping kids with homework, volunteering for school groups like the PTA, transporting kids from piano lessons to soccer practice, and so forth. In this chapter we'll look closely at creative solutions that real families have used so fathers can more easily share these responsibilities with their spouses. This communicates the message to the children that their father's role in their day-to-day lives remains strong and helps the children succeed in the realm of social and extracurricular activities—making friends, handling peer pressure, "fitting in," and doing well at school.

Make Homework a Shared Priority

Mothers (especially stay-at-home mothers) often see helping kids with homework as their responsibility, but I always counsel fathers to find some way to play a part even if they work until early to mid-evening. How can this be achieved? While you might designate one parent as the on-call parent who is primarily responsible for overseeing or supervising the homework (that does *not* mean *do* the homework), each parent can take a lead role in helping with subjects that interest them or that they're good at. One mom I know, a former nutritionist at a hospital who is now at home with her children, is an ace at science, math, and health; her husband, a feature writer for a newspaper, helps with English and history.

When mothers who arrive home first or are home during the

day are tempted to supervise all the homework without Dad's help, it often leads to their children thinking that their dad doesn't care about "school stuff." It also doesn't support the idea that fathers do have a role in educating the child. Both parents can check and discuss homework, or help review for quizzes and tests before bed. There is no reason to assume that this is mom's solo; research shows that kids whose fathers and mothers give consistent support, interest, and guidance do better in school and with their homework.

Gene often got home late, just as his wife, Aimee, was putting their seven- and ten-year-old girls to sleep. Instead of bowing out of the homework scene because of his schedule as a store manager, he would go into the girls' room with their workbooks in hand, and before they went to sleep, he would read or tell them a story, then go over any drills they needed for tests, such as multiplication tables or spelling words. The girls thought this was great, and they always practiced hard before their dad got home. On the weekends Gene would often take the girls to the library to find resource materials for their school projects. Even though he wasn't available after school on weekdays for help with homework, Gene found ways to maintain an influential role in his daughters' education.

Vernon sees fatherhood as a privilege; he says it's probably the most important thing he does even though he has a busy, exciting job managing entertainers and jazz musicians. He and his nine-year-old son, Ellington, do everything together, including homework, playing, and taking trips together. Ellington is very bright and doesn't need much help with homework; Vernon considers homework his son's responsibility but also feels it's the job of both parents to communicate the importance of a good education. So after Ellington finishes his homework, Vernon or his wife goes over it to check for mistakes and discuss the material.

Another unique way Vernon contributes to his son's education relates to the "affordances" theory talked about in chapter 6—that is, doing interesting things with your child during the time you spend together. Vernon travels often for his job and spends a lot of time in New York to meet with executives at record labels or to attend concerts and club performances. If the trips fall on the weekend, after school hours, or during school vacations, he lets Ellington accompany him. Ellington loves meeting the musicians and singers, and his favorite part is getting to visit different cities and going to concerts and performances with his dad. Vernon wants his son to see what he does when he's working, and Ellington soaks up the exposure. He knows all the artists his dad represents, and he's proud his dad knows more about music than any of his friends. Vernon wants to expose his son to as many positive experiences as he can and to let him know about all the possibilities in the world for people who get an education.

Stay Involved in School Issues

A friend of mine told me that the schools in his district make a strong effort to encourage fathers to attend class trips; in fact, the school requires at least one dad to go on each field trip to supervise the boys when they need to use the bathroom facilities (like most school districts, this one still has predominantly moms and female teachers for chaperones). Not all schools focus so actively on recruiting fathers, even for pragmatic reasons.

I am often amazed at how outmoded some school rules are. I always urge fathers to make waves and to shake up the system a little. One mom told me she learned at a school meeting that a school rule stated only mothers who had participated in fund-raising events during the school year would be allowed to accompany the children on the special end-of-the-year class trip. She pointed out that the rule unfairly excluded many dads (most of whom weren't available for weekday fund-raisers) and many working moms, too. As a result of that meeting, the school updated its bylaws to welcome fathers (and working moms) to attend the end-of-year trips, no matter what their level of involvement during the year.

I'm also reminded of a case of a young boy who had difficulty reading. The boy was very bright in math and no learning disabilities had been detected, yet the child's teacher suggested that he might need to be held back in the first grade. In some circumstances the teacher might have been on target, but this child's parents knew their son's capabilities very well, and the father, who had himself been a late reader, became an active advocate for his son. He talked on the phone with his wife even while at work about how they might approach the problem together, and on the day the child study team was scheduled to review the boy's record, the father took the day off to attend. I also met with the parents several times before the school review meeting to help them organize their thoughts and comments.

At the school meeting, the dad made several important contributions, unwaveringly supported his wife's statements, and let the educators know that he had every reason to believe his son would catch up in reading. The parents also decided to hire a tutor during the summer months before second grade started. In the end, the boy was allowed to go on to second grade, where he did quite well with some after-school help and hands-on learning materials.

As a social worker earlier in my career, I was involved in a number of cases such as this. Invariably, I observed that when both parents presented a thoughtful, united front, the needs of the child were much more likely to be met without hesitation. (There may also be power in numbers, and for single parents, something may be said for bringing along a parent advocate or member of the extended family for support.)

I also like to remind dads that another way they can be involved in their child's school life is to find ways to connect what they do for a living with the school curriculum. Paul, the father of my son Kevin's best friend, Sam, is a detective. He is an involved father who really gets into what his kids are into. Kevin and Sam are in the same class at school and had a science assignment to show a way that science is used in the real world. One weekend, as Kevin and Sam were trying to come up with an idea, they discovered that the kids' furniture in our backyard had been knocked over and damaged. Sam's dad brought them a professional fingerprint dusting kit, the same kind the police use. They dusted for fingerprints, and then Paul blew up the fingerprints on a big chart, adding all the forensic information his department uses to analyze fingerprints. I remember him telling me, "My wife called at seven-thirty to see what I was working on so late. I told her, 'That fingerprinting chart for Sam and Kevin.' She thought I was joking, but I was serious. I stayed after hours just to finish it."

After School: Latchkey Kids

I'll state quite firmly that I'm not in favor of leaving children ages seven to twelve home alone after school. Naturally, one has to consider the development and maturity of the individual child, but most kids I know, even twelve-year-olds, benefit from a loving, caring adult to talk to at the end of the school day. If a child must be alone, I recommend a call to Mom or Dad at work when he arrives home, and a second call from Dad or Mom before he or she leaves work to go home.

I have met many dual-career couples who have come up with creative, productive solutions, using friends, neighbors, art classes, sports programs, flextime, working at home, and other options to avoid a child's having to be home alone or to attend a poor-quality after-school program. I suggest that parents take the same care they took to find a preschool for their toddler, exploring every possible solution before deciding to leave a child alone after school. It's best to get both parents involved in solving this dilemma—two heads *are* better than one.

One dad I know who works for a very large company happens to have a small conference room next to his office that is almost never used. After school, the bus takes his kids to the office, where he has games, books, and a portable TV. (On snow days or when the kids have an unexpected day off, they spend the day there and have lunch with their dad.) Here are a few other solutions that dual-career families have used:

- Sonia, a home furnishings buyer for a department store, gets home at 5:30 P.M. Her husband, Will, a marketing director for a nonprofit theater, gets home at 6:00. Sonia has made an arrangement with the stay-at-home mom of one of their daughter Tory's classmates to watch Tory. The two girls walk home together from the bus stop and do homework or ride bikes.

▪ Cindy, a technical editor, and her husband, Phil, an advertising sales representative, have managed to work out a flextime arrangement. Cindy works from 7 A.M. to 2 P.M. three days a week, and 11 A.M. to 6 P.M. the other two. Phil works a similar schedule on different days. This enables one parent to be there when their children arrive home from school. Whichever parent doesn't have to go in early packs the lunches and takes the kids to school. Fortunately, their employers are willing to support this effort—-as will happen increasingly if parents and legislators continue to push for family-friendly work environments.

▪ Frederick and Althea run a small business. Money is tight, and no close relatives live nearby, but the district offers an excellent after-school program. Their children can do homework or art projects, spend time in the school library, or play sports in the gym until a parent arrives. Although the business stays open until 8 P.M., one parent always leaves by 5 P.M. to pick up the children and make dinner. Whenever there is a slow day, Althea or Frederick leaves the business early and picks up the kids at the after-school program.

As a stay-at-home dad, I often looked after a child whose mom worked full-time, and when something comes up for me or one of the other parents in our neighborhood, parents who are home are always there to help. This may not be feasible on a daily basis, but if working parents can arrange for their children to spend at least one or two days after school with another parent and child, it may be easier to fill in the other days with after-school programs.

Peer Groups and Peer Pressure

When children are young, it's easy to influence their social relationships; you choose a preschool, and you arrange play dates with children whose parents you know. But once children enter the school setting, they begin to make their own friendships. This is, of course, a healthy and natural part of social development.

Sometimes parents may disagree with their child's choices of friends, especially as they enter preadolescence, at around ten or eleven. Or they may observe that their child is unhappy with a particular friendship but doesn't seem to be doing anything about it. You and your spouse may also disagree on when to step in and when to let the child work things out on his own. It helps to keep in mind that when parents have a positive relationship with each other and have established clear rules and limits for their children, their children are less apt to go along with what their friends say and more likely to adhere to the principles their parents have taught. When parents themselves have a rocky relationship or are not actively involved in their child's life, the child tends to depend more on peers to guide him. This is when children begin to be negatively influenced by peer groups.

The classic problem that comes up in my conversations with parents is what to do when peers exert pressure to buy expensive clothes or to engage in activities that the parent doesn't feel the child is ready to handle. There is always the friend whose parents buy her expensive clothing (even at age ten!) or is allowed to go to the movies without an adult. I urge parents to discuss these issues and then stick to their decisions. Remember: You set the rules, not your kids. Kids this age will generally appreciate having limits, as they may secretly not really feel ready for the kind of freedoms they're requesting but think that since their friends are doing such-and-such, so should they. It's important to keep in mind that requests for expensive clothing may indicate that a child is having problems with self-esteem or fitting in. If a parent doesn't want to purchase high-end clothing, they should simply say so, without apology.

My clients Conner and Maeve had a twelve-year-old daughter, Genevieve, who repeatedly asked for expensive clothing. Maeve, who wanted her daughter to be accepted by the "in" kids, continued to buy it for her. Conner was outraged and felt his wife was caving in to Genevieve's demands. The two were constantly battling. It turned out that piling on fancy clothing was not getting to the root of Genevieve's problem, which, we found in the therapy sessions, was related to poor self-esteem. I asked Maeve to slow down on her spending until we could work on these problems.

Genevieve, who was very withdrawn, had trouble communicating with her peers and desperately needed to learn some social skills, such as what to say to a fellow player at the end of a game, how to introduce herself in a new setting, and how to call a friend and ask her to get together. As Genevieve's communication skills improved, she began to feel better about herself. Gradually, she began to focus more on her friendships and less on clothes.

Gender Issues in the Middle Years

When Kevin and A.J. were younger and brought friends over to the house, the children often did a double take when they saw that a dad was home—and, to boot, cooking in the kitchen or cleaning the house! But after a while they didn't even seem to take notice; it was just what was "normal" at the Frank home.

I have found that although children are likely to mimic all or some aspects of gender stereotypes they've picked up at school or learned from television or movies, the lessons they learn in their own homes will eventually hold the greater influence. Kids of stay-at-home dads are getting a crash course in fathers as caregivers and nurturers, and although we have no long-range studies to prove it yet, I'd be willing to predict that these kids are going to have an entirely different view of fatherhood when they grow up from that of children raised in families in which fathers are less involved.

Allen, a pharmacist and father of eight-year-old Colin, made a call to the mother of one of his son's friends. He needed to find out what type of toy her daughter wanted for a birthday present because he and Colin were about to go out and purchase the gift. Allen also accompanied Colin to the party. The mom commented to Allen how surprised she had been to hear from the father, admitting that usually mothers made that kind of inquiry. Whether he was aware of it or not, by making that call, Allen showed his son, his wife, and the other mom (who undoubtedly told her husband and other friends) that a father is capable of managing the myriad tasks that moms usually do.

Parents can also help their kids avoid falling into gender stereotypes through the activities they choose. A mom I know made a point of instilling a love of physical activity in her daughter from the time she learned to walk; today, at age twelve, she plays a number of team sports all through the school year. This not only keeps her busy after school, but it has helped her develop a fabulous sense of competence and confidence. Plus, she is so interested in playing sports that she doesn't care about going to the mall or watching TV when she's home, for which her parents are grateful. Her parents have also found that the other girls on the team are "just great kids"—honest, responsible, friendly, and fun to be with.

Fathers, too, can support the effort to break out of limiting roles. Granted, this doesn't always come easily for dads. Alfred, the father of one of my kid's friends, was extremely upset when his wife told him that their eight-year-old son, Rory, had announced he wanted to learn to play the clarinet. To Alfred, a construction worker who had been brought up in a very traditional, sports-oriented family and knew virtually nothing about music, playing an instrument in the school band was a girlish endeavor. He was afraid it would "feminize" his son, whom he would much rather have seen go out for football. Privately, he argued with his wife, a nurse, about the issue; she herself had played the piano as a child and thought that a love of music was one of the greatest gifts a child could have. Eventually, after much cajoling from his wife, Alfred finally agreed to let Rory take the lessons.

As it turned out, Rory excelled at playing the clarinet, and music gave him great pleasure. His talent also became a deep source of pride, particularly when the school holiday concert came and he lit up the stage with his excitement. After the show I happened to see Rory and his dad in the hall. Alfred had his arm around Rory's shoulder, and I could see from the broad smile on his face how very proud he was. Rory's experience had really changed his dad's perspective. To this day Rory still plays the clarinet, and his dad is always front and center at the school concerts. In fact, I've never observed a father who was more thrilled by his son's musical accomplishments.

Sports and Other Activities

During the middle childhood years, the push to get seriously involved in sports becomes a very big issue for many kids and their parents. This is the time when many parents begin hearing that it's very important for their child to join up with traveling teams and spend many hours practicing and perfecting their sport.

I completely disagree with the current trend of pushing young children into sports; sometimes it is too far and too soon. In fact, I believe that rather than extending their sports careers—if that is indeed what they really want—kids who are pushed too hard or too soon may have limited years of interest in sports. Interestingly, the late Dr. Benjamin Spock, a child care guru from the 1940s until his recent death, advised putting intense sports involvement off until age fourteen!

When A.J. was seven or eight, the pressure was on for her to join a traveling team, which would have involved many additional hours of games and practice. Linda and I sat down with A.J. to discuss the traveling team versus the league team. A.J. didn't seem too happy about all the practices and games with the traveling team, and Linda and I didn't really want to travel on the weekends to various schools. We agreed together that the benefits of the traveling team wouldn't outweigh the drawbacks. Now A.J. is having a great time playing league soccer. She's one of the best players on her team, and of course I'm proud of her. But she also has time for gymnastics, reading, and playing with her friends, and she isn't devoting all day long every summer to soccer camp.

In the cases of some of my clients, a child can also become a pawn for a parent's unfulfilled dream of going to the majors. I've also had clients, men and women, who have mistakenly and unconsciously pushed their children so hard that they begin to think the only way to gain approval and attention from their parents is through sports. When I see this obsessive approach to a sport developing, I suggest that the parent step back and consider what the relationship with their child will mean when the tennis or football or soccer game is over or if the child can no longer play because of a physical problem. Both parent and child need to identify other ways to enhance their bond and balance their lives.

Eight-year-old Robin was in a soccer league, and her father, Tom, was the coach. Tom was putting far too much pressure on Robin at practices and games, and their relationship was suffering. Robin started to have anxiety attacks and was afraid to go to school each morning, which prompted the family to come to me for counseling. After explaining to Tom that the pressure he was unconsciously putting on Robin was affecting her adversely, I suggested that he identify a noncompetitive activity he and Robin could do together in addition to soccer. That way their whole relationship wouldn't be founded on the soccer activity.

The next week Tom saw a flyer on the wall at the YMCA for an "Indian princess" group that was forming; activities included arts and crafts, nature survival skills, camping, and hiking. Both Tom and Robin ended up loving the group, and Robin's anxiety attacks and overall emotional state improved dramatically. The experience also had a positive effect on how Tom related to Robin during soccer.

Respecting Your Child's Choices

Make sure as you and your spouse make important decisions regarding your seven- to twelve-year-olds that you leave room for them to make some decisions on their own at appropriate times. Naturally we want to steer our kids in the direction we think best, but it's good for them to learn from their own experiences and mistakes. For instance, if a child shows an interest in a particular activity or sport, but you and your spouse don't approve, it may not be a bad idea to let your child try it out—unless, of course, there are safety or other serious concerns. Like the father who wasn't happy about his son's learning the clarinet, sometimes parents actually learn and grow from their kids' decisions.

One seven-year-old I know had a miserable season playing baseball and repeatedly told his parents he wanted to pursue gymnastics. The father finally took the boy to an "open workout" where he could sample the equipment; the child loved it, so the dad signed him up for classes. Although some classes met right after school, the father scheduled the class for an early evening so he could accompany his son and watch his lesson. This turned out to be a wonderful experience for both the boy and his dad.

Let your child take the lead. Your daughter's friends may be signing up for tennis, but she may really have more interest and talent in swimming or field hockey. Computer clubs, chess clubs, golf, canoeing, art classes, pottery, music, voice, or dance are some of the many possibilities. Also, fathers should not leave the pursuit of these interests up to moms only. Letting your child be a part of these decision-making skills lays the groundwork for positive parent-child dialogue later when other "life" decisions crop up, such as what college to attend, what to study, and what to do for a career.

Before signing up your child for an extracurricular activity such as a sport or music lessons, discuss the issue together and consider such factors as:

- How will the activity impact on family life, schoolwork, and time for free play?

- How much will the activity cost, including equipment such as shoes, helmets, instrument purchase or rental, and so on?

- Can the child take a sample or demo class to see if he or she really likes it?

- Who will take the child, stay with the child, or pick up the child? How can this responsibility be shared between mother and father?

- Will parents be required to supervise, coach, or contribute in some way to the activity, and how will each parent do so?

- How will you respond if traveling teams or special leagues are offered?

Attend Your Child's Events

We all live busy lives, and too often there seems to be very little time left over for anything but the basics. Nevertheless, I urge moms and dads to figure out ways for both to attend their children's special events or at least to tag-team their attendance so it isn't always the same parent the child sees watching his game, listening to his recital, chaperoning her scouting expedition, or attending her class play. When you know ahead of time that only one parent can make the event, it's easy to find ways for the other parent to be involved, such as taking the child to buy film and get the camera or camcorder ready, helping to make a costume or with batting practice, polishing those riding boots, or French-braiding a daughter's hair for a special performance. (Little girls are very impressed by a dad who knows how to braid hair.) After the event, make a special time to let your child tell you all about it; you might help her make a scrapbook page from the photos or write a letter about the event to send to her grandparents. You can put in a photo and go to the post office together. If you're the parent who attended the game, make sure you make time to tell your spouse about the game in front of the child; if you're the listening parent, stay away from comments like "Did you score a goal?"

Please note: I advise parents to avoid making promises; fathers, unfortunately, are prone to this. If you think there is any chance you may not be able to attend your child's recital, sporting event, or performance, tell her straight out so she won't be disappointed. Then make arrangements to speak with your child on the phone as soon as possible after the event or take one of the suggestions above.

Dave and Jenna had scheduled a meeting to discuss the upcoming Cub Scout trip. Their ten-year-old son, James, had missed every trip so far because his dad worked on weekends, and this time Jenna decided she would go on the trip even though mostly dads were going and only a few moms would be there. And although she knew Dave was working that weekend, she wondered if he could get up to the mountain for at least part of the trip. She didn't want to suggest this, though, because she suspected her husband would have a negative reaction. Instead, she asked him if they could set a time to discuss the trip and told him she had some concerns. After explaining to her husband that she was willing to take James up the mountain, set up the tent, and stay for the afternoon, she brought up the subject of whether Dave might want to drive up after work and join them. His initial reaction, as Jenna expected, was negative: "I'll be tired after work, and I don't know if I'll be able to locate your tent in the dark anyway."

Jenna wasn't happy with this outcome, so she asked Dave to give it a little more thought and if they might meet again the next evening. She added that it was very important to her. The next day the couple met again, and this time Jenna said she had thought a lot about the trip, and she knew it would mean a lot to James to have his dad there, too, even if for just part of the trip. Dave agreed but reiterated that he didn't want to drive up directly after work because he'd be too tired. He did offer, however, to get up at sunrise and be at the campsite in time for breakfast. This resolution suited everyone's needs and left Jenna confident that her husband had tried his best to be an involved partner.

Make Time for Connecting One-on-One

Many dads enthusiastically volunteer to coach a team or run a scout group, yet they hesitate when it comes to spending one-on-one time with their child. Granted, there are plenty of opportunities in most communities to become extremely involved in team sports, scouting, or other volunteer groups (the time some fathers and mothers spend on these pursuits can actually amount to the equivalent of a part-time job!). I commend these parents, but volunteering to coach the basketball team doesn't replace taking your child for a walk, reading together, or just talking together. Quite often I observe fathers on the weekend rushing from game to game (many dads serve as umpires for other games when they're not coaching their own team), and I wonder whether they've actually taken the time to have a conversation with their own child that day. While I applaud the efforts of parents to keep their kids actively involved in outside activities, I encourage dads not to lose their perspective and become too enmeshed in the "team" effort.

I like to take Kevin to the library or bring A.J. with me when I go for a jog. Linda plays chess with Kevin or rides bikes with A.J. One-on-one time can be part of an ordinary day, and the results of talking and exchanging ideas can be extraordinary. One dad took his seven-year-old daughter to buy a new mattress; the girl came home and told her mom, "He couldn't have done it without me!" All she had really done was carry the twine that her dad used to secure the mattress to the roof of the car, but she felt that she had really helped in the task.

Stress and the "Hurried" Child

As you might imagine, I see a lot of troubled children in my practice, some of whom are overburdened, rushed, and pushed to grow up too fast. There is a very clear set of signals that indicates a child is stressed, and some of these symptoms can become quite serious. Kids who have too much to deal with may be depressed or lethargic without being sick; some may develop eating or sleeping disorders, complain about imagined injuries or illness, or seem unusually distracted, tired, or hyperactive. Unfortunately, the parents who are allowing the child to do too much or do things that are too strenuous or "grown-up" may not recognize these signs until a teacher, coach, or friend points them out.

As adults we rush from place to place, from job to home and back again, often taking on more than we can comfortably handle. Regrettably, this same urge to rush and overload has been extended into childhood. As David Elkind, a renowned expert in child development, writes in *The Hurried Child*, the consequences for the emotional health of children can be severe when we allow—and sometimes even encourage—them to grow up too quickly.

One child I know was taught by her parents to read at a very early age. By three or four, Ellie was able to decode words fluently. In grade school her parents continued to push her academic achievements, but they allowed very little time for Ellie to play with friends or to be active outdoors. Instead, Ellie was always inside, buried in books. Her parents thought this was just wonderful until, at about age eight or nine, Ellie stopped reading entirely. She had had enough and began doing poorly in school. Ellie was a "burned-out" nine-year-old. We had to work very hard to balance this child's life and restimulate a love of learning. Much had been lost and very little gained by the great rush to push this child so far ahead of her classmates.

In academics, in sports, in just about everything, there is a fine line between dedication and taking things too far. I think it's very important for parents to encourage their child's interests and to allow kids this age to sample a variety of pursuits. But it's also necessary to keep a close eye on how your child's schedule is shaping up and how great are the demands placed on the child. It's essential for parents to discuss this together and to arrive at mutual decisions in order to make sure their child is not overloaded or overwhelmed.

Recently, as I was signing up A.J. for soccer at her school, I overhead a mother and father disagreeing as they stood in line. The father was instructing his wife to sign their son up for soccer, but I could tell from their discussion that the boy's plate was already full with involvement in football practice and a swim team. The mother agreed without saying a word, and I wondered if they had actually discussed their decision or had just taken it for granted that the child could handle yet another commitment. Another dad, when his son was offered an opportunity to join the same soccer league, discussed the issue with his wife and told the coach, "No, thanks." When I asked his reason, he said that his son had plenty to do already and needed some downtime. Here was one dad who was putting his kid's needs first.

One of my clients once told me that her nine-year-old son had turned down an opportunity to attend a week-long tennis camp because his dad had Fridays off from work in the summer and the family (including two younger siblings) usually went to the beach on that day. I thought that revealed quite a bit about the child's honest priorities. While the mom at first thought it surprising that her son didn't prefer to be with his peers, she realized that his decision revealed how deeply her son valued the time with his father, herself, and his siblings. Sometimes children don't communicate so directly how much they really do need their parents.

When we rush our children from place to place or push them to excel or succeed at the expense of their health or emotional development, there is very little time for listening. And as you may remember from chapter 3, listening is the keystone to effective communication—not just between spouses but also between parents and children. I try to spend some time during my parenting seminars encouraging parents to slow down a little (it's also the perfect excuse to take some pressure off yourself as a parent). I talk about the value of focusing on getting to know the fascinating person your little boy or girl has become in the middle years of childhood. Before you know it, the teen years will be here—and that's quite a different ball game!

Fathers Can Teach Sons to Nurture

Just the other day when I was on a hike with my family, we passed another family on the trail. The father had taken his newborn baby out of the Snugli and was cradling the infant in his arms as he walked (the baby was really soaking up the woods and fresh air, as well as his dad's love). The mom was holding the hand of the couple's four-year-old. I thought this was lovely to see and a good lesson for my kids as well as for other families hiking the trail that day. I suspect that my kids and the other kids who passed by will remember that dad on the trail.

The best way for kids—and especially for boys—to learn that men can be strong and still be loving, caring, and nurturing is for fathers and other male role models to show in their words and actions that this is so. The dads I have seen in my seminars and in private practice who aren't afraid to be affectionate with their children, who hold hands with their daughters and embrace their sons, and who keep an open dialogue seem to have established ties that reach into the teen years and beyond. Often these are the same men who are also willing to share child care tasks with their wives.

Just as Linda does, I tell Kevin and A.J. "I love you" each day as they leave for school. Kevin has learned that it is normal and natural for men to express their feelings and to be open about the love they feel for their children and others. It is especially important, I believe, for boys to understand that their emotional lives—their feelings of love and kindness, or fear and sadness—are real, valid, accepted, and understood. There is a great deal of literature today (some are listed in the bibliography) that shows how male stereotypes are still being perpetuated. For example, William Pollack, author of *Real Boys,* talks about "the Boy Code"—the fact that boys today are still encouraged to deny and cloak feelings of sadness, fear, vulnerability, and love and to "act tough" instead. As a result, many boys still feel disconnected from their own deepest feelings. I encourage fathers to take the lead in teaching their sons that emotions—love, sorrow, fear—are equally important facets of the definition of "man" as are strength, courage, and independence. It is essential as well for girls to learn this about their fathers so that they will grow up to expect these qualities in the men they choose as partners.

A common response I get from dads after thinking about this is "Okay, I think I'm comfortable with this. But how do I get started?" I say a good way to begin is to do the following:

- Learn who your child's friends are—what their names are, where they live, what your child likes about them, and what your child likes to do with them. Who doesn't he like and why?

- Find out which activities he's involved in and how his schoolwork is going. Kids like to know that you're interested in what they're doing and what they like—even if at times they don't show it or act as if they don't care.

- Ask specific questions and have meaningful discussions. Even if you're talking about school, you're making an important connection with your children when you talk to them. Avoid asking vague questions like "What happened at school today?" A child invariably replies, "Nothing." With A.J., for example, I always start with the more mild "Who'd you play with at recess?" or "Who did you sit with at lunch?" Then I ask something a little more specific about one of her friends, such as "Did Megan hand in her project?" Then, I get more specific about A.J.'s schoolwork: "What were some of the questions on your history quiz?"

The more knowledgeable you are about the important arenas of your child's life, the more likely those lines of communication will remain open. Kids really do want to talk to their parents, even if it may not seem that they do at a given moment. I encourage both moms and dads to keep the dialogue open. There are benefits now in this prelude to the teen years when kids tend to clam up even more.

Popular Heroes

Many parents begin to worry during the middle childhood years that their child will be influenced by the "wrong" heroes in popular culture. It's inevitable that TV stars, sports figures, rock singers, and others begin to play a part during the middle childhood years. (Even if television is limited in the home, there are still the outside world and other friends' houses.) However, many kids still look to their parents as primary role models. I recently read about a class of fourth graders who were asked to write an essay about the person they most admire. Many of them wrote about their fathers, mothers, or grandparents. So even if your child seems dazzled by a pop culture hero, it's likely that she is still looking to her own immediate family as role models, too. My wife, for instance, was encouraged by her father not only to go into business but to take it a step further than he did (and although she didn't consciously set out to do this, it's exactly what she has accomplished). Our son, Kevin, is already interested in becoming a psychologist!

While I know that many parents worry about how their children will be influenced by the media—and, granted, there is much to fret about—the best defense is to create strong role models in our own families. Fathers and mothers can also help by pointing out other role models. For instance, when a father speaks at the dinner table or during a drive with the family about his admiration for a particular female governor or congressperson for her ideas or when a mother points out how graceful yet strong a male skater is during the Olympics, kids learn that there are other heroes to emulate besides pencil-thin models or macho movie stars. Talking about why we admire certain people and what their best qualities are—whether they're teachers, other parents, grandparents, friends, actors, dancers, or athletes—gives our children a chance to talk about (and think about) what they really like in someone they consider a hero.

The Teen Years:

Ages Thirteen to Eighteen

RESEARCH SHOWS THAT during the school week fathers spend an average of less than an hour a day with their teenagers and about an hour or two more on weekends. On paper this doesn't sound like very much time; it seems nonexistent to many of the young adults I see in my practice who are still attempting to resolve the rejection, disappointment, and hurt caused by the emotional abandonment of their dads. When fathers tell me the reason they don't spend time with their teens is that they are not important anymore to their teenage children, I can only respond with some of the stories I have heard from my young adult clients. Fathers are as important during the teen years as they are at every stage of a child's growth and development. The dynamics of the parent's involvement, however, need to reflect the developmental stage of the teen.

In spite of most parents' fears about the teen years, when a couple works together to support and guide the teenager in this crucial time of development, the outcome for all involved can be not only enjoyable but rewarding. That's not to say the challenge of staying connected to the teen isn't real. Parents of teens typically feel a deep concern for their teens' emotional life; this is compounded by the emotional conflicts often occurring at the same time in the parents themselves who are confronting their own personal mid-life issues. And as the teen establishes his independence, tests his boundaries, explores his identity, defines his beliefs and values, and begins to address what life as an adult will mean, parents need to be supportive, instructive, and yet nonintrusive. This is no easy task.

For the teen, living with parents who do not share parenting responsibilities can lead to unresolved emotional issues—even stress and depression—that do not surface until the early adult years. As the child becomes an adolescent, it is essential that both parents find ways to be involved in the bridge from childhood to young adulthood.

Here is a glimpse into two families with a teen. In the first, both Mom and Dad are actively involved; in the second, the teen is left to go it alone.

- Alex, a sophomore in high school, is on the basketball team and plays saxophone in the high school band. His parents attend his games and concerts, although they try to remain somewhat inconspicuous since Alex tells them he feels embarrassed if they hoot or clap too much. Alex has several close friends who are interested in in-line skating and computers, and the boys often get together after school and on weekends. While his parents sometimes miss the years when Alex wanted to spend most of his free time with them, they respect his newfound independence. Alex and his father enjoy canoeing together, and occasionally they plan a Saturday outing. While Alex likes to be with his friends, he knows he must keep his parents apprised of his whereabouts. During the school week, Alex knows he is expected to be at the dinner table at six when the family eats together. Both his parents work, but Ellen, a librarian, is home by three two days a week, and Sonny, a public relations manager, leaves work early on Fridays.

▪ Justin, who is sixteen, has been given free rein by his parents, whom he rarely sees. His parents, Art and Denise, have decided Justin is old enough to fend for himself. He spends from 3 P.M. to 7 P.M. alone every day after school and has no extracurricular activities other than hanging out at a strip shopping center in town, smoking cigarettes. On weekends Justin often stalks out of the house for no apparent reason, angry at his parents, who suddenly ask where he is going. Justin has been suspended from school twice for fighting and has a lot of time on his hands. Art thinks that Justin is old enough to "take care of himself," and whenever Denise brings up the subject of Justin's after-school schedule, her husband points out that by the time he was seventeen he was working two jobs after school. Both parents feel that Justin is a disappointment, but neither is willing to explore ways to improve their relationship with their son.

The Teen Question: Who Am I?

The teens in the previous scenarios were both coping with the question all adolescents face during this exciting and turbulent time: Who am I? As the teen begins to sort out his definition of self, his cognitive skills are expanding. He can now hypothesize and problem solve, and he's beginning to establish his own moral sense. As a result, the teen is often argumentative and won't necessarily accept his parents' word as the final rule. Parents can either act as supportive mentors while the teen negotiates his entry into adulthood, or they can wring their hands and cry, "We give up!" I always urge parents to stay actively involved in the teen's life, though discretion is required, and they can't be involved in the same ways they were when their child was four or six or even ten. Doing something, however, is so much more constructive than sitting back and watching a situation snowball out of control, and this chapter is full of families' stories that show the myriad ways parents can rethink their involvement with their teen.

Involvement can be challenging during the teen years, and one reason for that is teens in general are very self-centered. It's normal for adolescents to feel that they stand center stage, yet they need to be reminded of other people's interests, too. Not long ago I told my preteen son that I wanted him to visit his mom in the hospital after she had some minor surgery. Kevin didn't really want to go, but I pointed out to him, "This isn't about you, it's about Mom." Parents of teens may find themselves making this sort of statement quite often.

Parents need to nurture a connection that allows the teen to feel supported, valued, and safely moored. During these years, parents and teens will grapple with a number of issues: curfew decisions, dating, learning to drive a car, preparation for college or a vocation, issues surrounding sex, and possibly problems relating to experimentation with drugs and/or alcohol. It is crucial for fathers to remain involved in these issues and for spouses to work together to agree on and enforce limits and guidelines as well as provide—as a team—love and acceptance. Never forget, especially on your most frustrating days, that the teen deserves the respect and affection of both parents.

The Father-Teen Relationship During Puberty

What parents haven't rolled their eyes at the amount of time their daughter spends in the bathroom combing her hair or the time their son spends changing his shirts before school? While it's great for parents to stress that it's what's inside that counts, it's quite normal for teens to focus on their physical appearance. How teens feel about their own body and appearance can dramatically affect their sense of self-esteem and self-confidence. In my practice, I have seen hundreds of young women who are coping with what they saw as rejection from their fathers during the teen years. I can't stress enough how important it is for dads to be supportive of their daughter's physical appearance as well as her achievements. "You look great in that dress!" or "I'm really proud that you aced that math test!" goes a long way; likewise, when dads make no comments or negative comments about a girl's appearance, the outcome can be seriously damaging to her self-esteem. It's very important for parents, and especially dads to their daughters, to show support and approval for their teen's physical appearance while, of course, keeping the main focus on "what's inside."

Anabelle came to see me when she was about twenty-four. She had been dating and, to my astonishment, was considering marrying a man with whom she had an emotionally abusive relationship. After talking to Anabelle several times, I determined that her very low self-esteem originated during a period of her adolescence when she perceived that her father had rejected her. Anabelle had idolized her dad, and until she was twelve or thirteen, the two had shared a very close relationship. When Anabelle began to develop into a young woman, however, her father became mysteriously distant. He refused to give her a hug or to be affectionate, and he rarely had a conversation with her. She now felt rejected and confused. She began hanging out with a group of kids who drank and took drugs, and the chasm between her and her father continued to widen. Her mother saw what was happening but felt powerless to change the situation. It wasn't until many years later and some long-term therapy that Anabelle was able to forgive her father and to understand that his remoteness had been caused by his fear of his daughter's emerging sexuality and his confusion about how to deal with it. Through counseling I was able to help Anabelle improve her self-esteem and confidence, though I lost track of her and am not sure she married the man who was abusive.

Although Anabelle's case is somewhat extreme, this derailing of the father-daughter relationship occurs to varying degrees in many families when a girl reaches puberty. Fathers often feel baffled or confused by a daughter's sexuality and developing female physique. It is my perception that this doesn't happen in general with moms and their sons because women aren't as likely as men are to view things in a sexual context. Males in our society—and especially men who have not had positive relationships with women in the past—are likely to make decisions and determine actions within sexual parameters.

In the therapy setting I work with fathers like Anabelle's to help them understand that they can love and value their daughters—for their kindness, their intelligence, their special talents, and even for their beauty—without their feelings of pride and affection being interpreted or expressed in a sexual context. Because it's so important for fathers to be emotionally supportive of their children, I encourage them to seek therapy if they feel this sexual conflict emerging in a disturbing way during their children's adolescence. Often the mother sees what is happening; if this is the case, perhaps she can encourage her spouse to seek counseling. Otherwise, the problem can have serious repercussions for these youngsters in their adult lives.

On the other hand, sometimes a father is still comfortable hugging his daughter or sitting close to her, but the daughter is uncomfortable with these signs of physical affection from her father. In this situation I advise dads to respect their daughter's feelings. They can verbalize their feelings of love and support by saying "I love you!" or "I think you're great!" It's even okay to say "I know you may be uncomfortable about hugging me now that you're growing up, but I want you to know how proud I am of you." Expressing these emotions with words may be difficult for some men, but it's so important for a girl to know that her father loves, values, and admires her even if on the outside she shrugs off the words or says, "Oh, Dad," or "Yeah, right." Keep praising her and focus on communicating these messages as sincerely as they're meant.

It's important for dads to let their sons know they support and value them, too. I also have young adult male clients who never received their father's approval during the adolescent years. It is essential for a young man to gain his father's approval and to know in his heart that his worth is validated by the most important male figure in his life. I've met a surprisingly large number of fathers who simply assume that their sons know how much they value them—to which I reply: Yes, but you still need to express these feelings verbally.

One of my clients spoke very highly of his son whenever he wasn't around, but as soon as the teen was within earshot, the dad was more likely to criticize him than to praise him. This young man was unaware that his father held him in high esteem. Don't be afraid to hug your teen, praise him, or rumple his hair; all human beings are validated when they receive affection.

Bernard had two sons, Adam, fifteen, and Andrew, twelve. Shortly after Adam turned fifteen at the beginning of the summer, he repeatedly made comments that he was "too scrawny." Bernard took his son's concerns seriously and called the pediatrician to ask if it would be okay for Adam and his younger brother to begin weight lifting. Following the physician's guidelines, Bernard bought appropriate weights for himself and his two sons and began a summer workout program every other morning before he went to work. Before long, Adam had visibly increased his muscle mass. By the time school started in the fall, both Bernard and Adam were in excellent shape (Andrew had lost interest), and the teen no longer felt physically inferior to his friends, many of whom were on the football team. That fall he was accepted on the wrestling team.

Drugs, Alcohol, and Sexual Issues

Sex, drugs, driving fast, skiing fast, doing anything fast, in excess, or in an unsafe manner—here are the teen years in living color. If two involved parents have laid a supportive foundation with positive parent-child communication, it is more likely that no harmful activity or circumstances will occur. As you address these issues, keep in mind that teens think they are invincible. It's quite natural for adolescents to think "It won't happen to me." They can't imagine they will ever get in a car accident or hurt themselves skiing wildly on the ski slopes. And so they may drive fast and recklessly, drink without a thought as to how much is too much, or try any manner of crazy stunts. (Recent brain research indicates that teenagers are actually more prone to react instinctively, so their impulsiveness may be a result of brain function and development rather than obstinacy.)

The call to action for parents? A calm, united front when problems arise. It's vital to talk to your kids about these issues even though the discussions may be difficult. Talk that is constructive and not demeaning or berating can have a positive influence on your teen's behavior. Teens need information about the dangers of alcohol and drugs and the risks of unprotected sex (and it is up to parents whether they want to advocate abstinence or safe sex). Even though most of the parents who attend my seminars have young children, I always talk about the teen years and explain that it's a mistake to assume teens and even younger kids are going to get the "right" information from their friends. One public health study concluded that when parents discussed safe sex with their teens, the kids were more likely to use condoms when they engaged in their first sexual encounter.

Teens also need accurate information about their bodies and their emerging sexuality. I have suggested some good books geared for teens in the bibliography. Fathers or mothers—whoever is most comfortable—can talk to their child about puberty and sexual topics, including the very real threat of AIDS, sexually transmitted diseases, and, of course, pregnancy.

Sixteen-year-old Nick had arrived obviously drunk at a school dance. His parents, Hillary and Bart, were horrified when the principal called and told them. They decided to sit down with Nick and discuss the repercussions of what he had done (including the fact that he was suspended from the football team). They had also noticed on several occasions that Nick's clothing smelled of cigarette smoke. Having ignored this in the past, they now decided to discuss the smoking as well as the dance incident with Nick. They scheduled a family meeting with Nick and firmly, but without yelling, talked with him. They also listened to what he had to say and learned that other kids had been drinking and smoking but hadn't been caught.

Hillary and Bart understood that most teens go through a phase of experimentation, but they weren't hesitant to sit down and talk to Nick as soon as they sensed that he might be headed for trouble. Nick admitted that having a beer once in a while at a party was not quite the same as showing up drunk at a school function, and he revealed that he had been drinking that day because he had blown an important test. I recommended to Hillary and Bart, as I do to lots of parents of teens who feel their child is doing poorly on tests, that they speak to Nick to help identify the problem or trigger: Does the child feel the material was covered well in class? Did the child study enough? Did he study the correct things? It can be helpful to encourage the teen to talk to the teacher. Research shows that a strong parent-child-teacher relationship can help improve grades and test scores.

Hillary and Bart talked to Nick, and he finally admitted that he felt he did poorly on the test because he didn't have enough time to study. With this information, the three of them could begin to work out a plan to avoid the problems of poor test scores and drinking in the future. I encourage parents to let the child initiate and "manage" the plan. If that doesn't seem to work, then the parents may manage the plan. Nick said he was willing to put the plan into action. He asked his dad to drive him to the library after dinner, especially on the two or three days before a test, or to drive him to group study sessions instead of the after-school impromptu soccer games he had been going to with his friends. Hillary's part in the plan was to give Bart verbal support and to remind him without nagging that she and Bart were available to help him study or to drive him places, and so on. She also tried to open up communication on a daily basis with Nick so that he would feel comfortable telling his parents when a test or important school deadline was coming up.

Parents can't forget that their own behavior becomes a kind of model with respect to drugs, alcohol, smoking, and so forth. For example, if a parent has a few beers now and then or a glass of wine with dinner a few times a week, that is moderation; but when alcohol is used excessively in the home, the teen may think it's acceptable. This holds true even if one parent engages in the behavior and the other doesn't. One mom told me she finally quit smoking for good when her son entered middle school because she would have felt even guiltier smoking around him at an age where he might be likely to pick up the habit himself. Remember, too, to give praise when a teen makes the right decisions in these areas.

Friends and Peers

The peer group is extremely important at this age, and it's essential to make an attempt to steer your teen toward a good group of kids. "Steer" is the operative word here; you can't make his decisions for him. Parents often come to me worrying that their child is hanging out with "bad" kids who may lead him or her into trouble. Invariably I have found that when teens do not meet other kids with similar interests and get involved in healthful, enjoyable activities, they are drawn as if by a magnet to a group that is not a positive influence. A high school teacher once told me that the kids who have nothing to do are the kids who inevitably get into trouble. I encourage parents to help their teens find the right group—whether the group is associated with sports, the school yearbook or paper, band, church, choir, drama club, or another activity.

Sometimes when parents are scratching their heads about what to do with their teen, I recommend that the mom and dad schedule a parent-to-parent meeting and brainstorm resources; coaches, teachers, extended family, church leaders, scout leaders, and others may be able to encourage your teen or give you some ideas. Also, the YMCA, scouts, Boys Club, Girls Club, recreation departments, and the public library may have brochures, flyers, or newsletters that help direct parents to ideas for constructive, enjoyable extracurricular activities. If you have successfully encouraged your child during the middle childhood years to try soccer, baseball, scouting, or something else he is interested in, he should now be able to apply himself to something he is charged up about. If your teen doesn't seem to be interested in anything but "hanging," it's time to sit down as a family and discuss possible avenues to explore.

One dad mentioned to the band director during back-to-school night that his daughter was hesitant to join an after-school club and had recently given up flute lessons because she had lost interest. A month later the teen came home and announced that Mr. Antonelli, the band director, had said he really needed her to play in the orchestra for the school musical.

I also encourage parents to allow their teen to find another adult in his life—down the street, at school, or a relative—who is what I call "intuitive." Some adults just seem to have a natural, relaxed attitude about them that teens are drawn to and feel comfortable with. For example, there's a girl on my daughter's soccer team who always comes over and talks to me as if I'm her best friend; she senses that I'm approachable. I also know a woman whose thirteen-year-old son, Eric, likes to chat with her best friend from college, Carla, if he answers the phone when she calls (although, like most boys, he is not a big phone talker). Eric got to know Carla during his childhood and even occasionally e-mails her. Carla is a high school teacher, and Eric knows she's in touch with the latest music and trends; he feels comfortable talking with her about what is going on in his life.

Letting your teen spend time with intuitive adults can be a positive experience and in some cases can help him or her discover a new interest or activity that would be a good thing; at the very least it is a receptive ear for the emotional highs and lows of adolescence. Don't feel threatened that your teen can talk to other adults, and don't jump to judge them until you know them better.

I recommend that both moms and dads make every effort to get to know their teen's friends. One mom encourages her son to invite his friends over on a regular basis. The dad grills hamburgers or orders pizza, and the kids watch a sports event on TV or play touch football in the backyard. Let your teen invite a friend to come along for a long weekend away with your family. You'll understand that kid afterward.

Choose Your Battles

Parents of teens may find themselves arguing over what the teen is wearing, whether he can get his ear (or belly button!) pierced or dye his hair, or whatever. It's pointless to obsess about these issues, but if something really bothers you, it's okay to set limits: "You can go to the dance, but not wearing those skin-tight jeans." It's a communication issue again. What is it that bothers you? You're entitled to express your opinion, but is it worth pressing the issue? I always encourage parents of teens to choose their battles carefully; otherwise they'll be battling all the time, and their concerns or fears about the big issues will be diluted. Are the teen's friends dressing that way? Is it a gang-related thing or just the style?

It's a good idea to talk to your teen about the issues that are of concern, but it's more important for the parents to sit down and discuss what they want the outcome to be. Rather than one parent picking on the teen because of her hairstyle, and another bringing up the subject of her friends, it's more productive for parents to focus on the positive aspects of their teen's life and to express to each other what is really bothering them about the negative aspects. Discuss together what about a particular friend, hairstyle, or activity disturbs you, and why. Share your feelings with your spouse first and then decide whether it's something really worth discussing with your teen. If you want to communicate openly with your adolescent, schedule a time to talk, use "I statements," approach your teen with respect, and follow all the rules of effective communication presented in chapter 3. If parents have been practicing these communication skills with each other, it shouldn't be difficult to use them with their teen.

Keep the Lines of Communication Open

It is difficult to talk to a closed door or to someone wearing headphones, so choose your time to talk to your teen wisely—but by all means do choose a time. A.J. and I often talk while I'm driving her to soccer practice; although she's not a teen yet, I suspect that the car will always be a place where she feels comfortable to chat. One of my clients, a sixteen-year-old, revealed to me that she talks to her mom about some subjects and to her dad about others. (She wouldn't tell me what; another hallmark of adolescence is secrecy!) It's great when a teen knows she can go to one or the other parent for comfort or advice, depending on the subject or situation.

If you've been talking regularly with your child since she was very young, chances are that the lines of communication will continue, although they may falter now and then. Often when I speak with a parent who is having difficulty talking to a teenager, I recommend that the parent really be on the lookout for that window of opportunity and take advantage of that moment. One mom told me her son never speaks willingly at dinner anymore; he is in a hurry to eat and get to his homework. Often, however, he initiates a conversation late at night when she's ready to go to sleep, so she stays up and talks because she recognizes that window.

Teens are on a slightly different timetable than the rest of the world. Some school systems, in fact, have accommodated that scientific reality by beginning the high school day an hour or so later than the elementary school. I'm always amazed at how we, as parents, sweat about the big effort, the big event that will greatly impact our children's lives, yet time after time it is a little scrap of a conversation at an unforeseen moment and place that has served to spark the parent-child connection. Sometimes the smallest efforts result in surprising rewards. I suspect that that boy who talks to his mom late at night will remember those talks when he is away at college or out on his own in the world even more than a lot of things his mom did for him.

Pay attention to when your teen seems ready to talk. It may be before bed, after dinner, or driving in the car (but usually not first thing in the morning). Not every conversation must be deeply significant, nor should you ask a battery of questions. A casual, off-the-cuff comment such as "How are things going? What happened with that math project?" shows that you care. Don't let the teen steer the conversation into a silent void, and resist the temptation to throw up your hands in defeat. Engage your teen in conversation without asking grueling questions. Expect your teen to respond to your salutations, however, and explain that it's not an inquisition—

you, too, are a human being and merit a respectful response. Listen when the opportunity arises; don't be vindictive and say, "Well, he wouldn't talk when I was ready, so I'm going to keep my lips shut now!" I encourage parents to get to know whether their teen is a morning person or a night person or maybe a weekend afternoon person; then one or both parents should let the teen know they are available. Also, don't make your kid have your timetable. Dads often seem to be more stubborn than moms about this sort of thing, wanting their teen to talk when *they* want to talk. That's just plain counterproductive.

Respect and Communication

A lot of parents don't make the connection between respect and positive communication with their children. Agree with your spouse that you will both model respect, and show your teen how you feel in ways that are appropriate. When a teenager comes home past his curfew, it's much better to say, "We were really worried about you. Please call when you're going to be late or make sure you're here at the time we agreed on," than to rant and rave. Yelling just slams the door shut for any opportunity for communication or for allowing your teen to feel comfortable sharing information; he'll likely just clam up.

This does not mean there are no consequences. Decide with your spouse what they will be in advance. For instance, tell your teen that if he misses his curfew, he will not be able to go out the following evening or the curfew will be shortened by one-half hour, or whatever you as a couple decide is appropriate. The important thing here is to let your teen know that next time there will be consequences; this way you are always giving your child an opportunity to make a change before suffering consequences. This is a good approach at any age, even with toddlers who are just beginning to be disciplined.

One couple with a fifteen-year-old girl told me that they had sat together for an entire hour worrying about their daughter, who had gone to the movies with some friends and had not returned home on time. While they waited, they decided together how they would respond when she walked in the door. Thankfully the girl was okay; there had been some confusion about the bus home. The parents told her how important it was that she find a phone and call if she was going to be late, and the teen appreciated the fact that they didn't scream at her or assume she had been doing something wrong. If you find that you and your spouse react very differently in front of your teen, meet with your spouse and, using the communication tactics described in chapter 3, come to some agreement about how you will both talk to your teen when she has broken a house rule.

Communication After Hours

If your teenager is going to be home alone after school on a regular basis, I suggest that you set a rule about phoning in to the on-call parent. One teenage girl beeps her dad whenever she changes locations: "I'm over at Judy's now, and then I'm headed for the library." Parents of teens may not need an account of where a teen is at every moment of the day, but it's important to give your teenager the message that you do expect to know where she is. I also recommend that mothers and fathers share the on-call responsibility for the teen so that (1) the teen knows she is accountable to both parents, which helps avoid such thinking as "Oh, my mom won't care" or "If my dad's home, I never have to bother calling," and (2) neither parent has to shoulder the on-call responsibility every day.

I also recommend that parents of teens who are not yet driving tag-team all the picking up and dropping off. When one parent has to do this all the time, resentment brews. Jess, a fifteen-year-old, was attending a party at a friend's house. His mother, Tina, a midwife, and his father, Ivan, an anesthesiologist, both worked at the same hospital. Tina and Ivan had arranged for the mother of one of Jess's friends to take him to the party. Ivan had promised to pick up the boys on his way home from his shift at the hospital, at about

11 P.M. Tina, who had worked a twelve-hour shift at the hospital that day, was able to go to bed early, knowing that her husband would accompany the boys safely home.

Teens Watch Their Parents as a Couple Even if They Don't Show It

I got a wonderful e-mail message recently, one of those lists of things that people zing around through cyberspace to one another. It was a list of life's little instructions, and number 31 said, "If you have kids, improve your marriage." Indeed, a classic inquiry by a therapist during the early stage of therapy is "Tell me about your parents' marriage." Like it or not, our parents are our first role models about relationships, and many of us spend a good portion of our adult lives trying to figure out why having a relationship is so difficult for just that reason. Although they act as if they don't register anything, teens carefully observe their parents' relationship to see how to behave in their own emerging relationships with the opposite sex. Further, teens are always concerned about their parents' relationship. It helps their own emotional development if they know that their parents are well loved by each other and taken care of and respected.

Teens observe how the father interacts with the mother and how the parents share parenting responsibilities. Involved fathers present a positive role model for teens of both genders by showing that males are partners in nurturing and emotionally supporting the family. As your child sits on the cusp of her own adult life, this message should continue to be strong. Seeing one's mom and dad being respectful to and supportive of each other and observing how they talk to resolve their differences are invaluable examples for all teens. When you and your spouse verbalize your feelings, both positive and negative, your teen learns that it is acceptable and normal to talk about emotions and the challenges of family living. This is particularly important for boys, who may think they need to act tough or cool all the time.

Spending Time with Your Teen

Although many teenagers resist spending time with their parents or siblings, I suggest that parents make a real effort to use some family activities to keep the connection solid. You may not spend as much time together as a family as when your child was younger, but that's normal. Try to find activities that your teen likes to do. I know one mom and daughter who, when they go on vacations to the shore, like to read on the beach; then they switch books and later talk about the books. Other perennial favorites are attending a sporting event together and eating out.

Lots of parents I know get their teens to attend a family event by informing them well in advance and letting them bring a friend. An elderly woman in my neighborhood always encourages her teenage grandchildren to bring a friend to dinner. I think this is a nice way to guarantee the teen's presence! Another couple allowed their teenage daughter to bring her best friend (who was practically part of the family anyway) on the family's summer vacation. Moans and groans were quickly stifled when the dad said, "Let's invite Rachel to come with us this year."

Arranging to spend one-on-one time with a teen may be tricky, but I encourage both mothers and fathers to find a pastime to share with your teen, whether it's shopping, boating, hiking, building furniture, or just sharing a meal at a favorite restaurant. Often this time together naturally brings about those little moments of connection and communication that parents of teens so crave, and that teens need, too.

■ When Zoe was a little girl, her father always brought her trout fishing. They didn't go often, but it was a ritual that lasted throughout her childhood and even into her college years when her friends actually thought it was cool that she went fishing with her dad. Zoe and her father talked mostly about fish when they were on their excursions, but they also shared the beauty of nature together. And their silences were not uncomfortable as they sat and waited for a bite. Zoe always remembered the times fishing with her father as special, peaceful, and meaningful.

■ When his wife works late at the office, Alan, a banker, often brings his seventeen-year-old son, Cole, out to a favorite restaurant that serves the Catalan cuisine of Spain. Cole's favorite subject in school is Spanish, and he really enjoys reading the menu and chatting in Spanish with the waiters. Alan and his son have made this dinner out a favorite ritual. While enjoying the food, they talk about a variety of subjects, including Cole's plans for college.

Support Your Teen's School and Extracurricular Life

Many teens may claim they would rather not ever see their parents on school grounds—or anywhere out of the house! Nevertheless, most teenagers value their parents' support of their academic and extracurricular careers even if they keep it a secret. I'm reminded of one young woman who complained that her mom had never attended her track meets when she was a junior in high school. The mom, who was in her forties, had given birth to a baby and thought that her older daughter didn't need or want her attention so much anymore. While there was no question that the teen loved her new sibling, she was also jealous of the attention the baby received. Years later she confessed that she felt her parents had ignored her sports success and that she resented her parents being so focused on the new baby.

My advice to the parents of teens is to maintain a discreet presence at school. Parents can join the PTA, the band parents' organization, or the football boosters, or they can chaperone the choir trip, sell T-shirts at the school flea market, and so on. Parents can communicate with teachers through e-mail or by phone, help the teen locate a college (the Internet is a great place to start), take her to visit prospective colleges, meet with the guidance counselors when she's experiencing problems, attend back-to-school night and curriculum seminars, volunteer for committees, run for the school board, and so on. Your teenager may claim she doesn't want to "see" you at school, but that doesn't mean she won't notice (and won't be privately disturbed or disappointed) when her parents ignore her educational progress and activities. The more involved both parents are, the clearer will be the message that school is important. Remember that college or vocational decisions are extremely weighty and stressful for the teen; the support, attention, and encouragement of both parents is crucial.

I also encourage both parents to find ways to stay involved in the teen's homework. Obviously, you won't sit with her as you did when she was seven, but when a teenager has a special report or gets stuck on a chemistry assignment, it's perfectly appropriate to help guide her to the answer—if, indeed, you can figure it out! Teens may also sometimes need help getting organized. Joan, the mom of fourteen-year-old Ellen, purchased a daily planner for her daughter when she became a freshman in high school; Ellen was a bit overwhelmed with all her classes and keeping track of books she needed to read, homework deadlines, and long-range assignments. Joan bought an assortment of inserts for the planner, and she and Ellen sat down together and organized the planner into separate sections, including a calendar and a floor plan of the high school. They met every Sunday night to review the week's upcoming activities and assignments. Frank, Ellen's father, was an Internet whiz and helped Ellen find and bookmark helpful reference Websites for her school research.

While I don't suggest chasing your teen around like a toddler, I don't buy the theory that boys and girls must take complete and total charge of their lives as soon as they turn thirteen. I do think it's reasonable to be knowledgeable and interested in your adolescent's schoolwork. After all, you'll soon be footing the bill for college if that's the route your teenager decides to take.

Some teens may want to get jobs or drive cars—often both. Parents must approach these issues together. One dad told me he absolutely did not want to purchase a car for his daughter when she turned seventeen, but once she proved to be an excellent, responsible driver, he couldn't resist buying her an inexpensive used car so she could be more independent. Whether a teen works depends largely on family income, the teenager's interest in pursuing a job, and what is available in your community. These questions need to be weighed and discussed as a family, and parents need to consider how the teenager's schoolwork will be affected, how he will get to and from the job, when he will be required to work, safety and health issues, and how each parent can support the effort if that is what is agreed on. It's essential for dads to be involved in these discussions. Since many teens stay up late, a parent-teen conference after working hours and when other siblings are asleep is a feasible option.

Recently, I attended a school event at which a senior girl gave a wonderful speech. Afterward I saw the girl's mom and asked where her daughter was going to college. The mom told me her daughter had applied to a couple of schools, but she couldn't remember which ones. I was saddened that this bright and conscientious teen didn't appear to have the active support of her parents, and I could only hope that she was strong enough to find her direction on her own.

On the other hand, I had a young woman as a client who told me of a special trip her father took her on to visit colleges in the Northeast. The father had worked out all the particulars of the itinerary, set up interviews and campus tours, and even arranged for his daughter to spend one night in a dorm while he stayed at a local bed and breakfast. The young woman remembered all the details and effort her father had put into making the trip a positive experience. Interestingly, ten years later the two of them planned a trip to Italy together, on the daughter's suggestion. The father said he would pay for food and lodging and plan the itinerary (he had traveled often in Europe on business before he retired) if the daughter paid her airfare and provided her own spending money. The daughter saved for two whole years, and their delightful two-week trip became a poignant and special memory for both of them. The young woman, who was especially close with her mom, shared with me that she might not have had the confidence about having a good time while traveling with her dad were it not for the college trip so many years ago.

After the Teen Years

Once your teen goes off to college or out on his own, the recommendations I've made in this chapter still hold for maintaining a connection as your child enters adulthood. As a college professor I have had the privilege of meeting dozens of students who have confirmed for me the value of positive communication and involvement between parent and child. Some of them keep in touch with their parents by calling or writing on a regular basis. Parents come in for games and go out to dinner, or dads or moms come in separately for special events. On the flip side, I have seen plenty of other kids who have no ongoing contact with their parents, who don't even want to go home for Thanksgiving.

When the communication triangle of mother-father-child is strong, children take the initiative to keep in touch with their parents and maintain the familial relationship. I had a student from California a couple of years back who had a terrific relationship with both her parents. She proactively worked to keep the connection strong, as did her parents. Knowing what her parents had done for her when she was growing up, she tried to reciprocate now that she was a young adult. She worked part-time to pay for her flights home and spoke to them often on the phone. I have a very strong philosophy about this "triangle": If in infancy and childhood you attach to Mom and Dad, and then you learn to detach, you are then able as a young adult to reattach and form positive adult relationships—with friends, coworkers, and a spouse. Those primary relationships of mother-child and father-child lay the foundation for your relationship skills for the rest of your life.

We're Not There Yet

ONE DAY I'D like to arrive at the park on a sunny afternoon and discover five dads with their children and five moms with their children, and no one would ask the fathers, "Are you babysitting today?" or "Are you helping your wife out today?" or "Why aren't you working?" No one bats an eye when a mother brings a baby and her two older children to the dry cleaner or the bank; I'd like to see dads running the family errands with all the kids in tow— and no one taking notice! Sure, we see this sometimes, but we still think, oh, what a great dad. Do we ever see a mom with kids at the playground and think, oh, what a cool mom?

Far too many people still assume that caring for children is "woman's work" or "mother's work" and that dads need only pick up the slack when absolutely necessary. I may relax about this one day—when I hear most mothers agreeing with the statement that they have parenting partners, not just "helpers," and when fathers across the board pay as much attention to the day-to-day aspects of family living as do moms. Some people may think this vision isn't realistic, but I know plenty of couples who are living in this type of family structure right now. I predict that in the future many more parents will join the ranks.

Fathers Do Matter

While reading newspapers, books, and magazine articles, I occasionally come across pop-psychology articles that question whether fathers—or even parents—really matter. The fact is, there are plenty of data on the negative effects of fatherlessness, but the positive data on men as nurturers and child rearers is scarcer. Nevertheless, throughout this book I have cited research which clearly reveals that fathers' play styles enhance cognitive skills, that fathers can positively affect their children's self-esteem, and that dads who are involved in their children's schooling raise better learners. Research aside, any father who has witnessed the joy his child shows when he lifts her into his arms knows that he matters.

As a family counselor I can assure you that both mothers and fathers do matter greatly in deep, enduring ways. It is completely worth the effort to overcome the obstacles to increasing the daily involvement of fathers. Instead of asking whether fathers matter or whether parents matter, I believe it's time to ask how fathers and mothers can work as a team to share equally the commitment of raising their children.

Often when I'm speaking to a class of college students about the value and goals of fathers being as involved as mothers in the daily lives of their children, I'm approached afterward by a student who tells me a story of being abandoned by his or her father in some way. Either the dad cut his child off emotionally during adolescence, or he was an alcoholic or a workaholic; in some way he was not present in a consistent, positive way in his child's life. Sometimes we don't see the results of a father's lack of involvement as clearly when a person is young as when the person is an adult and remembers the loss and rejection. Human beings are the most attached of any mammal; look at how many years it takes us to raise our young. When a mother and father love and attach to their child, and vice versa, that child begins the process of evolving into a caring, emotionally healthy adult who learns to love, learns to detach, then learns to love and attach again as a grown man or woman. A friend of mine whose father died more than a decade ago often refers to how positively he influenced her life; she speaks often of the love of learning and literature her father instilled in her. This sort of value just can't be measured in a research study.

I remember when I was learning to drive, at sixteen or seventeen, how surprised I was when I went out in the car alone one day and realized I was driving with my left hand on the steering wheel and my right arm flung across the top of the seat. This was exactly the way my own dad always sat when he drove, though he certainly never told me to do so. It's just that I had watched my dad drive this way for sixteen years, and so when it was my turn to get into the driver's seat, I unconsciously imitated him. We learn so many things—small and big—from our parents, who are indeed the most important role models in our lives. Peers may seem more important for a while, particularly during the teen years, but those years pass swiftly and peer groups can change often; what remains to guide us through our most important decisions and life transitions are the lessons and examples passed on to us by our parents.

Fathers who are involved with their children on a day-to-day basis are, I believe, the role models and trailblazers for a new generation of boys who have been taught and have learned firsthand that fathers can be nurturing, equally involved parenting partners to their wives. I'm convinced that my kids will have different expectations because I stayed home with them when they were growing up and because of the type of work I do. If nothing else, they will certainly remember that I was there and their mother was there, and that we cared. Those two seemingly small factors can bear magnificent fruit as a child grows into an adult.

Just recently A.J. smiled at me while I was bandaging her knee after a tumble on her bike and said, "You know, Dad, you always take care of me when I get hurt." She was just talking about scraped knees, of course, but the message I heard was that she knows she can count on me no matter what. I happen to be a stay-at-home dad, but any dad who does these kinds of things for their kids at any time of the day or night knows how good it feels to have a child look at you and say, "I'm so glad you're here."

Raising children is a twenty-four-hour-a-day commitment. It seems obvious that such a tremendously important mission is best shared by the two individuals who first agreed to become parents. The puzzle is not so intricate, after all; it seems only logical that when possible both mother and father should contribute in a balanced manner to their child's care and well-being. We no longer live in a world in which women automatically stay home and men are the sole breadwinners; nor would we want to return to a world in which women are limited in their options, and men are denied the full rewards of family and fatherhood. It is no longer feasible or desirable for women to shoulder all or most of the child care responsibility. (In my opinion, this was never the best answer for couples or for children.) In our continuing challenge of trying to balance work and family life, I would like to see fathers *and* mothers fulfilling both their own professional and personal goals, as well as their family goals, so that children can receive the myriad benefits of two involved parents.

Changing the Language of Parenting

As a stay-at-home dad I have a unique perspective on what it means to be involved in the daily management of a family. I'm well aware that laundry, housework, cooking, and all the family-related tasks are not a thrill a minute. But I don't really see these aspects of my life as drudgery, either. Perhaps because we live in such a busy, hectic, competitive world, there is a sense that *everything* is hard work. But what would be the other option to spending time with your child? I really can't think of any other pastime that would be more rewarding.

If we would relinquish the language of parenting as a job, work, or a second shift, and focus instead on compromising with our partners so that men make a greater effort to share the caregiving, there would be more opportunities for us to *enjoy* what we're doing, to take pleasure in reading to our kids, talking with them, bathing them, or just holding them. When we're having a good time raising our kids and don't feel the entire responsibility rests on our shoulders alone, that "negative" language isn't really on our minds. When parents use negative language, it frequently is an indication that their relationship is out of balance; one person is feeling too much pressure to be responsible for the day-to-day tasks required to run the family.

Sometimes even involved fathers refer to parenting as their main "job." Simply rephrasing that sentiment—saying, for example, as I often do, that fathering is my highest priority, my greatest reward, and one of my most important and fulfilling ongoing experiences—is a good place to start. I believe that when parents share a balanced parenting relationship, they can better enjoy their children and feel more positive about themselves, their marriages, their families, and their work.

Signs of Change

Surveys by the Families and Work Institute indicate that while working men are spending more time with children and doing household chores, it is still not anywhere comparable to the amount of time working women spend on these activities. Further, data from these studies may be flawed due to the fact that time estimates from study participants are self-reported and may reflect what the participant thinks is socially acceptable, or they may reflect "combination" efforts such as talking to your child while you do the dishes. I am still bolstered, however, by these positive signs of change. Men are beginning to see that their role as breadwinner is limited and doesn't fulfill all their personal needs. And men are not the only breadwinners in most families today. Flexible work settings for both men and women are on the rise, and some two million fathers have chosen to be stay-at-home dads—a fairly uncommon option twenty years ago.

Young couples today are discussing child care options even before they have children. As one young woman wrote in a *New York Times* op-ed piece, she and her husband have planned their careers to prepare for parenthood and are discussing who will care for the baby. The writer said she sought a husband who would sacrifice some career ambition and share the role of breadwinner; they have already had experience taking turns supporting each other's career moves. The husband went to law school while the wife took responsibility for the home; then, while she got a master's degree, he took a low-key position in a law firm and ran the household as well. Even before becoming parents, this couple is aware that their lives will change dramatically when they have children, and they are hoping to meet the challenges they will face together in a balanced manner. Talking and thinking about these matters right from the start certainly is progress.

Men's attitudes are also changing; as one professionally successful father who manages some high-profile musicians told me: "Fatherhood is the most important aspect of my life. My work, my clients, my travel—all are secondary to raising my son." While this terrific attitude is mirrored by lots of fathers today, the reality is still that many fathers are not involved on a daily basis with their kids. Practical, everyday matters of home and family are still primarily the realm of women even though they are working in greater numbers outside the home. In my efforts as an educator, professor, counselor, and friend to other dads, I am heartened when I see signs of change such as an article I read recently about Generation X dads. We all know Gen-Xers generally get a bad rap, but this article, like that op-ed piece, focused on the fact that many dads who are now in their twenties express a new perspective on fatherhood, and many who are not yet fathers are looking forward to that stage in their lives with greater expectations for involvement. Generation X dads expect to have a more hands-on role with their children and possess an egalitarian attitude toward marriage; they plan to share child care, housework, shopping, and involvement in their children's education and activities.

Women's Roles Are Changing

In the 1990s, 75 percent of women with school-age children were in the labor force, according to the U.S. Bureau of Labor Statistics. Women today can choose to combine work and family in creative ways that were not available even a decade ago. Take an informal survey of the working mothers you know, and you're likely to hear that one of them works at home one or two days a week or goes into the office early, leaving her husband to pack the kids off to school, and leaves early to meet her children after school. Many young women are looking for mates who will share child care and parenting responsibilities and who will not expect their wives to relinquish their careers when they have children.

Still, many women with children who have been married for a time are wondering why their lives seem unbalanced. They can't seem to draw their spouses into becoming more involved in their children's daily lives. At best, most of these women are depressed to some degree, although many don't even know it; at worst, some have fallen into a pattern of "learned helplessness" and are convinced there is nothing they can do to change their situation. These women need to examine the factors contributing to their unique family situation. I hope the stories in this book—examples of couples from dual-income families and from families in which one parent stays home—have illustrated the myriad creative solutions to achieving the goal of spouses being more involved.

The Workplace Must Change

A philosophical shift toward involved fatherhood won't occur unless the American workplace changes. It is changing, but it's a grassroots effort, I think, more than a government-directed one. It's no secret that dual-career families are on the rise. In 1997 the Bureau of Labor Statistics reported 352,000 more dual-worker families than in the previous year and 145,000 fewer "traditional" families in which only the husband was employed. Workplace flexibility will gain more attention with more parents in the workplace.

I encourage working parents to push for family-friendly work environments in the companies they work for and to explore and design alternatives to the classic Monday-to-Friday, nine-to-five schedule. Flextime, compressed time, shift work, job sharing, and telecommuting are all viable options for parents, whether they work for a company of ten or ten thousand employees. We need to look at the employer-employee relationship as a mutually beneficial contract.

Sometimes it takes only one voice to make a positive change. One dad, a salesman who works for a large office supplies corporation, cut his hours to twelve hours a day, three days a week; he spends the other days at home with his kids. He spent two years working out this arrangement, but he finally convinced his employer he could do it. One of my neighbors who works for a small software company recently negotiated a flextime arrangement with her employer: She goes to work at 8:00 A.M. and is home by 2:30 P.M. so she can be there for her kids after school. She often works on her computer from home and occasionally makes calls in the afternoon, but she's able to supervise their homework as well, so the evenings are free for them to enjoy one another as a family.

There is no better time to start establishing a husband's involvement in his family than from the moment his wife becomes pregnant—or even before that. Fathers need to plan to take paternity leave or be the first to set a precedent if no company policy exists. Fathers need to demand flexible, family-friendly work hours. This can no longer be a mothers-only agenda. Dads need to speak out and let employers know that the more involved they are with and the better they feel about their families, the better they'll feel about and perform at work. Just as working moms request time off to attend school conferences, doctor appointments, personal family days, or their children's sick days, fathers must do the same without fear of reprisal. The workplace, now equally comprised of men and women in many professions, must change to accommodate these goals.

One dad I know, a detective, adjusts his hours so he can attend school conferences, functions, and other school events. This means that he often has to work at night or drive to and from his workplace twice a day instead of once. The trade-off is worth it to him. The day after a recent election I was impressed to see a story on television about a senator on his first day of work. The first order of business on his agenda was to see his daughter off at the school bus stop. No doubt this was orchestrated by his PR people, but I still think it sent a good message that men with "important" jobs see fathering as a high priority.

A few years ago I was invited to appear on a national talk show. I had just returned with my wife from a three-day vacation without our kids; we had left A.J. and Kevin with their grandparents and gone on a rare weekend alone. This was great for us, but when we got back, we were thrilled to be with the kids and didn't want to leave them again so soon. I informed the talk show host that I'd be happy to fly to California if the company would foot the bill for the whole family to travel; I told her I simply couldn't leave our young children again without their parents. Much to my surprise, the company agreed to fly my whole family to Los Angeles; all that was required was the asking.

Based on what I hear from many of my clients, the majority of men are still worried that they won't be taken seriously as employees if they openly place family first, but I believe the trend is headed toward acceptance of more involved fathers. Until men begin to question the rules and policies that have limited their lives and deprived them of family time, progress can go only so far. One of my clients decided that his job was too demanding; the hours denied him any family time at all, and he got very little personal satisfaction out of his job. He finally just decided to quit and found another job, one that didn't pay as much but had greater flexibility. I believe that when men begin to speak up and insist on family-friendly work environments without apology or to forge career paths that allow for a reasonable amount of family time, we'll eventually achieve across-the-board change. And certainly both men and women can vote for representatives who support family-friendly work issues.

The seventy-hour work week must come to an end, as should the sixty, fifty, and possibly even the forty-hour work week. The Families and Work Institute reports that men typically work forty-nine hours a week, and women forty-two; men with children under eighteen work slightly longer hours. Yet, 63 percent of the men and women surveyed said they would like to work fewer hours. Interestingly, the U.S. Census Bureau reports that men in service occupations, such as firemen, policemen, and maintenance workers, are about twice as likely as fathers in "white collar" occupations to be taking care of their preschoolers while the mothers are working. Isn't it interesting that these occupations involve nontraditional or shift schedules? Men with traditional work hours and higher incomes were the least likely to be caring for their preschoolers while their wives worked, the Census Bureau found.

Most of All, Parents' Attitudes Must Change

I had a wonderful opportunity not long ago to visit Elisabeth Kübler-Ross, whom I mentioned earlier. What strikes such a deep chord within me about her work is this: When people who are dying from a terminal illness, and therefore *know they are dying*, reflect back on their lives, they express major regret at having spent too much time on work and career and not enough time on meaningful personal relationships with their children, spouse, and friends. This regret is as emotionally painful and wrenching as the physical manifestations of their illness. I see the seeds of such regret in some of my patients who, while they are not dying of a terminal illness, are suffering in other ways.

I recently had as a patient a mom with debilitating depression. Her illness was wasting away her life and her time with her children. It was hurting her family and her experience as a parent. I spent a good deal of time counseling her and helping her focus on the issues that Kübler-Ross studied. And I am happy to say this mom was able to effect a complete turnaround and recovery. Parenting is a unique, personally rewarding experience. I am saddened by the number of men and women I see in my practice who wish, years after their children are grown, that they had given parenting, not work, their "all." To all parents I say, "Begin now to make the changes necessary to spend more time involved in the daily lives of your children. Not tomorrow or next year or after that next promotion. Begin now."

I have never heard an older person say they wished they could have worked more. Each and every person I've ever asked this question has regretted not having spent more time with their kids and families. I was talking the other day to a man in his fifties who was looking back at how, imperceptibly over time, he had lost connection with his daughter. This man is typical of many of the older fathers I talk to who wish that they had made more time for their families. I urge fathers to evaluate their lives now and to make the necessary changes while there is time. After a certain point you just can't bring childhood—and the opportunity to be with your child—back.

Communication Is the Ticket

I dedicated a whole chapter in this book, chapter 3, to building and practicing effective communication skills between you and your spouse. Parenting well and sharing responsibilities equitably requires compromise skills and healthy two-way communication. One day when A.J. and Kevin were having a sibling squabble, Kevin turned to me and asked why I didn't solve the problem for them. I answered, "You can work it out yourselves," to which Kevin complained, "Dad! We're not therapists!"

Of course not all of us are psychologists, but the good news is that good communication skills can be learned. I'm convinced that the better a couple communicates, the better chance they have of realizing the goal of having the father as involved in the daily lives of the children as the mother most likely is. A natural question for me to focus on in the early stages of working with women who are having trouble in this arena is "How well are you communicating with each other, and are you communicating your wishes for him to be more involved in a way that will make him receptive?"

So many women who are frustrated that their husbands aren't more involved admit that they don't really appoint a time and place to talk to their spouse about important issues on a regular basis. They also admit that certain issues or activities in their children's lives are handled solely by one spouse or the other, with little conversation between the two parents. Further muddying the waters may be the fact that some dads want to be more involved but perceive that there isn't space for them in the picture. Most of these marriages are rampant with assumptions. One spouse simply assumes from the get-go (and I do mean from the day the child is born) that the mother will "take care of" so much of the child's daily care. This is no way to increase father involvement. I urge couples to sit down together and share the concerns, challenges, issues, problems, as well as the joys of parenthood. Just start talking.

Schedule Regular Parent-to-Parent Meetings

Whether it's after the kids go to bed, before they get up, while the baby is napping, or when Grandma or a sitter can come by for an hour, get together with your spouse and discuss the issues—the little day-to-day ones as well as the big ones—of raising your children. No detail is too minor to be shared! These are your children—they belong to both of you—and there is no reason that mom should be the only one who knows all about what's making the baby fussy or how best to get him to go down for a nap. In that event Dad won't have an inkling of how to care for the baby when Mom goes out or is taking care of other personal or professional commitments.

My wife and I are able to do this each night from 9:00 to 9:30 or 10:00. And if my wife tries to ditch out of it, as she does if she's really tired or has had a hard day, I insist that we talk for at least ten minutes about one particular thing that is going on with A.J. or Kevin. Inevitably she is glad that we talked, and more often than not, her fresh eye on the issue helps us change our tack or plan an important activity. Like a good team, she sees things I miss, and vice versa. Some couples work shifts or evenings and aren't able to sit down together at night; nevertheless, I'm confident that you will be able to find a time to discuss the family you have created and are raising together once you decide to make it a priority. Tackle one topic at a time. If you can't finish in a half hour or an hour, schedule another meeting. Keep the dialogue about your family issues going with your spouse forever.

Spend Time with Your Spouse and Children as a Family

Again, I realize that we're all busy people, but when you decide to make family time a priority, you will find a way to do it. I encourage families to eat dinner together as often as possible, although I know that some work schedules do not allow for this. If it can possibly be arranged, however, the family dinner is one of those vestiges from the Leave It to Beaver days that actually makes a lot of sense. Connections are made, conversations occur, and each member recognizes his or her part in the working whole. I can't emphasize how important it is to share a meal together (even breakfast!) on a regular, consistent basis.

In addition, I encourage families to develop hobbies together, to get involved in sports, to read together, to walk together, to plan outings together, to spend time just enjoying each other's company.

It's so easy for parents to get caught up in all the many other responsibilities, and children themselves are so busy with sports teams, extracurricular activities, friends, schoolwork, and so forth. These are all important pursuits, but we need to keep an eye on how much time we also spend together.

Spend Time with Your Children One-on-One

In order to keep communication in the family healthy and to help build trust and understanding between the child and each parent as an individual caregiver and friend, I believe it's essential for both the mother and the father to spend occasional one-on-one time with their child. Ideally, this pattern will begin early—during infancy—and continue through adolescence. As a child grows, I encourage parents to find special things they like to do with their child. Whether it's reading and talking about books, riding bikes, playing a sport, or just taking a drive as I do with A.J. to talk, we need to make time to be with our children and get to know them deeply. When they are teenagers, they will of course begin to draw away and may not be so happy to jump in the car with Mom or Dad. But there are ways to remain connected, and as we saw in chapter 9, some dads are quite inventive about getting their teen to talk to them—even if they need to take a fishing trip or go out to eat at a special restaurant to do so.

The Involved Father: The New Parenting Paradigm, Part I

I am often asked by the media, my clients, my students, and parents who attend my seminars to give them in a nutshell the ingredients for creating ways for fathers to be more involved in the daily lives of their children. Here are my suggestions:

- Put kids first. I encourage parents to form strong, stable attachments with their children, especially during the crucial first three years of life.

- Working mothers need their spouses to be involved dads. The working world puts increased stress and demands on mothers, and working fathers must be ready to step in and share the child care and housework. I've yet to see a working mother who refuses to be involved with the kids or housework, yet I see plenty of working dads who seem to believe they are too tired or busy to contribute to home life.

■ Stay-at-home mothers need their spouses to be involved dads. Just because a mother is home with the kids does not relieve the father of his responsibilities for being intimately involved in the daily business of raising his children. Stay-at-home moms need breaks, too; every parent needs time off. When working moms come home to a stay-at-home dad, my studies show, they pitch right in, helping to prepare dinner and bathing and putting the children to bed. Working dads can do the same when moms stay home.

■ Children deserve the benefit of their father's attention and involvement. Research confirms that children benefit in myriad ways—socially, cognitively, and emotionally—when their fathers are actively involved in their lives.

■ Fathers, just like mothers, learn by on-the-job training. It isn't enough to say you know how to do it—you need to *do* it. No baby comes with a manual—don't we all wish they did?— and mothers do not possess all the answers the moment they give birth. Quite the contrary. They learn as they go by reading a lot and talking to other moms; dads can do this, too.

■ Fathers need to share the role of the on-call parent. That means being completely responsible for the daily care of the child several times a week, for a whole day or part of a day or evening, in order to become knowledgeable about the child's schedule and changing needs, temperament, and developmental stage. The picture a father sees when he is on call is very different from the picture a father sees when he comes and goes.

■ Get rid of the archaic idea that raising and caring for a child is a gender-specific responsibility or gender-related set of skills. Aside from giving birth and breastfeeding, a father can nurture and care for his baby in exactly every way a mom can, from packing a lunch to giving a bath to soothing a child's hurt feelings to driving a child to school.

The Involved Father: The New Parenting Paradigm, Part II

In order for all this to work, fathers as much as mothers need to be "in tune" with the child at each stage of the child's development, which is why I chose to fashion the core chapters of this book in an ages and stages format. The ways in which fathers can most successfully be involved in the daily lives of their children must necessarily change with each developmental stage. Then, within the context of that stage, fathers need to be knowledgeable about and involved in:

- the child's interests, day-to-day schedule, and activities. Sharing the on-call role helps achieve this goal, as do parent-to-parent meetings and spending one-on-one time with your child.

- the child's friends. When the child is young, there is no reason a dad can't arrange play dates. As the child grows, fathers can play an important role in keeping an open dialogue with their child about friends and peer relationships, particularly as peers take on more importance during the teen years, and can encourage their child to have friends over.

- the child's caregivers or after-school activities. Fathers need to feel comfortable communicating with the child's caregivers if the child is in a day care setting. I strongly recommend that dads and moms together research, interview, and choose a caregiver for an infant or toddler, or find and evaluate an after-school care program or situation for an older child. Fathers need to feel comfortable contacting the caregiver during the day for a report of what or how his child is doing.

- the child's school and educational issues. From choosing a preschool to helping with homework to communicating with teachers to supporting his child's academic goals and extracurricular interests and activities, a father can find ways to stay involved in his child's educational growth.

Parents Who Share the Care of Their Children

We hear a lot about such things as "Father of the Year" awards. I'd rather see "Parents of the Year," parents who are equally involved and active in raising their children. Some neighbors of mine down the block fit that description. The dad works an evening job from 10 P.M. until 6 A.M. Then he comes home and catches a few hours of sleep before spending the morning with his toddler and getting his older kids off to school; sometimes the dad and toddler nap in the early afternoon, too. The mother works full-time but during the day calls home often to check in with her husband on how the kids are doing and what is going on. They're both very involved in their children's school and extracurricular activities; the dad even coaches a soccer team. And in spite of their busy, hectic lives, I never hear them complain; they're doing what they wanted to do, raising their children together, and they're supportive of each other's interests and needs. Their roles as parents are definitely not typecast.

When I was a young man, I certainly never aspired to be a stay-at-home dad, nor did I ever really give much thought to how I would raise my family. But when I did get married and we had a baby, I realized I was the natural one to stay home with Kevin and then with A.J. I was able to pursue my studies at home and to continue my private practice around the children's schedules, and Linda was able to maintain her full-time job, which she loves. Yet she has always remained a devoted and active mother, pitching in with the family as soon as she comes in the door at night and spending one-on-one and family time with the kids on the weekends.

Having fathers equally involved as mothers in the parenting partnership lies at the very core of what it means to be a family. Mothers will feel less stressed and taken for granted, and will be able to explore their careers and/or pursue and enjoy their personal interests, knowing that a competent, caring father is available.

Mothers have a legitimate need and right to an involved partner, even though it may be difficult for some to achieve this goal. Women as well as men often feel hesitant to make changes, or they may worry about what will happen if they upset the apple cart. If your parenting relationship has been out of balance for some time, you may feel that you have no choice but to continue to shoulder most of the responsibility. However, all you need to do is take one step in the right direction. Decide to try a new communication technique; identify your issues and prioritize them in writing; or schedule a parent-to-parent meeting to figure out how you can get some free time each week. Just do one thing: Don't get overwhelmed by trying to "fix" everything overnight; instead, work toward gradual improvement.

I encourage moms to think about all the possible choices and options that will bring about more involvement from their spouses and a healthier family life overall. Explore every choice, every option, and don't settle for anything less than what will be best for you, for your spouse, and for your child.

As the on-call parent, I'm the one who takes the kids to their after-school activities, who plans and makes the dinners, who replenishes the laundry soap, who runs to the school if there's a problem, who helps with homework, and who keeps track of how the kids are getting along with peers. And though at times I feel overwhelmed by this responsibility, I maintain my own career, my own goals, and my personal life. I wouldn't be able to do it all or nearly so well if I didn't have an equal partner who communicates with me, who helps me make decisions, who is cognizant of our children's schedules and changing needs, who is equally committed to their upbringing, and who can step in to be the on-call parent at any time because she is fully in tune with her children's lives.

In the majority of two-parent families across our country, mothers either work and retain the responsibility of the on-call parent or are the stay-at-home caregiver. I look forward to the day when the typical father will be proud to say that his role as an involved parent is his most significant priority and his greatest joy. I have met hundreds of fathers like that, and I look forward to meeting hundreds more as I go through life. The beneficiaries of this movement will clearly be our children, our families, and ourselves.

Bibliography and

Recommended Readings

Chapter 1

Bowlby, John. *Attachment*. Basic Books, 1969.

Bronstein, Phyllis, and Carolyn Pape Cowan, eds. *Fatherhood Today: Men's Changing Role in the Family*. John Wiley, 1988.

Canada, Geoffrey. *Reaching Up for Manhood: Transforming the Lives of Boys in America*. Beacon Press, 1998.

Griswold, Robert L. *Fatherhood in America: A History*. Basic Books, 1993.

Harlow, H. F. "The Nature of Love" in *American Psychologist* 13 (1958): 673–85.

Kübler-Ross, Elisabeth, M.D. *On Death and Dying*, rep. ed. Touchstone Press, 1997.

Lamb, Michael. *The Role of the Father in Child Development*, 3rd ed. John Wiley, 1997.

———. *The Father's Role: Applied Perspectives*. John Wiley, 1986.

———. *The Father's Role: Cross-Cultural Perspectives*. Lawrence Erlbaum Associates, 1987.

O'Connell, M. "Where's Papa! Fathers' Role in Childcare" in *Population Trends and Public Policy* 20. Population Reference Bureau, 1993.

Silverstein, Louise B. "Transforming the Debate About Child Care and Maternal Employment" in *American Psychologist* 46 (1991): 1025–32.

Chapter 2

Barnett, Rosalind C., and Caryl Rivers. *She Works/He Works: How Two-Income Families Are Happy, Healthy, and Thriving*. Harper San Francisco, 1996.

Beebe, Steven, and John Masterson. *Family Talk: Interpersonal Communication in the Family*. Random House, 1986.

Carter, Jaine, and James D. Carter. *He Works, She Works: Successful Strategies for Working Couples*. American Management Association, 1995.

Coltrane, Scott. *Family Man: Fatherhood, Housework, and Gender Equity*. Oxford University Press, 1996.

Cooksey, E., and M. Fondell. "Spending Time with His Kids: Effects of Family Structure on Fathers' and Children's Lives" in *Journal of Marriage and the Family* 58 (August 1996): 693–707.

Erikson, Erik. *Childhood and Society*. W. W. Norton, 1950.

Glennon, Will. *Fathering: Strengthening Connection with Your Children No Matter Where You Are*. Conari Press, 1995.

Goldberg, W. A., "Material Quality, Parental Personality, and Spousal Agreement About Perceptions and Expectations for Children" in *Merrill-Palmer Quarterly* 36 (1990): 531–56.

Hochschild, Arlie Russell. *The Time Bind: When Work Becomes Home and Home Becomes Work*. Metropolitan Books, 1997.

Kantrowitz, Barbara, and Claudia Kalb. "Boys Will Be Boys" in *Newsweek*, May 11, 1998: pp. 55–60.

Kindlon, Daniel J., and Michael Thompson. *Raising Cain*. Ballantine, 1999.

Klein, Arthur C. *Dad and Son: A Memoir About Reclaiming Fatherhood and Manhood*. Tortoise Books, 1996.

Koestner, R.; C. Franz; and J. Weinberger. "The Family Origins of Empathic Concern: A 26-Year Longitudinal Study" in *Journal of Personality and Social Psychology* 58 (1990): 709–17.

Lawhon, T. "Responsible Fathering: An Educational Approach" in *Journal of Family and Consumer Science*, Winter 1996.

Levine, James A., and Todd L. Pittinsky. *Working Fathers: New Strategies for Balancing Work and Family*. Harvest Books, 1998.

Marsiglio, William. *Fatherhood: Contemporary Theory, Research, and Social Policy*. Sage Publications, 1995.

Popenoe, David. *Life Without Father*. The Free Press, 1996.

Silverstein, L. "Fathering Is a Feminist Issue" in *Psychology of Women Quarterly* 20 (1996): 3–37.

Williams, Edith; Norma Radin; and Theresa Allegro. "Sex Role Attitudes of Adolescents Reared Primarily by Their Fathers: An 11-Year Follow-Up" in *Merrill-Palmer Quarterly* 38 (1992): 457–76.

Chapter 3

Dimitrius, Jo-Ellen, and Mark Mazzarella. *Reading People*. Random House, 1998.

Elium, Don and Jeanne. *Raising a Son: Parents and the Making of a Healthy Man*. Celestial Arts, 1994.

Gray, John. *Men Are from Mars, Women Are from Venus*. HarperCollins, 1992.

Chapter 4

Bronfenbrenner, Uri. "Toward an Experimental Ecology of Human Development" in *American Psychologist* (July 1977): 513–31.

Doherty, W.; E. Kouneski; and M. Erickson. "Responsible Fathering: An Overview and Conceptual Framework," in *Journal of Marriage and the Family* 60 (May 1998), 277–92.

Chapter 5

Baylies, Peter; Curtis Cooper; and Barry Reszel, eds. *At-Home Dad Handbook*. AHDH, 1998.

Eisenberg, Arlene; Heidi E. Murkoff; and Sandee E. Hathaway. *What to Expect During the First Year*. Workman, 1994.

———. *What to Expect When You're Expecting*, rev. ed. Workman, 1994.

Ferber, Richard. *Solve Your Child's Sleep Problems*. Simon & Schuster, 1985.

Fox, Isabella, and Norman M. Lobsenz. *Being There: The Benefits of a Stay-at-Home Parent*. Barron's Educational, 1996.

Greenspan, Stanley. *First Feelings*. The Book Press, 1985.

Healy, Jane M., Ph.D. *Your Child's Growing Mind*, rev. ed. Doubleday, 1994.

Klaus, Marshall, and Phyllis Klaus. *Your Amazing Newborn*, rev. ed. Addison-Wesley, 1998.

Klaus, Marshall; John Kennell; and Phyllis Klaus. *Bonding: Building the Foundations of Secure Attachment and Independence*. Perseus Press, 1996.

Lewis, M., and L. A. Rosenblum, eds. *The Child and Its Family*. Plenum, 1979.

Piaget, Jean, and Barbel Inhelder. *The Psychology of the Child*. Basic Books, 1969.

Pryor, Karen, and Gale Pryor. *Nursing Your Baby*. Pocket Books, 1991.

Sweet, O. Robin, and Thomas Bloom. *The Well-Fed Baby: Easy Healthful Recipes for the First 12 Months*. Macmillan, 1994.

Turecki, Stanley. *The Difficult Child*. Bantam Books, 1985.

Chapter 6

Beal, Carole R. *Boys and Girls: The Development of Gender Roles*. McGraw-Hill, 1994.

Bushman, B. J., and R. G. Green. "Role of Cognitive-Emotional Mediators and Individual Differences in the Effects of Media Violence on Aggression" in *Journal of Personality and Social Psychology* 58 (1990): 156–63.

Fagot, B. I., and R. Hagan. "Observation of Parents' Reactions to Sex-Stereotyped Behaviors: Age and Sex Effects" in *Child Development* 60 (1991): 617–28.

Greenspan, Stanley, and Nancy Thorndike. *The Essential Partnership.* Viking, 1989.

Goleman, Daniel. *Emotional Intelligence.* Bantam Books, 1995.

Osofsky, J. D. "The Effects of Exposure to Violence on Young Children" in *American Psychologist* 50 (1995): 782–88.

Rogoff, Barbara. *Apprenticeship in Thinking.* Oxford University Press, 1990.

Trelease, Jim. *The Read-Aloud Handbook.* Penguin, 1995.

Chapter 7

Brazelton, T. Berry, M.D. *Touchpoints: Your Child's Emotional and Behavioral Development.* Perseus Press, 1994.

Fraiberg, Selma H. *The Magic Years: Understanding and Handling the Problems of Early Childhood,* reissue. Fireside, 1996.

Frankel, Fred H. *Good Friends Are Hard to Find: Help Your Child Find, Make and Keep Friends.* Perspective, 1996.

Herman, Doris. *Doris Herman's Preschool Primer for Parents: A Question-and-Answer Guide to Your Child's First School Experience.* Tarcher/Putnam, 1998.

Hyman, Irwin A. *The Case Against Spanking: How to Discipline Your Child Without Hitting.* Jossey-Bass, 1997.

Nathanson, Laura Walther, M.D. *The Portable Pediatrician for Parents,* HarperCollins, 1994.

———. *The Portable Pediatrician's Guide to Kids: Your Child's Physical and Behavioral Development from Age Five to Age Twelve.* HarperCollins, 1996.

Phelan, Thomas W. *1-2-3 Magic: Effective Discipline for Children 2–12.* Child Management, 1996.

Chapter 8

Bassoff, Evelyn S. *Cherishing Our Daughters: How to Raise a Healthy, Confident Daughter.* Dutton, 1997.

Biddulph, Steve. *Raising Boys.* Celestial Arts, 1998.

Elkind, David. *The Hurried Child.* Addison-Wesley, 1998.

Gurian, Michael. *The Wonder of Boys*. Tarcher/Putnam, 1996.

Mackoff, Barbara. *Growing a Girl*. Dell, 1996.

Marone, Nicky. *How to Father a Successful Daughter*. McGraw-Hill, 1988.

Pollack, William. *Real Boys: Rescuing Our Sons from the Myths of Boyhood*. Random House, 1998.

Chapter 9

Elkind, David. *All Grown Up and No Place to Go: Teenagers in Crisis*. Addison-Wesley, 1998.

Kamin, Ben. *Raising a Thoughtful Teenager: A Book of Answers and Values for Parents*. Dutton, 1996.

McCoy, Kathy, Ph.D., and Charles Wibbelsman, M.D. *The New Teenage Body Book*. Perigee, 1992.

Chapter 10

Brazelton, T. Berry, M.D. *Working and Caring*. Perseus Press, 1992.

Casper, Lynne M. "My Daddy Takes Care of Me!: Fathers as Care Providers" in *Current Population Reports*, Bureau of the Census, September 1997.

Families and Work Institute. *National Study of the Changing Workforce*. April 1998.

Hochschild, Arlie Russell, and Anne Machung. *The Second Shift*. Avon, 1997.

Holcomb, Betty. *Not Guilty!: The Good News About Working Mothers*. Scribner, 1998.

Kübler-Ross, Elisabeth, M.D., and Todd Gold. *The Wheel of Life: A Memoir of Living and Dying*. Touchstone Books, 1998.

Snarey, John R. *How Fathers Care for the Next Generation: A Four-Decade Study*. Harvard University Press, 1993.

U.S. Department of Labor, Bureau of Labor Statistics. *Employment Characteristics of Families in 1997*, May 1998.

INDEX

About the Author

DR. ROBERT FRANK is one of the nation's leading researchers on fatherhood, parenting, and childcare issues. He holds a Ph.D. in educational psychology and has had a private practice in psychotherapy, specializing in family therapy, since 1985. He holds the position of Assistant Professor of Psychology at Oakton Community College (Des Plaines, Illinois), where he teaches classes in human and child development, and he hosts parenting seminars in the Chicago area.

Dr. Frank first drew national media attention in 1996 with the publication of his groundbreaking research on the impact of stay-at-home dads on the American family. He has been interviewed on various parenting topics by *The New York Times*, *The Wall Street Journal*, *USA Today*, *The Daily Telegraph* (London), *The Chicago Tribune*, *The Christian Science Monitor*, *The Boston Globe*, *U.S. News & World Report*, *Working Mother*, *American Baby*, *Child*, *Parenting*, and *New Woman*, among others. He has appeared on *ABC Nightly News*, *Extra!*, *CBS This Morning*, CNN, and several Chicago-area stations. Dr. Frank lives with his wife, son, and daughter in Glenview, Illinois.

KATHRYN E. LIVINGSTON has been writing on parenting issues for the past fifteen years. Her work has appeared in *Parenting*, *Working Mother*, *Redbook*, *Child*, *Parents*, *Country Living*, *Sesame Street Parents* and other national publications. She lives in Bergen County, New Jersey, with her husband and three sons.